THE MILITARY BALANCE 1978-1979

The International Institute for Strategic Studies
18 Adam Street London WC2N 6AL

ISBN 0 86079 022 3

ISSN 0459-7222

Printed in Great Britain by
Adlard & Son Ltd, Bartholomew Press, Dorking

CONTENTS

PREFACE

The Military Balance is an annual, quantitative assessment of the military power and defence expenditure of countries throughout the world.

It examines the facts of military power as they existed in July 1978, and no projections of force levels or weapons beyond this date have been included, except where specifically stated. The study should not be regarded as a comprehensive guide to the balance of military power; in particular, it does not reflect the facts of geography, vulnerability or efficiency, except where these are explicitly touched upon.

In general, national entries are grouped geographically, but with special reference to the principal regional defence pacts and alignments. Information about some smaller countries, whose military forces are of a size which has not seemed to warrant fuller description at this stage, has been set out in a tabular form. Other tables give comparative information on nuclear delivery vehicles and static measurements of the strategic nuclear balance, defence expenditure (with historical trends), military manpower (active and reserve), light missile craft, some army divisional establishments and arms-transfer agreements. Those tables which, by their nature, change only slightly from year to year, are not always repeated in every edition. A separate essay assesses the European theatre balance between NATO and the Warsaw Pact and summarizes the statistics of forces and weapons in Europe which are in position or might be used as reinforcements. An essay on the naval balance is included for the first time.

Notes, which follow this Preface, will help the reader to use the current edition of *The Military Balance*. It is important to read them, since they amplify and give precision to the data in the national sections and tables. In addition, because some items have not appeared annually, an index is given on p. 119 which provides a guide to such occasional features in this and previous editions.

The Institute assumes full responsibility for the facts and judgments which this study contains. The co-operation of governments has been sought and, in many cases, received. Not all countries have been equally co-operative, and some figures have necessarily been estimated. The Institute owes a considerable debt to a number of its own members and consultants, who have helped in compiling and checking material.

The Military Balance is complemented by the Institute's other annual handbook, *Strategic Survey*, published each spring, which reviews the most significant issues of international security and strategic policy in every major country and area of the world during the previous calendar year and is designed to enable subsequent events to be followed.

September 1978

READERS' NOTES

Regions and Countries

The main geographical regions are indicated in the Table of Contents on p. iii. An alphabetical list, showing where each country entry is to be found, is on p. 2, following these notes. To the extent that national variations permit, each country entry (with the exception of those for some smaller countries) is arranged in a standard form: general information about population, military service, total military manpower strength, Gross National Product (GNP) and defence expenditure is followed by separate sections on the main armed services (army, navy, air force), each of which contains, where the information is available, sub-sections on reserves and para-military forces and, where relevant, on deployment of forces of a significant size.

Defence Pacts and Agreements

A short description of multilateral and bilateral pacts and military aid agreements introduces each of the main regional sections of the study. Defence assistance given under less formal arrangements is also noted. Agreements which cover only economic aid are not included.

Defence Expenditure

For defence expenditure the latest available budget figures are quoted. Table 4 on pp. 88–9 shows current and past expenditures, expressed in United States dollars so as to afford international comparisons; however, since many countries update these each year, the figures will not necessarily correspond with those shown in previous editions of *The Military Balance*. In Table 3 there are comparisons of NATO defence expenditures 1960–1977 in current and constant prices. In this table, and for the NATO countries in Table 4, a NATO definition of defence expenditure is used, but in all other cases national definitions are used. The defence expenditures of the Soviet Union and the People's Republic of China are estimates. The problem of arriving at Soviet defence expenditure and at a suitable exchange rate to afford comparability is discussed on p. 11, whilst a note on p. 57 gives an indication of the difficulty of arriving at a figure for China.

Gross National Product (GNP)

GNP figures are usually quoted at current market prices (factor cost for East European countries). Where figures are not currently available from published sources, estimates have been made, and Table 4 uses both published and estimated GNP figures. Wherever possible, the United Nations System of National Accounts has been used, rather than national figures, as a step towards greater comparability. For the Soviet Union GNP estimates are made in roubles, following R. W. Campbell, 'A Shortcut Method for Estimating Soviet GNP' (*Association for Comparative Economic Studies*, vol. XIV, no. 2, Fall 1972). East European GNPs at factor cost are derived from Net Material Product, using an adjustment parameter from T. P. Alton, 'Economic Growth and Resource Allocation in Eastern Europe', *Reorientation and Commercial Relations of the Economies of Eastern Europe*, Joint Economic Committee, 93rd Congress, 2nd Session (Washington: USGPO, 1974). For the People's Republic of China two estimates of GNP have been given in a note on p. 57.

Currency Conversion Rates

To make comparisons easier, national currency figures have been converted into United States dollars, using the rate prevailing at the end of the first quarter of the relevant year. In all cases the conversion rates used are shown in the country entry but may not always be applicable to commercial transactions. An exception has been made in the case of the Soviet Union, since the official exchange rate is unsuitable for converting rouble estimates of GNP. Various estimates of more appropriate conversion rates have been made, but they have shortcomings too great to warrant their being used here; the official rate is, however, given in the country section. Further exceptions are certain East European countries which are not members of the IMF and Romania (which is), for which the conversion rates used are those described in Alton's study mentioned above.

Manpower

Unless otherwise stated, the manpower figures given are those of active forces, regular and conscript. An indication of the size of militia, reserve and para-military forces is also included in the country entry where appropriate. Para-military forces are here taken to be forces whose equipment and training goes beyond that required for civil police duties and whose constitution and control suggest that they may be usable in support, or in lieu, of regular forces. Further manpower information is also included in Table 5.

Equipment

The equipment figures in the country entries cover total holdings, with the exception of combat aircraft, where front-line squadron strengths are normally shown. Except where the contrary is made clear, naval vessels of less than 100 tons structural displacement have been excluded. The term 'combat aircraft' comprises only bomber, fighter-bomber, strike, interceptor, reconnaissance, counter-insurgency and armed trainer aircraft (i.e. aircraft normally equipped and configured to deliver ordnance); it does not include helicopters. Basic technical details of the nuclear delivery vehicles (missiles, artillery and aircraft) available to NATO and Warsaw Pact countries are given in Table 1 on pp. 80–86.

Strength of Military Formations

The table below gives the average establishment strength of the major military formations used in the text (further information about certain of the divisions is given in Tables 9–11 on pp. 101–3). The figures should be treated as approximate, since military organization is flexible, and formations may be reinforced or reduced. The manning of formations may, of course, be well below these levels.

	Division					Brigade				Squadron
	Armoured		Mechanized		Airborne	Armoured		Mechanized		Fighter aircraft
	Men	Tanks	Men	Tanks	Men	Men	Tanks	Men	Tanks	
United States	16,850	324	17,840	216	15,000	4,500	108	4,800	54	12–24
Soviet Union	11,000	325[a]	13,000	266[a]	7,000	1,300[b]	95[b]	2,300[b]	40[b]	10–14
China	10,000	270	12,000[c]	30[c]	9,000	1,200[b]	90[b]	2,000	—	9–10
Britain[d]	8,500	148	—	—	—	—	—	—	—	8–15
Germany	17,000	300	17,500	250	8–9,000	4,500[e]	108[e]	5,000[e]	54[e]	15–21
India	15,000	200	17,500[c]	—	—	6,000	150	4,500	—	12–20
Israel	—	—	—	—	—	3,500	80–100	3,500	36–40	15–20
Egypt	11,000	300	12,000	190	—	3,500	96	3,500	36	10–12

[a] These tank strengths are for Soviet divisions in Eastern Europe; other Soviet divisions have fewer.
[b] Strength of a regiment, which is the equivalent formation in the Soviet and Chinese command structures. (The term 'regiment' is, however, often employed, particularly in West European countries, to describe a battalion-size unit, and it is so used in *The Military Balance*.)
[c] Infantry division.
[d] Britain has eliminated the brigade. Armoured division strength will rise to 11,500 on mobilization. New infantry formations of about brigade size, known as Field Forces, have been formed; their establishments vary according to role.
[e] Proposed new armoured brigades will have 3,026 men and 99 tanks, mechanized brigades 3,730 men and 66 tanks.

Divisional strengths cover organic units only and exclude support units or services outside the divisional structure. Warsaw Pact formations and squadrons have establishments similar to those of the Soviet Union. NATO formations and squadrons not included in the table above have similar totals to those of Germany unless otherwise mentioned in the text. Iran, Pakistan, the Philippines, Thailand, Japan, South Korea and Taiwan have tended to adopt American military organization, while Australia, New Zealand, Malaysia and Singapore have generally followed British practice.

Arms Transfers

Major arms supply agreements identified as being made during the year which ended on 1 July 1978 are listed, under geographical regions, in Table 12 on pp. 104–7. Because the actual transfer of arms may take place outside that year, an indication is also given there of expected delivery dates, where these are known. Licensing arrangements, which are very widespread among the larger countries, are not normally included.

Abbreviations and Terms

A list of the abbreviations used in the text is on p. viii, immediately following these notes. For the convenience of the reader, certain important abbreviations are explained again when first used. Where a $ sign appears it refers to United States dollars, unless otherwise stated. The term billion equals 1,000 million. The symbol (–) indicates that part of a unit's or formation's establishment is detached.

ABBREVIATIONS

AA	Anti-aircraft		LPH	Landing platform, helicopter
AAM	Air-to-air missile(s)		LRCM	Long-range cruise missile(s)
AB	Airborne		LSD	Landing ship, dock
ABM	Anti-ballistic missile(s)		LSM	Landing ship, medium
Ac	Aircraft		LST	Landing ship, tank
AD	Air defence		Lt	Light
AEW	Airborne early warning			
AFV	Armoured fighting vehicle(s)		M	Million
ALBM	Air-launched ballistic missile(s)		MARV	Manoeuvrable re-entry vehicle(s)
ALCM	Air-launched cruise missile(s)		MCM	Mine counter-measures
Amph	Amphibious		Mech	Mechanized
APC	Armoured personnel carrier(s)		Med	Medium
Armd	Armoured		MGB	Motor gunboat
Arty	Artillery		MICV	Mechanized infantry combat vehicle(s)
ASM	Air-to-surface missile(s)		MIRV	Multiple independently-targetable re-entry vehicle(s)
ASW	Anti-submarine warfare			
ATGW	Anti-tank guided weapon(s)		Mor	Mortar(s)
ATK	Anti-tank		Mot	Motorized
AWACS	Airborne warning and control system		MR	Maritime reconnaissance
AWX	All-weather fighter		MRBM	Medium-range ballistic missile(s)
			MRV	Multiple re-entry vehicle(s)
Bbr	Bomber		Msl	Missile
Bde	Brigade		MT	Megaton (1 million tons TNT equivalent)
Bn	Battalion *or* billion			
Bty	Battery		MTB	Motor torpedo boat(s)
Cav	Cavalry		n.a.	Not available
Cdo	Commando			
CEP	Circular error probable		OCU	Operational Conversion Unit
COIN	Counter-insurgency			
Comd	Command		Para	Parachute
Comms	Communications		Pdr	Pounder
Coy	Company		PSMM	Patrol ship, multi-mission
Det	Detachment		RCL	Recoilless rifle(s)
Div	Division		Recce	Reconnaissance
			Regt	Regiment
ECM	Electronic counter-measures		RL	Rocket launcher(s)
Engr	Engineer		RV	Re-entry vehicle(s)
Eqpt	Equipment			
EW	Early warning		SAM	Surface-to-air missile(s)
			SAR	Search and rescue
FB	Fighter-bomber		Sig	Signal
Fd	Field		SLBM	Submarine-launched ballistic missile(s)
FGA	Fighter, ground-attack		SLCM	Sea-launched cruise missile(s)
Flt	Flight		SP	Self-propelled
FPB	Fast patrol boat(s)		Spt	Support
FPBG	Fast patrol boat(s), guided-missile		Sqn	Squadron
			SRAM	Short-range attack missile(s)
GDP	Gross Domestic Product		SRBM	Short-range ballistic missile(s)
GNP	Gross National Product		SSBN	Ballistic-missile submarine(s), nuclear
GP	General purpose		SSM	Surface-to-surface missile(s)
Gp	Group		SSN	Submarine(s), nuclear
GW	Guided weapon(s)		Sub	Submarine
Hel	Helicopter(s)		Tac	Tactical
How	Howitzer(s)		Tk	Tank
Hy	Heavy		Tp	Troop
			Tpt	Transport
ICBM	Inter-continental ballistic missile(s)		Trg	Training
Indep	Independent			
Inf	Infantry		UNDOF	United Nations Disengagement Observation Force
IRBM	Intermediate-range ballistic missile(s)			
			UNEF	UN Emergency Force
KT	Kiloton (1,000 tons TNT equivalent)		UNFICYP	UN Force in Cyprus
			UNIFIL	UN Interim Force in Lebanon
LCT	Landing craft, tank		UNTSO	UN Truce Supervisory Organization
LHA	Amphibious general assault ship(s)			
Log	Logistic		Veh	Vehicle(s)
LPD	Landing platform, dock		V(/S)TOL	Vertical (/short) take-off and landing

1

_____

COUNTRIES AND PRINCIPAL PACTS

COUNTRY INDEX

The United States and the Soviet Union

Strategic Forces

As negotiations to limit offensive forces continued at the Strategic Arms Limitations Talks (SALT), the two super-powers modernized, and in some areas expanded, their capabilities within the limits imposed by the 1972 five-year Interim Agreement and the guidelines for a second accord reached at Vladivostok in 1974. The Interim Agreement, which set ceilings on numbers of sea- and land-based missile launchers, was scheduled to lapse on 3 October 1977 but has been extended for the duration of the SALT II negotiating process.

The United States concentrated on improvements to the existing triad of ICBM, SLBM and bombers and continued to fund development programmes for new systems for deployment in the 1980s. The size of the ICBM force – 550 *Minuteman* III (each with 3 MIRV), 450 single-warhead *Minuteman* II and 54 single-warhead *Titan* II – did not change. Plans to improve *Minuteman* III yield and accuracy with procurement of the 370KT Mk 12A MIRV warhead and NS-20 guidance system went ahead. These programmes, together with improvements to *Minuteman* software, would increase accuracy (measured in CEP) from about 0.25 nautical miles (nm) to 700 feet by the end of the decade and significantly enhance the ability to destroy hardened targets. Development of MARV proceeded, and component development has started on an 8–10-MIRV mobile ICBM, the MX, to replace parts of the *Minuteman* force in the 1980s and further enhance hard-target capability, but no decision has yet been taken to proceed to production of either.

At sea, the SLBM force of 496 *Poseidon*, each with 10–14 MIRV, in 31 submarines and 160 *Polaris*, each with 3 MRV, in 10 submarines remained in operation. Construction of the first four 24-tube *Trident* boats continued (initial funding has been approved for others), but delays in building have been reported. Testing began on the 4,000nm C4 *Trident* I missile, which will also be retrofitted in 12 in-service SSBN. When operational in 1979, the C4, armed with 8×100KT MIRV, will almost double the effective range of American SLBM and increase their accuracy to a CEP of less than 1,500ft. A second-generation SLBM for the *Trident* class, the 6,000nm D5, with up to 14×150KT Mk 500 *Evader* manoeuvrable warheads, was under early development.

In the air, structural and avionics improvements were made to the B-52G/H bomber force and plans were pushed forward to adapt about 120 B-52G/H bombers to carry ALCM. Flight testing continued on three B-1 bomber prototypes, and a fourth is under construction, but plans to procure further aircraft have been cancelled.

Flight testing proceeded of versions of the air-launched cruise missile (ALCM) for deployment aboard the B-52 and possibly other aircraft. The terminally-guided version for possible deployment in the early 1980s would have a maximum range of 1,500nm. Cruise missiles were also tested from other platforms. The *Tomahawk* sea-launched cruise missile (SLCM) has been fired from surface vessels and submarines, and feasibility studies were continued for adapting this 2,000nm-range missile for ground and air launch. Limitations on the ranges of cruise missiles are under discussion in SALT II.

American ICBM, SLBM and long-range bombers totalled 2,142, over 168 fewer than in 1967. However, this force had the capability to deliver over 11,000 warheads, almost twice as many as a decade earlier. Future capabilities obviously depend upon the outcome of SALT II.

The improvement of strategic defensive forces continued at a slower pace. Interceptor aircraft were held at six active and ten reserve (air national guard) squadrons. Development of an advanced bomber and missile attack radar went on, but the *Seafarer* submarine communications system has had to be modified during development as a result of domestic political pressures. Several programmes to enhance satellite survivability have begun, including satellite 'hardening', manoeuvrability and, possibly, development of an anti-satellite capability.

The Soviet Union proceeded with broad modernization of ICBM, SLBM and bomber capabilities. Although total ICBM numbers fell to a little over 1,400 (as older ICBM were replaced by new SLBM), at least 370 new ICBM – SS-17, SS-18 and SS-19 – were deployed in MIRV and single-warhead modes. These were said to be notably more accurate than the SS-9 and SS-11, SS-19 accuracy reportedly approaching that of existing US systems. Deployment of the SS-16 in silos is ready to begin, but it has not been deployed in a mobile mode or in silos pending the outcome of SALT II. Deployment of the SS-20 (the first two stages of the SS-16) as a mobile MIRV MRBM has begun in the Western USSR, and possibly in the Eastern USSR also. A new ICBM family for possible late 1980s deployment has been reported in the early development stage.

Soviet SLBM increased to 1,015 in 90 submarines. Thirteen *Delta* II and III submarines are in service, most with 16 4,800nm-range SS-N-8. Two new SLBM have been tested: the SS-NX-17, a solid-propellant replacement for the SS-N-6, and the SS-N-18, a 3-MIRV replacement for the SS-N-8. The first SS-N-18s are reported operational on *Delta* II SSBN. Development of a longer-range replacement for the SS-N-3 SLCM continued.

Deployment of the *Backfire* B bomber continued at a rate of approximately 25 per year, and development proceeded on new ASM.

Compared with 837 in 1967, Soviet ICBM, SLBM and long-range bombers numbered approximately 2,550. This force can deliver roughly 4,500 warheads against the United States. With the replacement of the remainder of the ICBM force with the new MIRV-equipped missiles, this total would rise to over 7,500 in the early 1980s, individual warheads having significantly higher yields than US ones.

Both air defence interceptors and SAM have been modernized. The 64 ABM launchers around Moscow remained in operation, and tests have been reported of new transportable radars and endo-atmospheric missiles. Civil defence activities and satellite interceptor tests continued.

General-Purpose Forces

Numbers in the American and Soviet armed forces remained roughly at last year's levels of 2.07 million and 3.64 million respectively, compared with roughly 3 million for each in the mid-1960s. Both steadily improved conventional capabilities. One US infantry division is also being mechanized. Programmes concentrated on new direct- and indirect-fire anti-armour weapons. The procurement of *TOW* and *Dragon* missiles continued. Cannon-launched guided projectiles and scatterable mines were under development, as were new precision-guided munitions for helicopters, and procurement of new surveillance and target-acquisition aids continued. Tank production was increased, but the number of medium tanks (around 10,000) was roughly the same as in 1967. The XM-1 tank has been accepted for service and the first 110 tanks are due to be delivered in FY 1979, to be followed by 569 in FY 1980. Plans to develop a new Mechanized Infantry Combat Vehicle (MICV) have been dropped. A less costly alternative is under consideration; as an interim measure, 1,200 more M-113 APC will be produced in FY 1979 and FY 1980.

The Soviet Union continued to increase holdings of BMP MICV and T-62 and T-72 tanks, and tank numbers rose to some 50,000 compared with some 34,000 in 1967. The deployment of helicopters, SAM, ATGW and self-propelled artillery also continued.

In the US Navy plans were made to reverse the decline in major surface combatants from over 300 to 172 in a decade. The building of a new nuclear-powered carrier was undecided, however, and planning concentrated on a new class of smaller, conventionally-engined carrier. Four 688-class attack submarines have been delivered, and three more should be delivered in FY 1979. Development continued of the *Aegis* ship defence system (to be deployed aboard a new strike cruiser), and deployment of the *Harpoon* anti-shipping missile has started, together with a tactical version of the *Tomahawk* SLCM. Research continued on the development of a new generation of naval VTOL aircraft and sea mines.

The Soviet Navy continued its gradual growth in size and quality. The first of three *Kiev*-class aircraft carriers is operational, construction of *Kara*- and *Kresta*-II-class missile cruisers, and development of a class of missile cruiser for the 1980s was also reported. Procurement of nuclear V- and T-class and diesel F-class attack and C-II-class cruise-missile submarines proceeded. New anti-shipping and anti-submarine missiles were under development and being deployed, and the naval air force received more *Forger* VTOL and *Backfire* aircraft.

The United States continued deployment of the Air Force F-15 and the Navy F-14 fighters, began to build the F-16, and continued development of the less costly F-18 in order to enable combat aircraft force levels to be kept above 2,500 as older aircraft are retired. Production of the

A-10 close air support aircraft continued and is to be completed by the early 1980s. Procurement of 19 E-3A AWACS aircraft was approved (but no decision to buy it was taken by NATO). Modification of the F-4C and development work on converting the F-111A for electronic warfare roles proceeded.

The deployment of new Soviet fighters with improved range, payload and avionics continued, including the Su-17 *Fitter* C, MiG-23 *Flogger* B and Su-19 *Fencer*. With the introduction of more multi-role aircraft, the Soviet Union has over twice as many fighters suitable for ground-attack missions as in the 1960s, many nuclear capable. There were reports of new air-to-air and air-to-surface missiles under development, and of work on ECM equipment to enhance aircraft penetration.

THE UNITED STATES

Population: 218,630,000.
Military service: voluntary.
Total armed forces: 2,068,800 (115,000 women).
Estimated GNP 1977: $1,890 bn.
Defence expenditure 1978–79: $115.2 bn.*

Strategic Nuclear Forces:†

OFFENSIVE:

(a) *Navy:* 656 SLBM in 41 SSBN.
  31 SSBN (*Lafayette*-class), each with 16 *Poseidon* C3 (12 to be retrofitted with *Trident* C4 msls).
  10 SSBN (5 *Washington*-, 5 *Allen*-class), each with 16 *Polaris* A3.
  (4 *Ohio*-class SSBN, each with 24 *Trident* C4, building.)

(b) *Strategic Air Command* (SAC): Some 600 combat aircraft.
  ICBM: 1,054.
    450 *Minuteman* II, 550 *Minuteman* III, 54 *Titan* II.
  Aircraft:
    Bombers: 432.
    66 FB-111A in 4 sqns ⎫ with
    241 B-52G/H in 15 sqns ⎬ 1,250 SRAM
    75 B-52D in 5 sqns. ⎭
    Training: 50 B-52D/F.
    Storage or reserve: 125, incl B-52D/F.
    Tankers: 487 KC-135 in 30 sqns.
    Strategic Reconnaissance and Command: 10 SR-71A in 2 sqns; 10 U-2C/K; 4 E-4A/B; 19 RC/EC-135.

DEFENSIVE:

North American Air Defense Command (NORAD), HQ at Colorado Springs, is a joint American-Canadian organization. US forces under NORAD are in Aerospace Defense Command (ADCOM).

ABM: Safeguard system (msls deactivated).
Aircraft (excluding Canadian and tac units):
  Interceptors: 331
    (i) Regular: 6 sqns with 141 F-106A.
    (ii) Air National Guard (ANG): 3 sqns with 60 F-101B, 2 with 40 F-4D, 5 with 90 F-106A.
  AEW aircraft: 1 reserve sqn with 10 EC-121.

Warning Systems:

(i) *Satellite-based early-warning system:* 3 DSP satellites, 1 over Eastern Hemisphere, 2 over Western; surveillance and warning system to detect launchings from SLBM, ICBM and Fractional Orbital Bombardment Systems (FOBS).

(ii) *Space Detection and Tracking System* (SPADATS): USAF *Spacetrack* (7 sites), USN *SPASUR* and civilian agencies. Space Defense Center at NORAD HQ: satellite tracking, identification and cataloguing control.

(iii) *Ballistic Missile Early Warning System* (BMEWS): 3 stations (Alaska, Greenland, England); detection and tracking radars with ICBM and IRBM capability.

(iv) *Distant Early Warning* (DEW) *Line:* 31 stations roughly along the 70° N parallel.

(v) *Pinetree Line:* 24 stations in Central Canada.

(vi) *474N:* 3 stations on US East, 1 on Gulf, 3 on West coast (to be replaced by *Pave Paws* phased-array radars: 1 on East, 1 on West coast); SLBM detection and warning net.

(vii) *Perimeter Acquisition Radar Attack Characterization System* (PARCS): 1 north-facing phased-array 2,000-mile system at inactive ABM site in North Dakota).

(viii) *Cobra Dane Radar:* phased-array system at Shemya, Aleutians.

(ix) *Back-up Interceptor Control* (BUIC): system for AD command and control (all stations but 1 semi-active).

(x) *Semi-Automatic Ground Environment* (SAGE): 6 locations (2 in Canada); combined with BUIC and Manual Control Centre (MCC) in Alaska (to be replaced by Joint Surveillance System (JSS) with 7 Region Operations Control Centres, 4 in US, 1 in Alaska, 2 in Canada); system for co-ordinating surveillance and tracking of objects in North American airspace.

(xi) *Ground radar stations:* some 51 stations manned by Air National Guard, augmented by

---

* Expected Outlay in Fiscal 1979. Budget Authority $125.6 bn; Total Obligational Authority $126.0 bn.
† Manpower included in Army, Navy and Air Force totals.

the Federal Aviation Administration (FAA) stations (to be replaced as surveillance element of JSS).

Army: 774,200 (50,700 women).
4 armd divs.
5 mech divs.*
5 inf divs (1 inf div to be mech in 1979).*
1 airmobile div.
1 AB div.
1 armd bde.
1 inf bde.
3 armd cav regts.
1 bde in Berlin.
2 special mission bdes.
Army Aviation: 1 air cav combat bde, indep bns assigned to HQ for tac tpt and medical duties.
1 *Honest John*, 3 *Pershing*, 8 *Lance* SSM bns.

Tanks: some 10,500 med, incl 3,300 M-48, 7,150 M-60 (540 M-60A2 with *Shillelagh* ATGW); 1,600 M-551 *Sheridan* lt tks with *Shillelagh*.
AFV: some 22,000 M-577, M-114, M-113 APC.
Arty and Msls: about 2,500 105mm, 155mm towed guns/how; 3,000 175mm SP guns and 105mm, 155mm and 203mm SP how; 3,000 81mm, 3,000 107mm mor; 6,000 90mm and 106mm RCL; *TOW, Dragon* ATGW; *Honest John, Pershing, Lance* SSM.
AA arty and SAM: some 600 20mm, 40mm towed and SP AA guns; some 20,000 *Chaparral/Vulcan* 20mm AA msl/gun systems, *Redeye, Stinger* SAM; *Nike Hercules* and *Improved HAWK* SAM (to be replaced by *Patriot*). (*Roland* SAM on order.)
Aircraft/Hel: about 500 ac, incl 300 OV-1/-10, 200 U-8/-21, 40 C-12; 9,000 hel, incl 1,000 AH-1G/Q/S, 4,000 UH-1/-19, 15 UH-60A, 700 CH-47/-54, 3,600 OH-6A/-58A, H-13 (148 AH-1S hel on order). Trainers incl 310 T-41/-42 ac; 700 TH-55A hel.

DEPLOYMENT:
Continental United States
Strategic Reserve: (i) 1 armd, 1 mech, 3 inf, 1 airmobile, 1 AB divs. (ii) To reinforce 7th Army in Europe: 1 armd, 2 mech divs, 1 armd cav regt.† (iii) Alaska 1 bde. (iv) Panama 1 bde.

Europe: 198,400.
(i) Germany: 189,000. 7th Army: 2 corps, incl 2 armd, 2 mech divs, 1 armd, 2 mech bdes plus 2 armd cav regts; 3,000 med tks.‡
(ii) West Berlin: 4,400. HQ elements and 1 inf bde.
(iii) Greece: 800.
(iv) Italy: 3,000.
(v) Turkey: 1,200.

Pacific
(i) South Korea: 30,000. 1 inf div, 1 AD arty bde (to be reduced by 1 bde in 1978).
(ii) Hawaii: 1 inf div less 1 bde.

RESERVES: 556,000.
(i) Army National Guard: 366,000; capable after mobilization of manning 2 armd, 1 mech, 5 inf divs, 22 indep bdes§ (3 armd, 9 mech, 10 inf) and 4 armd cav regts, plus reinforcements and support units to fill regular formations.
(ii) Army Reserves: 190,000 in 12 trg divs, 3 indep combat bdes; 49,000 a year do short active duty.

Marine Corps: 191,500 (3,700 women).
3 divs.
2 SAM bns with *Improved HAWK*.
575 M-60 med tks; 950 LVTP-7 APC; 175mm SP guns; 105mm, 155mm how; 155mm, 203mm SP how; 230 81mm and 107mm mor; 106mm RCL; *TOW, Dragon* ATGW; *Redeye* SAM.
3 Air Wings: 364 combat aircraft.
  12 FGA sqns with 144 F-4N/S with *Sparrow* and *Sidewinder* AAM.
  13 FGA sqns: 3 with 80 AV-8A *Harrier*, 5 with 60 A-4F/M, 5 with 60 A-6A/E.
  1 recce sqn with 10 RF-4B, 1 ECM sqn with 10 EA-6B.
  2 observation sqns with 36 OV-10A.
  3 assault tpt/tanker sqns with 36 KC-130F.
  3 attack hel sqns with 54 AH-1J.
  4 lt hel sqns with 96 UH-1E/N.
  9 med hel sqns with 162 CH-46F.
  6 hy hel sqns with 126 CH-53D.

DEPLOYMENT:
(i) *Continental United States:* 2 divs, 2 air wings.
(ii) *Pacific:* 1 div, 1 air wing.

RESERVES: 29,700.
1 div and 1 air wing: 2 fighter sqns with 24 F-4N, 5 attack sqns with 60 A-4E/F, 1 observation sqn with 18 OV-10A, 1 tpt/tanker sqn with 12 KC-130, 7 hel sqns (1 attack with 18 AH-1G, 2 hy with 24 CH-53, 3 med with 54 CH-46, 1 lt with 21 UH-1E), 2 tk bns, 1 amph assault bn, 1 SAM bn with *HAWK*, 1 fd arty gp.

Navy: 532,300 (21,600 women); 172 major combat surface ships, 75 attack submarines. A further 38 major surface combat ships and 4 attack submarines are in reserve.

Submarines, attack: 70 nuclear, 5 diesel.

Aircraft carriers: 13; 3 nuclear-powered (2 *Nimitz*, 91,400 tons; 1 *Enterprise*, 89,600 tons).
  8 *Forrestal/Kitty Hawk*-class (75/80,000 tons).

---

* One National Guard bde is incorporated in 1 mech and 3 inf divs.
† One armd div, 1 mech div, 1 armd cav regt have hy eqpt stockpiled in W. Germany.
‡ Includes those stockpiled for the strategic reserve formations.
§ Including 4 indep bdes and 11 bns incorporated in active army divs.

2 *Midway*-class (64,000 tons).

These normally carry 1 air wing (85–95 ac, 75 in *Midway* class) of 2 fighter sqns with 24 F-14A or 24 F-4J, 3 attack sqns (1 AWX) 2 with A-7E, 1 with 10 A-6E; 1 recce with 3 RA-5C or 3 RF-8G; 2 ASW sqns (1 with 10 S-3A, 1 with 8 SH-3A/D/G/H hel); 1 ECM sqn with 4 EA-6B; 1 AEW sqn with 4 E-2B/C; 4 KA-6D tankers and other specialist ac.

Other surface ships:

7 nuclear-powered GW cruisers with SAM, ASROC (2 *Virginia*, 2 *California*, 1 *Truxtun*, 1 *Long Beach*, 1 *Bainbridge*).

20 GW cruisers with SAM, ASROC, 8 with 1 hel, (8 *Belknap*, 9 *Leahy*, 2 *Albany*, 1 *Cleveland*).

37 GW destroyers with SAM, ASROC (10 *Coontz*, 4 *F. Sherman*, 23 *C. F. Adams*).

30 gun/ASW destroyers, most with SAM or ASROC, (12 *Spruance*, 13 *F. Sherman*, 5 *Gearing*).

7 GW frigates with SAM, ASROC, hel (1 *O.H. Perry*, 6 *Brooke*).

58 gun frigates with ASROC (52 with 1 hel; 46 *Knox*, 10 *Garcia*, 2 *Bronstein*).

6 *Asheville*-class patrol gunboats, 4 with SSM.

1 patrol msl hydrofoil.

64 amph warfare ships (1 *Raleigh*, 2 *Blue Ridge* comd, 2 *Tarawa* LHA, 7 *Iwo-Jima* LPH, 12 *Austin*, 2 *Raleigh* LPD, 5 *Anchorage*, 8 *Thomaston* LSD, 20 *Newport* LST, 5 *Charleston* amph cargo ships).

3 MCM ships.

38 replenishment and 76 depot and repair ships. (13 SSN, 1 nuclear-powered carrier, 1 nuclear-powered GW cruiser, 12 destroyers, 7 GW frigates, 3 LHA building.)

Ships in reserve:

4 subs, 7 aircraft carriers, 4 battleships, 7 cruisers, 2 comd ships, 18 amph warfare, 8 MCM ships, 46 log support and 41 troop, cargo and tanker ships. (239 cargo ships, 162 tankers could be used for auxiliary sea-lift.)

Aircraft: 12 attack carrier air wings; some 1,100 combat aircraft.

26 fighter sqns: 14 with 168 F-14A, 12 with 144 F-4.

36 attack sqns: 11 with 110 A-6E, 25 with 300 A-7E.

10 recce sqns with 30 RA-5C or RF-8.

24 land-based MR sqns with 280 P-3B/C.

13 ASW sqns each with 10 S-3A.

13 AEW sqns each with 4 E-2B/C.

12 ASW hel sqns each with 8 SH-3A/D/G/H.

17 misc support sqns with 12 C-130F/LC-130, 7 C-118, 12 C-9B, 12 CT-39, 13 C-131, 6 C-117, 20 C-1, 15 C-2, 36 EA-6A/B ac; 30 RH-53D, CH-46, SH-3, SH-2B/C hel.

1 aggressor trg sqn with 13 F-5E/F.

19 trg sqns with T-1A, T-2B/C, T-28/-29B/-34/-38/-44, TA-4J/F, TA-7C, TS-2A, TE-2 ac; TH-1, UH-1D, TH-57A hel.

DEPLOYMENT (average strengths of major combat ships; some in Mediterranean and Western Pacific based overseas, rest rotated from US):

Second Fleet (Atlantic): 5 carriers, 62 surface combatants.

Third Fleet (Eastern Pacific): 4 carriers, 65 surface combatants.

Sixth Fleet (Mediterranean): 2 carriers, 15 surface combatants, 1 Marine Amphibious Unit (MAU).*

Seventh Fleet (Western Pacific): 2 carriers, 20 surface combatants, 1 MAU, 1 Marine Bn Landing Team.*

RESERVES: 94,100. Ships in commission with the Reserve include 28 destroyers, 3 patrol gunboats, 3 amph warfare, 22 MCM ships.

2 carrier wings: 6 A-7A/B attack, 4 F-4N fighter, 2 RF-8G recce, 3 EA-6A and EKA-3 ECM, 2 E-2B AEW sqns.

13 MR sqns with P-3A.

2 tac spt sqns with C-9B, C-118B.

2 composite sqns with TA-4J.

7 hel sqns: 4 ASW with SH-3A/G, 2 lt attack with HH-1K, 1 SAR with HH-3A.

Air Force: 570,800 (39,000 women); about 3,400 combat aircraft.†

81 FGA sqns: 48 with 1,100 F-4, 2 with 48 F-105G (*Wild Weasel*), 2 with 48 F-4G (*Wild Weasel*), 13 with 282 F-111E/F, 9 with 216 F-15, 4 with 96 A-7D, 3 with 48 A-10A.

9 tac recce sqns with 192 RF-4C.

1 AWACS sqn with 3 E-3A (19 on order).

1 defence system evaluation sqn with 21 EB-57 (2 with 40 EF-111A due).

11 tac air control sqns: 6 with 88 OV-10 and O-2E, 1 with 7 EC-130E, 1 with 11 EC-135 ac, 3 with 27 CH-3 hel.

5 special operations sqns: 4 with 20 AC-130 ac, 1 with CH-3, UH-1 hel.

4 aggressor trg sqns with 55 F-5E.

16 OCU: 7 with F-4, 1 with F-5, 2 with F-15, 2 with F-101/-106, 3 with A-10, 1 with RF-4C.

1 tac drone sqn with 7 DC-130A.

15 tac airlift sqns with 234 C-130.

17 hy tpt sqns: 4 with 70 C-5A, 13 with 234 C-141.

5 SAR sqns with 30 HC-130 ac, 76 HH-3/-53, 11 HH-1 hel.

3 medical tpt sqns with 17 C-9.

3 weather recce sqns with 14 WC-130, 29 WC-135.

---

* Marine Amphibious Units are 5–7 amph ships with a Marine bn embarked. Only 1 in Mediterranean and 1 in Pacific are regularly constituted. 1 Battalion Landing Team (MAU less hel) also deployed in the Pacific; 1 occasionally formed for the Atlantic.

† Excluding ac in SAC and NORAD; incl ac in Air National Guard and Air Force Reserve.

Hel incl 138 UH-1N, 21 HH-3E, 51 HH/CH-53.
28 trg sqns with 113 T-33, 700 T-37, 900 T-38, 135 T-39, 50 T-41, 20 T-43, C-5A, C-130E, C-141A.

DEPLOYMENT:

Continental United States (incl Alaska):
(i) Tactical Air Command: 82,000. 9th and 12th Air Forces. 43 fighter sqns, 5 tac recce sqns.
(ii) Military Airlift Command (MAC): 64,500. 21st and 22nd Air Forces.
Europe: US Air Force, Europe (USAFE): 76,000. 3rd Air Force (Britain), 16th Air Force (Spain; units in Italy, Greece and Turkey), 17th Air Force (Germany and Netherlands). 1 AD sqn in Iceland. 25 fighter sqns (plus 4 in US on call) with 312 F-4C/D/E, 20 F-5E, 72 F-15, 156 F-111E/F; 3 tac recce sqns (plus 3 in US on call) with 60 RF-4C; 2 tac airlift sqns (plus 6 in US on call) with 32 C-130.
Pacific: Pacific Air Forces (PACAF): 31,100. 5th Air Force (Japan, Okinawa, 1 wing in Korea), 13th Air Force (Philippines, Taiwan). 9 fighter sqns, 1 tac recce sqn.

RESERVES: 139,900.
(i) Air National Guard: 92,500; about 1,000 combat aircraft.

10 interceptor sqns (under ADCOM, see p. 5); 29 fighter sqns (11 with 283 F-100C/D, 3 with 84 F-105B/D, 2 with 40 F-4C, 11 with 256 A-7, 2 with 49 A-37B); 8 recce sqns (1 with 20 RF-101, 7 with 135 RF-4C); 19 tac tpt sqns (18 with 150 C-130A/B/C, 1 with 16 C-7); 6 tac air spt sqns with 120 O-2A; 13 tanker sqns with 104 KC-135, 1 ECM sqn with 10 C/EC-121; 1 defence system evaluation sqn with 20 EB-57B; 2 SAR sqns with 8 HC-130.
(ii) Air Force Reserve: 47,400; about 190 combat aircraft.
3 fighter sqns with 69 F-105D; 4 attack sqns with 91 A-37B; 17 tac tpt sqns (11 with 121 C-130 A/B, 4 with 63 C-123K, 2 with 31 C-7); 1 AEW sqn with 10 EC-121 (ADCOM), 3 tanker sqns with 24 KC-135; 2 special operations sqns with 10 AC-130, 7 CH-3; 4 SAR sqns (2 with 13 HC-130, 2 with 20 HH-3E, HH-1H); 1 weather recce sqn with 4 WC-130. 18 Reserve Associate Military Airlift sqns (personnel only): 4 tpt for C-5A, 13 tpt for C-141A, 1 aero medical for C-9A.
(iii) Civil Reserve Air Fleet: 220 long-range commercial ac (124 cargo/convertible, 96 passenger).

THE SOVIET UNION

Population: 261,310,000.
Military service: Army and Air Force 2 years, Navy and Border Guards 2–3 years.
Total armed forces: 3,638,000.*
Estimated GNP 1977: 516 bn roubles.†
Estimated defence expenditure: see p. 11.

Strategic Nuclear Forces:‡

OFFENSIVE:
(a) *Navy:* 1,015 SLBM in 90 subs.
13 D-II/-III-class SSBN, each with 16 SS-N-8/-18.
15 D-I-class SSBN, each with 12 SS-N-8.
34 Y-class SSBN, 33 with 16 SS-N-6 *Sawfly,* 1 with 12 SS-NX-17.
1 H-III-class SSBN with 6 SS-N-8.
7 H-II-class SSBN, each with 3 SS-N-5 *Serb.*
11 G-II-class diesel, each with 3 SS-N-5.§
9 G-I-class diesel, each with 3 SS-N-4 *Sark.*§
(b) *Strategic Rocket Forces* (SRF): 375,000.‖
ICBM: about 1,400.
190 SS-9 *Scarp* (converting to SS-18).
780 SS-11 *Sego* (converting to SS-17 and SS-19).
60 SS-13 *Savage.*
60 SS-17.
110 SS-18.
200 SS-19.

IRBM and MRBM: some 690 deployed (most in Western USSR, rest east of Urals).
90 SS-5 *Skean* IRBM.
100 SS-20 IRBM (mobile).
500 SS-4 *Sandal* MRBM.

(c) *Long-Range Air Force* (LRAF): 756 combat aircraft.¶
Long-range bombers: 135.
100 Tu-95 *Bear* A.
35 Mya-4 *Bison.*
Medium-range bombers: 491.
305 Tu-16 *Badger* with ASM.
136 Tu-22 *Blinder* with ASM.
50 Tu- *Backfire* B with ASM.

---

* Excludes some 750,000 uniformed civilians.
† See Readers' Notes: official exchange rate 1977, $1=0.75 roubles.
‡ Characteristics of nuclear delivery vehicles and notes on numbers and types under construction and test are given in Table 1 on pp. 80–86.
§ These 60 launchers are not considered strategic missiles under the terms of the Strategic Arms Limitation (Interim) Agreement.
‖ The SRF and *PVO-Strany,* separate services, have their own manpower.
¶ About 75 per cent based in the European USSR, most of the remainder in the Far East; there are also staging and dispersal points in the Arctic.

Tankers: 53.
9 Tu-16 *Badger*.
44 Mya-4 *Bison*.
ECM: 94.
94 Tu-16 *Badger*.
Recce: 36.
4 Tu-95 *Bear*.
22 Tu-16 *Badger*.
10 Tu-22 *Blinder*.

DEFENSIVE:
Air Defence Force (PVO-Strany): 550,000:‖ early
warning and control systems, with 6,000 early
warning and ground control intercept radars;
interceptor sqns with SAM units.
Aircraft: about 2,720.
Interceptors: incl some 80 MiG-17 *Fresco*,
170 MiG-19 *Farmer* B/E, 650 Su-9 *Fishpot* B,
Su-11 *Fishpot* C, 320 Yak-28P *Firebar*, 150
Tu-28P *Fiddler*, 850 Su-15 *Flagon* A/D/E/F
200 MiG-23 *Flogger* B, 300 MiG-25 *Foxbat* A.
Airborne Warning and Control Aircraft: 12
modified Tu-126 *Moss*.
Trg ac incl 30 Su-7, 40 Su-11, 120 Su-15, 20 MiG-
15, 60 MiG-17, 50 MiG-23, 50 MiG-25, 10
Yak-28.
ABM: 64 AMB-1 *Galosh*, 4 sites around Moscow,
with *Try Add* engagement radars. Target acquisi-
tion and tracking by phased-array *Dog House*
and *Cat House*, early warning by phased-array
Hen House radar on Soviet borders. Range of
Galosh believed over 200 miles; warheads
nuclear, presumably MT range.
SAM:
Fixed-site Systems: some 10,000 launchers, at
over 1,000 sites. SA-1 *Guild*, SA-2 *Guideline*,
SA-3 *Goa*, SA-5 *Gammon*,

Army: 1,825,000.
46 tk divs.
115 motor rifle divs.
8 AB divs.
Tanks: 50,000 IS-2/-3, T-10, T-10M hy, T-54/-55/
-62/-64/-72 med and PT-76 lt (most tks fitted for
deep wading).
AFV: 55,000 BRDM scout cars; BMP MICV;
BTR-40/-50/-60/-152, MT-LB, BMD APC.
Artillery: 20,000 100mm, 122mm, 130mm, 152mm,
180mm and 203mm fd guns/how, 122mm, 152mm
SP guns; 7,200 82mm, 120mm, 160mm and
240mm mor; 2,700 122mm, 140mm and 240mm
multiple RL; 10,800 ASU-57 and ASU-85 SP,
76mm, 85mm and 100mm ATK guns; *Swatter*,
Sagger ATGW.
AA Artillery: 9,000 23mm and 57mm towed,
ZSU-23-4 and ZSU-57-2 SP guns.
SAM (mobile systems): SA-4 *Ganef*, SA-6 *Gainful*,
SA-7 *Grail*, SA-8 *Gecko*, SA-9 *Gaskin*.

SSM (nuclear capable): about 1,300 launchers
(units organic to formations), incl *FROG*, SS-21
Scud B, SS-12 *Scaleboard*.

DEPLOYMENT AND STRENGTH:
Central and Eastern Europe: 31 divs: 20 (10 tk) in
East Germany, 2 tk in Poland, 4 (2 tk) in
Hungary, 5 (2 tk) in Czechoslovakia; 10,500 med
and hy tks.*
European USSR (Baltic, Byelorussian, Carpathian,
Kiev, Leningrad, Moscow and Odessa Military
Districts (MD)): 64 divs (about 22 tk).
Central USSR (Volga, Ural MD): 6 divs (1 tk).
Southern USSR (North Caucasus, Trans-Caucasus,
Turkestan MD): 24 divs (1 tk).
Sino-Soviet border (Central Asian, Siberian, Trans-
baikal and Far East MD): 44 divs (about 6 tk),
incl 3 in Mongolia.

Soviet divs have three degrees of combat readiness:
Category 1, between three-quarters and full
strength, with complete eqpt; Category 2,
between half and three-quarters strength, complete with fighting vehicles; Category 3, about
one-quarter strength, possibly complete with
fighting vehicles (some obsolescent).
The 31 divs in Eastern Europe are Category 1.
about half those in European USSR and the Far
East are in Category 1 or 2. Most of the divs in
Central and Southern USSR are likely to be
Category 3. Tk divs in Eastern Europe have 325
med tks, motor rifle divs up to 266, but elsewhere
holdings may be lower.

Navy: 433,000, incl 59,000 Naval Air Force,
12,000 Naval Infantry and 8,000 Coast Arty and
Rocket Troops; 243 major surface combat ships,
243 attack and cruise-missile subs (85 nuclear,
158 diesel). A further 29 major surface combat
ships and 117 attack submarines are in reserve.
Submarines:
Attack: 40 nuclear (12 N-, 17 V-I, 5 V-II, 5 E-I,
1 A-class), 134 diesel (60 F-, 10 R-, 10 Z-,
40 W-, 4 B-, 5 T-class, 5 coastal Q-class).
Cruise Missile: 45 nuclear:
1 P-class.
15 C-class, each with 8 SS-N-7.
29 E-II-class, each with 8 SS-N-3 *Shaddock*.
24 diesel:
16 J-class, each with 4 SS-N-3.
6 W-*Long Bin* class, each with 4 SS-N-3.
2 W-*Twin Cylinder* class, each with 2 SS-N-3.
Surface Ships:
1 *Kiev*-class carrier (40,000 tons) with SSM, SAM,
12 VTOL ac, 20 hel (1 on trials, 1 building).
2 *Moskva*-class ASW hel cruisers with SAM, about
20 Ka-25 hel.

---

* Excluding from the area tks in reserve (replaced by
new ones but not withdrawn).

6 *Kara*-class ASW cruisers with SAM, 1 hel (more building).
10 *Kresta*-II-class ASW cruisers with SAM, 1 hel.
4 *Kresta*-I-class cruisers with SSM, SAM, 1 hel.
4 *Kynda*-class cruisers with SSM, SAM.
10 *Sverdlov*-class cruisers (3 with SAM, 1 with hel).
1 trg cruiser (*Chapaev*-class).
20 *Krivak*-I/-II-class ASW destroyers with SAM (more building).
8 *Kanin*-class ASW destroyers with SAM.
4 *Kildin*-class destroyers with SSM.
19 *Kashin*-class ASW destroyers with SAM (5 with SSM).
8 modified *Kotlin*-class destroyers with SAM.
38 destroyers (18 *Kotlin*-, 20 *Skory*-class).
107 frigates (20 *Mirka*, 48 *Petya*, 35 *Riga*, 3 *Kola*, 1 *Koni* with SAM).
1 *Sarancha*-class msl patrol ship with SSM, SAM.
15 *Nanuchka*-class msl patrol ships with SSM, SAM (more building).
279 sub-chasers (30 *Turya*, 25 *Pchela* hydrofoils, 30 *Grisha*, 64 *Poti*, 70 *Stenka*, 60 SO-1).
70 *Osa*-I-, 50 *Osa*-II-class FPBG with *Styx* SSM.
70 MTB (50 *Shershen*, 20 P-6).
About 435 minesweepers (160 coastal).
About 84 amph ships, incl 14 *Alligator*, 10 *Ropucha* LST (more building), 60 *Polnocny* LSM.
80 landing craft.
41 hovercraft (5 *Aist*, 11 *Lebed*, 25 *Gus*).
38 tankers, 20 fleet replenishment ships.
45 depot and repair ships.
80 supply ships.
54 intelligence collection vessels (AGI).

Ships in reserve:
2 nuclear-powered attack subs, 10 Z-, 90 W-, 15 Q-class subs, 2 *Sverdlov*-class cruisers, 15 *Skory*-class destroyers, 12 *Riga*-class frigates, 35 T-43 minesweepers.

NAVAL AIR FORCE: some 770 combat aircraft.
280 Tu-16 *Badger* med bbrs with ASM.
30 Tu- *Backfire* B med bbrs with ASM.
40 Tu-22 *Blinder* med bbrs, MR, ECM ac.
Some 30 Yak-36 *Forger* VTOL FGA, 30 *Fitter* C FGA.
40 Tu-16 *Badger* E/F recce, 30 Tu-16 ECM ac.
210 MR ac: 45 Tu-95 *Bear* D, 25 Tu-95 *Bear* F, 50 Il-38 *May* ac, 90 Be-12 *Mail* amphibians.
80 Tu-16 *Badger* tankers.
220 ASW hel: Mi-4 *Hound*, Mi-14 *Haze*, Ka-25A/B *Hormone*.
280 misc tpts and trainers.

NAVAL INFANTRY (Marines):
5 naval inf regts, each of 3 inf, 1 tk bn, one assigned to each of Northern, Baltic and Black Sea fleets, two to Pacific fleet. T-54/-55 med, PT-76 lt tks, BTR-60P, BMP-76 APC; BM-21 122mm RL; ZSU-23-4 SP AA guns; SA-9 SAM.

COASTAL ARTILLERY AND ROCKET TROOPS:
Hy coastal guns, SS-C-1B *Sepal* SSM (similar to SS-N-3) to protect approaches to naval bases and major ports.

DEPLOYMENT (average strengths, excl SSBN and units in reserve):
Northern Fleet: 120 subs, 55 major surface combat ships.
Baltic Fleet: 30 subs, 50 major surface combat ships.
Black Sea Fleet (incl Caspian Flotilla and Mediterranean Squadron): 25 subs, 73 major surface combat ships.
Pacific Fleet: 70 subs, 65 major surface combat ships.

Air Force: 455,000; about 4,650 combat aircraft.*
Tactical Air Force: aircraft incl 120 Yak-28 *Brewer*, 40 MiG-17 *Fresco*, 260 Su-7 *Fitter* A, 1,300 MiG-23/-27 *Flogger* B/D, about 1,450 MiG-21 *Fishbed* J/K/L/N, 530 Su-17 *Fitter* C/D, 190 Su-19 *Fencer* A FGA; about 250 *Beagle*, *Brewer*, 150 MiG-25 *Foxbat* B/D, 300 *Fishbed* recce; 60 *Brewer* E, 6 An-12 *Cub* ECM ac; 220 tpts; 3,700 hel, incl 800 Mi-1/-2 *Hare/Hoplite*, 420 Mi-4 *Hound*, 500 Mi-6 *Hook*, 1,660 Mi-8 *Hip*, 10 Mi-10 *Harke*, 310 Mi-24 *Hind*; 1,100 tac trg ac.
Air Transport Force: about 1,300 aircraft: 50 An-8, 735 An-12 *Cub*, 20 An-24/-26 *Coke/Curl*, 235 Il-14 *Crate*, 15 Il-18 *Coot*, 2 Il-62 *Classic*, 80 Il-76 *Candid*, 100 Li-2 *Cab*, 10 Tu-104 *Camel*, 8 Tu-134 *Crusty* med, 50 An-22 *Cock* hy.
1,300 Civil Aeroflot med- and long-range ac available to supplement military airlift.

DEPLOYMENT:
16 Tactical Air Armies: 4 (1,700 ac) in Eastern Europe and 1 in each of 12 MD in the USSR.

RESERVES (all services):
Soviet conscripts have a Reserve obligation to age 50. Total Reserves could be 25,000,000, of which some 6,800,000 have served in last five years.

Para-Military Forces: 450,000.
200,000 KGB border troops, 250,000 MVD security troops. Border troops equipped with tks, SP guns, AFV, ac and ships; MVD with tks and AFV. Part-time military training organization (DOSAAF) conducts such activities as athletics, shooting, parachuting and pre-military training given to those of 15 and over in schools, colleges and workers' centres. Claimed active membership 80 million, with 5 million instructors and activists; effectives likely to be much fewer.

---

* Excluding *PVO-Strany* and Long-Range Air Force.

SOVIET DEFENCE EXPENDITURE

No single figure for Soviet defence expenditure can be given, since precision is not possible on the basis of present knowledge. The declared Soviet defence budget is thought to exclude a number of elements such as military R&D, stockpiling and civil defence – indeed some contend that it covers only the operating and military construction costs of the armed forces. The problem of arriving at a correct budgetary figure was discussed in *The Military Balance 1973–1974*, pp. 8–9, and on pp. 109–110 of the 1976–1977 edition.

Furthermore, Soviet pricing practices are quite different from those in the West. Objectives are set in real terms with no requirement for money prices to coincide with the real costs of goods and services. The rouble cost of the defence effort may thus not reflect the real cost of alternative production forgone and, in turn, a rouble value of defence expressed as a percentage of Soviet GNP measured in roubles may not reflect the true burden.

If rouble estimates are then converted into dollars to facilitate international comparisons, the difficulties are compounded, because the exchange rate chosen should relate the purchasing power of a rouble in the Soviet Union to that of a dollar in the USA. The official exchange rate is considered inadequate for this purpose, and there is no consensus on an alternative.

An alternative approach – estimating how much it would cost to produce and man the equivalent of the Soviet defence effort in the USA – produces the index number problem: faced with the American price structure, the Soviet Union might opt for a pattern of spending different from her present one. This particular method tends to overstate the Soviet defence effort relative to that of the USA.

Accordingly, the estimates produced by a number of methods are given below, both in roubles and dollars, together with official figures for the defence budget published by the Soviet Union. Estimates produced by China are also given but their basis is not known.

SOVIET UNION

Source		Price base	Defence expenditure			1970–1977	
			1970	1975	1977	% annual growth rate	Burden (% of GNP)
Billions of Roubles							
CIA	(1)	1970	40–45	50–55	53–58	4·5	11–13
Lee	(2)	1970	43–49	72–79	84–93	8–10	14–15
Lee	(2)	Current	43–49	67–76	81–91	—	—
China	(3)	Current	49	72·5	85·5	8·26	15+
USSR	(4)	Current	17·9	17·4	17·2	n.a.	n.a.
Billions of Dollars							
CIA	(5)	1977	105	120	130	4·5	—
CIA	(6)	Current	66–99	105–108	130	—	—
Lee	(7)	1970	80–105	97–133	110–147	5	—

(1) *Estimated Soviet Defense Spending in Roubles*, CIA SR 78-10121, June 1978.

(2) W. T. Lee, 'Soviet Defense Expenditures in the 10th FYP', *Osteuropa Wirtschaft*, No. 4, 1977; W. T. Lee, *The Estimation of Soviet Defense Expenditures, 1955–75: An Unconventional Approach* (New York: Praeger, 1977).

(3) *Peking Review*, November 1975, January 1976. Extrapolation to 1977 using their growth rate.

(4) Official declared budget.

(5) *A Dollar Cost Comparison of Soviet and US Defense Activities 1966–1977*, CIA SR 78-10002, January 1978. 1970 and 1975 figures taken from diagram.

(6) *Ibid.*; 1977 prices converted to current ones using wholesale price index.

(7) W. T. Lee, 'Soviet Defense Expenditures' in W. Schneider and F. P. Hoeber (eds), *Arms, Man & Military Budgets, Issues for Fiscal Year 1977* (New York: Crane Russak, 1976). 1977 figures by extrapolation.

The Alliances and Europe

THE WARSAW PACT

Treaties

The Warsaw Pact is a multilateral military alliance formed by the 'Treaty of Friendship, Mutual Assistance and Co-operation' which was signed in Warsaw on 14 May 1955 by the Governments of the Soviet Union, Albania, Bulgaria, Czechoslovakia, East Germany, Hungary, Poland and Romania; Albania left the Pact in September 1968. The Pact is committed to the defence only of the European territories of the member states.

The Soviet Union is also linked by bilateral treaties of friendship and mutual assistance with Bulgaria, Czechoslovakia, East Germany, Hungary, Poland and Romania. Members of the Warsaw Pact have similar bilateral treaties with each other. The essence of East European defence arrangements is not therefore dependent on the Warsaw Treaty as such. The Soviet Union concluded status-of-forces agreements with Poland, East Germany, Romania and Hungary between December 1956 and May 1957 and with Czechoslovakia in October 1968; all remain in effect except the one with Romania, which lapsed in June 1958 when Soviet troops left Romania.

Organization

The Political Consultative Committee consists, in full session, of the First Secretaries of the Communist Party, Heads of Government and the Foreign and Defence Ministers of the member countries. The Committee has a Joint Secretariat, headed by a Soviet official and consisting of a representative from each country, and a Permanent Commission, whose task is to make recommendations on general questions of foreign policy for Pact members. Both are located in Moscow.

Since the reorganization of the Pact in 1969 the non-Soviet Ministers of Defence are no longer directly subordinate to the Commander-in-Chief of the Pact but, together with the Soviet Minister, form the Council of Defence Ministers, which is the highest military body in the Pact. The second military body, the Joint High Command, is required by the Treaty 'to strengthen the defensive capability of the Warsaw Pact, to prepare military plans in case of war and to decide on the deployment of troops'. The Command consists of a Commander-in-Chief and a Military Council. This Council meets under the chairmanship of the C-in-C and includes the Chief-of-Staff and permanent military representatives from each of the allied armed forces. It seems to be the main channel through which the Pact's orders are transmitted to its forces in peacetime and through which the East European forces are able to put their point of view to the C-in-C. The Pact also has a Military Staff, which includes non-Soviet senior officers. The posts of C-in-C and Chief-of-Staff of the Joint High Command have, however, always been held by Soviet officers, and most of the key positions are still in Soviet hands.

In the event of war, the forces of the other Pact members would be operationally subordinate to the Soviet High Command. The command of the air defence system covering the whole Warsaw Pact area is now centralized in Moscow and directed by the C-in-C of the Soviet Air Defence Forces. Among the Soviet military headquarters in the Warsaw Pact area are the Northern Group of Forces at Legnica in Poland; the Southern Group of Forces at Budapest; the Group of Soviet Forces in Germany at Zossen-Wünsdorf, near Berlin; and the Central Group of Forces at Milovice, north of Prague. Soviet tactical air forces are stationed in Poland, East Germany, Hungary and Czechoslovakia.

The Soviet Union has deployed short-range surface-to-surface missile (ssm) launchers and nuclear-capable aircraft in Eastern Europe. Most East Euroean countries also have short-range ssm launchers, but there is no evidence that nuclear warheads for their missiles have been supplied. Longer-range Soviet ssm and aircraft are based in the Soviet Union.

BULGARIA

Population: 8,850,000
Military Service: Army and Air Force 2 years, Navy 3 years.
Total regular forces: 150,000 (94,000 conscripts).
Estimated GNP 1977: $18.6 bn.
Defence expenditure 1978: 518 m leva ($432 m).
$1 = 1.2 leva.

Army: 115,000 (75,000 conscripts).
8 mot rifle divs.*
5 tk bdes.
1 AB regt.
3 SSM bdes with *Scud.*
4 arty regts.
3 AA arty regts.
1 mountain bn.
2 recce bns.
125 T-34, 1,800 T-54/-55 med tks; 290 BRDM-1/-2 scout cars; 1,500 BTR-60, 35 OT-62 APC; 200 85mm, 400 122mm, 95 152mm guns/how; 82mm, 350 120mm, 160mm mor; BM-21 122mm RL; 36 *FROG*-7, 20 *Scud* SSM; 76mm ATK guns; 130 82mm RCL; *Sagger, Snapper* ATGW; 57mm, 85mm AA guns; SA-6/-7 SAM.

RESERVES: 200,000.

Navy: 10,000 (6,000 conscripts).
4 submarines (ex-Soviet, 2 W- and 2 R-class).
2 *Riga*-class escorts.
3 *Poti*-, 6 SO-1-class coastal escorts.
4 *Osa*-I-class FPBG with *Styx* SSM.
4 *Shershen*- and 4 P-4-class MTB.
6 MCM ships (2 T-43-, 4 *Vanya*-class).
24 PO-2-class small patrol/minesweeping boats.
20 landing craft (10 *Vydra*-, 10 MFP-class).
6 Mi-4 ASW hel.

RESERVES: 15,000.

Air Force: 25,000 (13,000 conscripts); 263 combat aircraft.
6 FGA sqns with 72 MiG-17, some MiG-23/-27.
10 interceptor sqns: 4 with 53 MiG-21, 1 with 20 MiG-19, 5 with 64 MiG-17.
3 recce sqns with 10 MiG-21, 24 MiG-15.
1 tpt regt with 6 Il-14, 4 Il-18, 4 An-24, 2 Tu-134.
1 hel regt with 30 Mi-4, 30 Mi-2 and Mi-8.
Operational trainers incl 20 MiG-21U; other trg ac incl 80 L-29, Yak-11/-18, 50 MiG-15/-17/-21UTI.
AA-2 *Atoll* AAM.
26 SA-2, 8 SA-3 SAM bns.
1 para regt.

RESERVES: 20,000.

Para-Military Forces: 15,000 border guards with AFV; 12,000 construction troops; 12,000 security police; 150,000 volunteer People's Militia.

CZECHOSLOVAKIA

Population: 15,070,000.
Military service: 2 years.
Total regular forces: 186,000 (110,000 conscripts).
Estimated GNP 1977: $49.6 bn.
Defence expenditure 1978: 19.45 bn koruny ($1.82 bn).
$1 = 10.7 koruny.

Army: 140,000 (95,000 conscripts).
5 tk divs.*
5 motor rifle divs.*
1 AB regt.
3 SSM bdes with *Scud.*
2 ATK regts.
2 arty, 2 AA arty bdes.
3,400 T-54/-55 med tks; 680 OT-65, BRDM scout cars; 200 BMP MICV; 2,000 OT-62/-64/-810 APC; 300 100mm, 600 122mm, 50 130mm, 120 152mm guns/how; 122mm SP guns; 81mm, 120mm mor; 250 RM-70 122mm, M-51 130mm RL; 40 *FROG*, 27 *Scud* SSM; 125 82mm RCL; 125 *Sagger* ATGW; 200 57mm towed, M53/59 30mm SP AA guns; SA-4/-6/-7 SAM.

RESERVES: 300,000.

Air Force: 46,000 (15,000 conscripts); 613 combat aircraft.
13 FGA sqns with 80 Su-7, 36 MiG-15, 42 MiG-21, 12 MiG-23.
18 interceptor sqns with 240 MiG-21, 7 MiG-15.
6 recce sqns with 24 MiG-21R, 48 L-29.
Tpts incl 6 An-24, 53 Il-14, 1 Tu-134.
Hel incl 90 Mi-1/-2, 100 Mi-4, 20 Mi-8.
Operational trainers incl 6 Su-7B, 34 MiG-21U, 60 L-29, 24 L-39.
AA-2 *Atoll* AAM.
28 SA-2/-3 SAM bns.

RESERVES: 50,000.

Para-Military Forces: 10,000 border guards, some APC, 82mm RCL; about 120,000 part-time People's Militia, 2,500 Civil Defence Troops.

GERMAN DEMOCRATIC REPUBLIC

Population: 16,830,000.
Military service: 18 months.
Total regular forces: 157,000 (92,000 conscripts).
Estimated GNP 1977: $54.6 bn.
Defence expenditure 1977: 11.02 bn Ostmarks ($3.15 bn).
$1 = 3.5 Ostmarks.

* East European Warsaw Pact divs are of three categories with different manning (and hence readiness) levels. Category 1 formations are at up to three-quarters of establishment strength; Category 2 at up to half; Category 3 little more than cadres.

Army: 105,000 (67,000 conscripts).
2 tk divs.*
4 motor rifle divs.*
2 ssm bdes with *Scud*.
2 arty regts.
2 AA arty regts.
1 AB bn.
2 ATK bns.
About 2,500 T-54/-55 med tks (600 T-34 in storage);
about 120 PT-76 lt tks; 880 BRDM-1/-2,
FUG-66 scout cars; 1,500 BMP MICV, BTR-50P/
-60P/-152 APC; 335 122mm, 100 130mm, 72
152mm guns/how; 250 120mm mor; 108
BM-21 122mm, RM-70 122mm RL; 24 *FROG*-7,
16 *Scud* B SSM; 100mm ATK guns; *Sagger*,
Snapper ATGW; 130 57mm, 65 100mm towed, 105
ZSU-23-4 SP AA guns; SA-4/-7 SAM.

RESERVES: 250,000.

Navy: 16,000 (10,000 conscripts).
1 *Riga*-class frigate.
4 SO-1-, 14 *Hai*-class submarine chasers.
12 *Osa*-I-, 3 *Osa*-II-class FPBG with *Styx* SSM.
45 MTB (18 *Shershen*-, 27 *Libelle*-class).
24 coastal patrol craft (coastguard).
34 *Kondor*-class coastal minesweepers.
5 *Frosch*-, 3 *Robbe*-class LST, 7 *Labo*-class LCT.
2 *Kondor*-class intelligence collection vessels (AGI).
1 hel sqn with 8 Mi-4, 5 Mi-8.

RESERVES: 25,000.

Air Force: 36,000 (15,000 conscripts); 362 combat
aircraft.
3 FGA sqns with 35 MiG-17.
18 interceptor sqns with 270 MiG-21.
1 recce sqn with 12 MiG-21, 4 Il-14.
2 tpt sqns with 20 Il-14, 3 Tu-124, 8 Tu-134.
6 hel sqns with 46 Mi-1, 18 Mi-4, 40 Mi-8 hel.
41 MiG-21U, L-39 trainers.
AA-2 *Atoll* AAM.
5 AD regts with 120 57mm and 100mm AA guns.
2 SAM bns with 22 SA-2, 4 SA-3.
2 para bns.

RESERVES: 30,000.

Para-Military Forces: 71,500. 46,500 border
guards, some tks, AFV, 24 coastal craft; 25,000
security troops, 500,000 Workers' Militia.

HUNGARY

Population: 10,670,000.
Military service: 2 years (incl Border Guard).
Total regular forces: 114,000 (78,000 conscripts).
Estimated GNP 1977: $25.2 bn.
Defence expenditure 1978: 14.41 bn forints
($658 m).
$1 = 21.9 forints.

Army: 91,000 (70,000 conscripts).
1 tk div.*
5 motor rifle divs.*
1 ssm bde with *Scud*.
3 arty regts.
2 AA arty regts.
1 SAM regt with SA-6.
1 AB bn.
Danube Flotilla.
About 1,000 T-54/-55 med, 100 PT-76 lt tks; about
600 FUG-65/-66 scout cars; 1,500 PSZH APC;
250 122mm, 36 152mm guns/how; 300 82mm,
100 120mm mor; 75 BM-21 122mm RL; 24
FROG, 12 *Scud* SSM; 300 57mm and 85mm ATK
guns; 75 *Sagger*, *Snapper* ATGW; 200 57mm and
100mm towed, 40 ZSU-23-4 and ZSU-57-2 SP
AA guns; 20 SA-6, SA-7, 50 SA-9 SAM; 10 100-ton
patrol craft, river MCM, 5 small landing craft.

RESERVES: 130,000.

Air Force: 23,000 (8,000 conscripts); 180 combat
aircraft.
6 interceptor sqns with 116 MiG-21.
About 20 An-2/-24/-26, 10 Il-14, 10 Li-2 tpts.
About 30 Mi-1/-2, 35 Mi-8, Ka-26 hel.
53 MiG-15UTI, 11 MiG-21U, Yak-11/-18, 20
L-29/-39 trainers.
AA-2 *Atoll* AAM.
14 SAM bns with SA-2.

RESERVES: 13,000.

Para-Military Forces: 15,000 border guards (11,000
conscripts) with lt inf weapons; 60,000 part-time
Workers' Militia.

POLAND

Population 34,950,000.
Military service: Army, internal security forces,
Air Force 2 years; Navy, special services 3 years.
Total regular forces: 306,500 (190,000 conscripts).
Estimated GNP 1977: $86.1 bn.
Defence expenditure 1978: 58.8 bn zloty ($2.55 bn).
$1 = 23.1 zloty.

Army: 222,000 (166,000 conscripts).
5 tk divs.*
8 motor rifle divs.*
1 AB div.*
1 amph assault div.*
4 ssm bdes with *Scud*.
3 arty bdes, 1 arty regt.
6 AA arty regts.
3 ATK regts.
3,800 T-34/-54/-55 med, 300 PT-76 lt tks; 2,000
OT-65 and BRDM-1/-2 scout cars; BMP MICV;
OT-62/-64 APC; 400 76mm, 85mm, 700 122mm,

---

* See note on p. 13.

150 152mm guns/how; 122mm SP guns; 600 82mm, 120mm mor; 250 BM-21 122mm, 140mm RL; 52 *FROG*-3/-7, 36 *Scud* SSM; 76mm, 85mm towed, ASU-85 SP ATK guns; 73mm, 82mm, 107mm RCL; *Sagger* ATGW; 400 23mm, 57mm, 85mm, 100mm towed, ZSU-23-4, 24-ZSU-57-2 SP AA guns; SA-6/-7/-9 SAM.

DEPLOYMENT: *Egypt* (UNEF): 957; *Syria* (UNDOF): 90.

RESERVES: 500,000.

Navy: 22,500, incl Marines and 6,000 conscripts.
4 W-class submarines.
1 *Kotlin*-class destroyer with 2 *Goa* SAM.
13 *Osa*-class FPBG with *Styx* SSM.
22 large patrol craft (some coastguard).
21 MTB (15 *Wisla*-, 6 P-6-class).
12 *Krogulec*-, 12 T-43-class ocean minesweepers, 20 K-8-class minesweeping boats.
23 *Polnocny*-class LCT and 15 landing craft.
2 trg ships.
1 Naval Aviation Regt (60 combat aircraft):
  1 lt bbr/recce sqn with 10 Il-28.
  4 fighter sqns with 12 MiG-15, 38 MiG-17.
  2 hel sqns with some 25 Mi-1/-2/-4.

RESERVES: 45,000.

Air Force: 62,000 (18,000 conscripts); 725 combat aircraft.
1 lt bbr sqn with 6 Il-28.
15 FGA sqns: 14 with 160 MiG-17 and 30 Su-7, 1 with 28 Su-20.
33 interceptor sqns with 80 MiG-17, 340 MiG-21.
6 recce sqns with 72 MiG-15/-21, 5 Il-28, 4 Il-14.
Some 50 tpts, incl 22 An-12/-24/-26, 21 Il-14/-18/ -62, 4 Tu-134, 5 Yak-40.
165 Mi-1/-2, 19 Mi-4, 26 Mi-8 hel.
300 trainers, incl *Iskra*, MiG-15/-17/-21UTI, Il-28.
AA-2 *Atoll* AAM.
36 SA-2, 12 SA-3 SAM bns.

RESERVES: 60,000.

Para-Military Forces: 95,000: 18,000 Border Troops (Ministry of Interior), 77,000 Internal Security and Internal Defence Troops (incl 21,000 Construction Troops). Some tks, AFV, ATK guns; 34 small boats operated by coastguard; 350,000 Citizens' Militia.

ROMANIA

Population: 21,670,000.
Military service: Army and Air Force 16 months, Navy 2 years.
Total regular forces: 180,500 (110,000 conscripts).

Estimated GNP 1977: $51.4 bn.
Defence expenditure 1978: 12.0 bn lei ($923 m). $1 = 13.0 lei.

Army: 140,000 (95,000 conscripts).
2 tk divs.*
8 motor rifle divs.*
2 mountain bdes.
1 AB regt.
2 SSM bdes with *Scud*.
2 arty bdes.
3 arty regts.
2 ATK regts.
2 AA arty regts.
200 T-34, 1,500 T-54/-55 med tks; 1,000 BRDM scout cars; BTR-50/-60, TAB-70/-72 (BTR-60) APC; 60 76mm, 50 85mm, 600 122mm, 150 152mm guns/how; 130 SU-100 SP guns; 1,000 82mm, 200 120mm mor; 122mm, 150 130mm RL; 30 *FROG*, 20 *Scud* SSM; 57mm ATK guns; 260 76mm and 82mm RCL; 120 *Sagger*, *Snapper* ATGW; 300 30mm, 37mm, 250 57mm, 85mm, 100mm AA guns; SA-6/-7 SAM.

RESERVES: 300,000.

Navy: 10,500 (5,000 conscripts).
6 coastal escorts (3 *Poti*-, 3 *Kronstadt*-class).
5 *Osa*-class FPBG with *Styx* SSM.
13 P-4-class MTB, 12 *Hu Chwan*-class hydrofoils.
18 *Shanghai*-class MGB.
28 patrol craft (19 coastal, 9 river under 100 tons).
30 MCM craft.
4 Mi-4 helicopters.

RESERVES: 20,500.

Air Force: 30,000 (10,000 conscripts); 437 combat aircraft.
5 FGA sqns with 75 MiG-15/-17.
12 interceptor sqns with 27 MiG-15/-19, 210 MiG-21.
1 recce sqn with 15 Il-28.
2 tpt sqns with some 4 Il-14, 4 Il-18, 1 Il-62, 10 An-24, 2 An-26, 12 Li-2, 1 Boeing 707.
6 Mi-4, 20 Mi-8, 45 *Alouette* III hel.
Trainers incl 50 L-29, 50 MiG-15UT1, 10 MiG-21U, 60 IAR-823.
AA-2 *Atoll* AAM.
108 SA-2 *Guideline* at about 18 SAM sites.

RESERVES: 25,000.

Para-Military Forces: 37,000: 17,000 border, 20,000 security troops with AFV, ATK guns. About 700,000 Patriotic Guard.

---

* See note on p. 13.

THE NORTH ATLANTIC TREATY

Treaties

The North Atlantic Treaty was signed in 1949 by Belgium, Britain, Canada, Denmark, France, Iceland, Italy, Luxembourg, the Netherlands, Norway, Portugal and the United States; Greece and Turkey joined in 1952, and West Germany in 1955. The Treaty unites Western Europe and North America in a commitment to consult together if the security of any one member is threatened, and to consider an armed attack against one as an attack against all, to be met by such action as each of them deems necessary, 'including the use of armed force, to restore and maintain the security of the North Atlantic area'.

The Paris Agreements of 1954 added a Protocol to the Treaty aimed at strengthening the structure of NATO and revised the Brussels Treaty of 1948, which now includes Italy and West Germany in addition to its original members (Benelux countries, Britain and France). The Brussels Treaty signatories are committed to give one another 'all the military and other aid and assistance in their power' if one is the subject of 'armed aggression in Europe'.

Since 1969 members of the Atlantic Alliance can withdraw on one year's notice; the Brussels Treaty was signed for 50 years.

Organization

The Organization of the North Atlantic Treaty is known as NATO. The governing body of the Alliance, the North Atlantic Council, which has its headquarters in Brussels, consists of Ministers from the fifteen member countries, who normally meet twice a year, and of ambassadors representing each government, who are in permanent session.

In 1966 France left the integrated military organization, and the 14-nation Defence Planning Committee (DPC) was formed, on which France does not sit. It meets at the same level as the Council and deals with questions related to NATO integrated military planning and other matters in which France does not participate. Greece has announced her intention to leave the integrated military organization; her status is under discussion, but she left the DPC in autumn 1974.

Two permanent bodies for nuclear planning were established in 1966. The first, the Nuclear Defence Affairs Committee (NDAC), is open to all NATO members (France, Iceland and Luxembourg do not take part); it normally meets at Defence Minister level once a year to associate non-nuclear members in the nuclear affairs of the alliance. The Secretary-General is Chairman of the NDAC.

The second, the Nuclear Planning Group (NPG), derived from and subordinate to the NDAC, has seven or eight members and is intended to go further into the details of topics raised there. The composition consists, in practice, of Britain, Germany, Italy and the United States, plus three or four other member countries serving in rotation, each for a term of 18 months. On 1 July 1978 these were: Belgium, Denmark and Turkey. The Secretary-General also chairs the NPG.

The Eurogroup, which was set up by West European member states of the Alliance (with the exception of France, Portugal and Iceland) in 1968, is an informal consultative body acting to co-ordinate and improve the West European military contribution to the Alliance. Its activities have included the European Defence Improvement Programme (1970) and agreement on principles of co-operation in the fields of armaments (1972), training (1973) and logistics (1975). Discussion in the Eurogroup of the need to extend European armaments co-operation led to the formation in 1976 of the European Programme Group, open to all European members of the Alliance but independent of it. Its membership now includes France and ten member countries of Eurogroup.

The Council and its Committees are advised on politico-military, financial, economic and scientific aspects of defence planning by the Secretary-General and an international staff. The Council's military advisers are the Military Committee, which gives policy direction to NATO military commands. The Military Committee consists of the Chiefs-of-Staff of all member countries except France, which maintains a liaison staff, and Iceland, which is not represented; in permanent session the Chiefs-of-Staff are represented by Military Representatives, who are located in Brussels together with the Council. The Military Committee has an independent Chairman and is served by an integrated international military staff. The major NATO commanders are responsible to the Committee, although they also have direct access to the Council and heads of Governments.

The principal military commands of NATO are Allied Command Europe (ACE), Allied Command Atlantic (ACLANT) and Allied Command Channel (ACCHAN).

The NATO European and Atlantic Commands participate in the Joint Strategic Planning System at Omaha, Nebraska, but there is no Alliance command specifically covering strategic nuclear forces. The United States has, however, committed a small number of ballistic-missile submarines (and Britain all hers) to the planning control of SACEUR and a larger number to SACLANT.

The Supreme Allied Commander Europe (SACEUR) and the Supreme Allied Commander Atlantic (SACLANT) have always been American officers, and the Commander-in-Chief Channel (CINCCHAN), one of the two deputies to SACEUR and the Deputy SACLANT British; the other deputy to SACEUR is German. SACEUR is also Commander-in-Chief of the United States Forces in Europe.

(i) ALLIED COMMAND EUROPE (ACE) has its headquarters, known as SHAPE (Supreme Headquarters, Allied Powers in Europe), at Casteau, near Mons, in Belgium. It is responsible for the defence of all NATO territory in Europe except Britain, France, Iceland and Portugal, and for that of all Turkey. It also has general responsibility for the air defence of Britain.

The European Command has some 7,000 tactical nuclear warheads in its area. The number of delivery vehicles (aircraft, missiles and howitzers) is over 3,000, spread among all countries excluding Luxembourg. The nuclear explosives, however, are maintained in American custody, with the exception of certain British weapons (there are also French nuclear weapons in France). There is a large number of low-yield weapons, but the average yield of bombs is about 100 kilotons, and of missile warheads, 20 kilotons.

About 66 division-equivalents are available to SACEUR in peacetime. The Command has some 3,100 tactical aircraft, based on about 200 standard NATO airfields, backed up by a system of jointly financed storage depots, fuel pipelines and signal communications. Most land and air forces stationed in the Command are assigned to SACEUR, while naval forces are normally earmarked.

The 2nd French Corps of two divisions (which is not integrated in NATO forces) is stationed in Germany under a status agreement reached between the French and German Governments. Co-operation with NATO forces and commands has been agreed between the commanders concerned.

The following Commands are subordinate to Allied Command Europe:

(a) *Allied Forces Central Europe* (AFCENT) has command of both the land forces and the air forces in the Central European Sector. Its headquarters are at Brunssum in the Netherlands, and its Commander (CINCCENT) is a German general.

The forces of the Central European Command include 26 divisions, assigned by Belgium, Britain, Canada, West Germany, the Netherlands and the United States, and about 1,400 tactical aircraft.

The Command is sub-divided into Northern Army Group (NORTHAG) and Central Army Group (CENTAG). NORTHAG, responsible for the defence of the sector north of the Göttingen-Liege axis, includes the Belgian, British and Dutch divisions and four German divisions and is supported by 2nd Allied Tactical Air Force (ATAF), composed of Belgian, British, Dutch and German units. (One newly-formed American brigade is being stationed in the NORTHAG area.) American forces, seven German divisions and the Canadian battle group are under CENTAG, supported by the 4th ATAF, which includes American, German and Canadian units and an American Army Air Defense Command. Allied Air Force, Central Europe (AAFCE) was set up in 1974 to provide centralized control of air forces in the sector.

(b) *Allied Forces Northern Europe* (AFNORTH) has its headquarters at Kolsaas, Norway, and is responsible for the defence of Denmark, Norway, Schleswig-Holstein and the Baltic Approaches. The commander (CINCNORTH) has always been a British general. Most of the Danish and Norwegian land, sea and tactical air forces are earmarked for it, and most of their active reserves assigned to it. Germany has assigned one division, two combat air wings and her Baltic fleet. Apart from exercises and some small units, US naval forces do not normally operate in this area.

(c) *Allied Forces Southern Europe* (AFSOUTH) has its headquarters at Naples, and its commander (CINCSOUTH) is an American admiral. Its main responsibilities are to deter aggression, to safeguard the sea lanes of communication in the Mediterranean and to defend the territorial integrity of Greece, Italy and Turkey. It is also responsible for the air defence of the Southern Region in peace and war and for naval operations in the Mediterranean and Black Seas. Ground forces include 22 division-equivalents from Turkey, 13 from Greece and 8 from Italy, as well as the tactical air forces of these countries. Other forces have been earmarked for AFSOUTH, as have the US Navy's Sixth Fleet and naval forces from Italy. Naval forces from Greece and Turkey will act in support of NATO's plans in the Region. The ground-defence system is based upon two separate commands: the Southern, comprising Italy and the approaches to it, under an Italian commander (LANDSOUTH) and South-eastern (LANDSOUTHEAST), comprising Turkey, under a Turkish commander. Command arrangements for Greece await the resolution of Greece's relationship to the integrated military structure of NATO. There is also an overall air command (AIRSOUTH), and there are two naval commands (NAVSOUTH and STRIKFORSOUTH) responsible to AFSOUTH, with headquarters in Naples.

Maritime patrol aircraft from Southern Region nations and the United States operate in the Mediterranean, co-ordinated by Maritime Air Forces Mediterranean (MARAIRMED), a functional command of NAVSOUTH. French aircraft participate. Submarine Force Mediterranean (SUBMED), another functional command of NAVSOUTH, is responsible for the conduct of submarine operations throughout the Mediterranean. COMARAIRMED and COMSUBMED are American rear admirals.

The Allied Naval On Call Force Mediterranean (NAVOCFORMED) consists of a ship from each of the allied powers concerned with the Southern Region, including the United Kingdom and the United States, and is activated twice each year for a month.

(d) *United Kingdom Air Forces* (UKAIR) has its headquarters at High Wycombe, England.

(e) *ACE Mobile Force* (AMF), with headquarters at Seckenheim, Germany, has been formed with particular reference to the northern and south-eastern flanks. Found by seven countries, it comprises seven infantry battalion groups, an armoured reconnaissance squadron, six artillery batteries, helicopter detachments and ground-support fighter squadrons, but has no air transport of its own.

(II) ALLIED COMMAND ATLANTIC (ACLANT) has its headquarters at Norfolk, Virginia, and is responsible for the North Atlantic area from the North Pole to the Tropic of Cancer, including Portuguese coastal waters. The commander is an American admiral.

In the event of war, its duties are to participate in the strategic strike and to protect sea communications. There are no forces assigned to the command in peacetime except Standing Naval Force Atlantic (STANAVFORLANT), which normally consists, at any one time, of four destroyer-type ships. However, for training purposes and in the event of war, forces which are predominantly naval are earmarked for assignment by Britain, Canada, Denmark, Germany, the Netherlands, Portugal and the United States. There are six subordinate commands: Western Atlantic, Eastern Atlantic, Iberian Atlantic, Striking Fleet Atlantic, Submarine Command and STANAVFORLANT. The nucleus of the Striking Fleet Atlantic has been provided by the United States 2nd Fleet with some five attack carriers; carrier-based aircraft share the nuclear strike role with missile-firing submarines.

(III) ALLIED COMMAND CHANNEL (ACCHAN) has its headquarters at Northwood, near London. The commander (CINCCHAN) is a British admiral. The wartime role of Channel Command is to exercise control of the English Channel and the southern North Sea. Many of the smaller warships of Belgium, Britain and the Netherlands are earmarked for this Command, as are some maritime aircraft. There are arrangements for co-operation with French naval forces. A Standing Naval Force, Channel (STANAVFORCHAN) was formed in 1973 to consist of mine counter-measures ships from Belgium, Germany, the Netherlands and Britain; other interested nations might participate on a temporary basis. Its operational command is vested in CINCCHAN.

BELGIUM

Population: 9,930,000.
Military service: 8 or 10 months.*
Total armed forces: 87,100 (26,600 conscripts).
Estimated GNP 1977: $73.4 bn.
Defence expenditure 1977: 66.47 bn francs
    ($1.82 bn).
        $1 = 36.62 francs (1977).

Army: 63,400, incl Medical Service and 22,600
    conscripts.
1 armd bde.
3 mech inf bdes.
3 recce bns.
2 mot inf bns.
1 para-cdo regt.
3 arty bns.
1 SSM bn with 4 *Lance.*
2 SAM bns with 24 *HAWK.*
5 engr bns (3 fd, 1 bridge, 1 eqpt).
4 aviation sqns.
334 *Leopard,* 52 M-47 med, 136 *Scorpion* lt tks; 154
    Scimitar AFV; 1,229 M-75 and AMX-VCI, 174
    Spartan APC; 22 105mm, 15 203mm how; 96
    M-108 105mm, 25 M-44, 41 M-109 155mm, 11
    M-110 203mm SP how; 5 *Lance* SSM; 80 JPK C-90
    SP ATK guns; *ENTAC, Milan* ATGW; 41 *Striker*
    AFV with *Swingfire* ATGW; 114 20mm, 40mm,
    57mm AA guns; 60 *HAWK* SAM; 6 Piper *Super
    Cub,* 12 BN *Islander* ac, 74 *Alouette* II hel; 31
    Epervier RPV. (90 *Spartan* APC, 55 *Gepard* SP AA
    guns, *Swingfire* ATGW on order.)

DEPLOYMENT: *Germany:* 27,000; 1 corps HQ, 2 div
    HQ, 1 armd bde, 2 mech inf bdes.

RESERVES: 50,000: 10,000 train every year, 1 mech,
    1 mot inf bde train every three years.

Navy: 4,300 (800 conscripts).
4 frigates with *Exocet* SSM, *Sea Sparrow* SAM.
7 ocean minehunters (ex-US).
6 coastal minesweepers/minehunters.
14 inshore minesweepers.
2 log support and comd ships (for MCM).
6 river patrol boats.
3 *Alouette* III hel.

RESERVES: 4,400.

Air Force: 19,400 (3,200 conscripts); 148 combat
    aircraft.
2 FB sqns with 36 F/TF-104G.
3 FB sqns with 54 *Mirage* VBA/D.
2 AWX sqns with 36 F-104G, 4 TF-104G.
1 recce sqn with 18 *Mirage* VBR.
2 tpt sqns with 12 C-130H, 3 HS-748, 6 *Merlin*
    IIIA, 2 *Falcon* 20, 2 Boeing 727QC.
1 SAR sqn with 4 HSS-1, 5 *Sea King* Mk 48 hel.
37 *Magister,* 33 SF-260, 12 T-33 trainers.

Sidewinder AAM.
8 SAM sqns with *Nike Hercules.*
(116 F-16A/B fighters, 33 *AlphaJet* trg ac, *Super
    Sidewinder,* AIM-7E *Sparrow* AAM, 40 BDX APC
    on order.)

Para-Military Forces: 16,500 Gendarmerie with 62
    FN armd cars, 5 *Alouette* II, 3 *Puma* hel.

BRITAIN

Population: 56,700,000.
Military service: voluntary.
Total armed forces: 313,253 (14,649 women and
    8,100 enlisted outside Britain).
Estimated GNP 1977: $263.6 bn.
Defence expenditure 1978–79: £6.92 bn ($13.04 bn).
    $1 = £0.531 (1978), £0.582 (1977).

Strategic forces:
SLBM: 4 SSBN, each with 16 *Polaris* A3 missiles.
Ballistic Missile Early Warning System (BMEWS)
    station at Fylingdales.

Army: 160,837 (5,740 women and 7,400 enlisted
    outside Britain).
10 armd regts.
9 armd recce regts.
47 inf bns.
3 para bns (1 in para role).
5 Gurkha bns.
1 special air service (SAS) regt.
1 msl regt with *Lance* SSM.
3 AD regts with *Rapier* SAM.
1 hy, 13 field, 1 GW, 1 cdo, 1 ATK, 1 locating arty
    regts.
10 engr regts.
6 army aviation regts.
900 *Chieftain* med, 271 FV101 *Scorpion* lt tks; 243
    Saladin armd cars; 290 *Scimitar,* 178 FV438/
    FV712 AFV; 1,429 *Ferret,* 200 *Fox* scout cars;
    2,338 FV432, 600 *Saracen,* 60 *Spartan* APC; 100
    105mm pack how and lt guns; 155 *Abbot* 105mm,
    FH70 155mm, 50 M-109 155mm, 31 M-107
    175mm, 16 M-110 203mm SP guns/how; 12 *Lance*
    SSM; 84mm *Carl Gustav,* 120mm RCL; *Milan,
    Swingfire* ATGW; FV102 *Striker* with ATGW;
    L/70 40mm AA guns; *Blowpipe, Rapier/Blindfire*
    SAM; 100 *Scout,* 7 *Alouette* II, 20 *Sioux,* 150
    Gazelle, 20 *Lynx* hel. (FH70 155mm guns,
    TOW ATGW on order.)

DEPLOYMENT AND ORGANIZATION:
United Kingdom. United Kingdom Land Forces
    (UKLF): United Kingdom Mobile Force (UKMF) –
    6th Field Force with 5 (3 regular, 2 TAVR) inf

---

* Conscripts serve 8 months if posted to Germany, 10
months if serving in Belgium.

bns and log spt gp; 7th Field Force with 3 regular, 2 TAVR bns; 8th Field Force (3 regular, 2 TAVR bns for Home Defence); 1 bn gp (for ACE Mobile Force (Land)), 1 SAS regt (−), 1 Gurkha inf bn. HQ Northern Ireland: 3 inf bde HQ, 1 armd recce regt, variable number of major units in inf role,* 3 engr, 2 army aviation sqns and elements of SAS.

Germany. British Army of the Rhine (BAOR): 55,000: 1 corps HQ, 4 armd divs, 5th field force, 1 arty div. Berlin: 3,000 (Berlin Field Force).

Brunei: 1 Gurkha bn.

Hong Kong: Gurkha Field Force with 1 British, 3 Gurkha inf bns, 1 hel flt, 1 engr sqn, spt units.

Cyprus: 1 inf bn less 2 coys, 1 armd recce sqn, 1 hel flt and log support with UNFICYP; 1 inf bn plus 2 inf coys, 1 armd recce sqn, 1 hel flt in garrison at Sovereign Base Areas.

Gibraltar: 1 inf bn, 1 engr tp.

Belize: 1 inf bn, 1 inf bn (−), 1 armd recce tp, 1 arty bty, 1 engr sqn, 1 hel flt.

RESERVES: 116,800 Regular reserves. 60,700 Territorial and Army Volunteer Reserve (TAVR): 2 armd recce regts, 38 inf bns, 2 SAS, 2 med, 3 lt AD, 7 engr regts. 7,800 Ulster Defence Regiment: 11 bns.

Navy: 67,770, incl Fleet Air Arm, Royal Marines, 4,003 women and 400 enlisted outside Britain; 72 major surface combat vessels.

Submarines, attack:
10 nuclear, 17 diesel.

Surface ships:
1 aircraft carrier (30 ac, 9 hel).
2 ASW/cdo carriers (1 with *Seacat* SAM, hels; 1 in reserve).
2 assault ships with *Seacat* SAM (1 trg).
2 hel cruisers each with 4 *Sea King* hel, *Seacat* SAM.
11 GW destroyers (7 County-class with *Seaslug*, *Seacat* SAM, ASW hel, 4 with *Exocet* SSM; 1 Type 82 with *Sea Dart* SAM, *Ikara* ASW; 3 Type 42 with *Sea Dart* SAM, ASW hel).
55 frigates: 49 GP (8 Type 21 with *Exocet* SSM, *Seacat* SAM, 1 *Lynx* hel; 26 *Leander*-class, all with 1 *Wasp* hel, 14 with *Exocet* SSM, 8 with *Ikara* ASW, 25 with *Seacat* SAM, 1 with *Seawolf* SAM; 7 Tribal-, 8 *Rothesay*-class with *Seacat* SAM and 1 *Wasp* hel); 2 Type 41 AA; 2 Type 61 aircraft direction with *Seacat* SAM; 2 ASW (1 Type 12 (trg), 1 Type 14).
33 coastal minesweepers/minehunters (3 trg).
5 inshore minesweepers (trg).
5 *Island*-class offshore patrol vessels.
4 *Bird*-class patrol craft, 5 *Ton*-class coastal patrol, 1 FPB.
13 survey, 1 ice patrol, 1 Royal Yacht/hospital, 3 depot/support ships.
3 hovercraft (2 SRN-6, 1 BH-N7).

Included above are 1 nuclear, 6 diesel subs, 1 hel cruiser, 1 ASW/cdo carrier, 1 assault ship, 1 GW destroyer, 12 frigates, 4 minesweepers in reserve or undergoing refit. (2 ASW cruisers, 3 SSN, 7 destroyers, 4 frigates, 2 MCM, 2 offshore patrol building; *Ikara* ASW msls, *Sub-Harpoon* underwater-to-surface GW, *Sea Skua* ASM on order.)

THE FLEET AIR ARM:
1 strike sqn with 14 *Buccaneer* S2.
1 FGA sqn with 14 *Phantom* FG1.
1 AEW sqn with 7 *Gannet* AEW3, 1 COD4, 3 T5.
7 ASW hel sqns: 5 with 29 *Sea King* (4 sqns embarked), 1 of 39 *Wasp* flts, 1 of 6 *Wessex* 3 flts, 4 *Lynx* flts.
1 cdo assault sqn with 16 *Wessex* 5.
3 SAR flts: 2 with *Wessex* HAS-1, 1 with *Wessex* 5.
1 utility hel sqn with *Wessex* 5.
5 trg sqns with *Sea King, Wasp, Wessex* 3/5, *Lynx*.
(35 *Sea Harrier* VTOL ac, 21 *Sea King*, 60 *Lynx* hel on order.)

THE ROYAL MARINES: 7,468.
1 cdo bde with 4 cdo gps, 1 lt hel sqn, spt units.
120mm RCL; SS-11 ATGW; *Blowpipe* SAM; *Milan* ATGW; 12 *Gazelle* hel. (4 *Lynx* hel on order.)

DEPLOYMENT:
Malta: 1 indep cdo coy gp (to be withdrawn by April 1979).
Falkland Islands: 1 det.

RESERVES (naval and Marines): 29,100 regular and 6,500 volunteers.

Air Force: 84,646 (4,906 women and 300 enlisted outside Britain); about 511 combat aircraft.
6 strike sqns with 48 *Vulcan* B2.
4 strike sqns with 50 *Buccaneer* S2.
3 close support sqns with 48 *Harrier* GR3.
6 attack and close support sqns with 72 *Jaguar* GR1.
9 interceptor sqns: 2 with 24 *Lightning* F6, 7 with 72 *Phantom* FG1/FGR2.
5 recce sqns: 1 with 8 *Vulcan* SR2, 2 with 24 *Jaguar* GR1, 2 with 22 *Canberra* PR7/9.
1 AEW sqn with 11 *Shackleton* AEW Mk 2 (to be replaced by *Nimrod*).
4 MR sqns with 28 *Nimrod* MR1.
1 ECM sqn with 3 *Nimrod* R Mk 1, 4 *Canberra* B6.
2 tanker sqns with 16 *Victor* K2.
1 strategic tpt sqn with 11 VC-10.
4 tac tpt sqns with 40 C-130.
3 lt comms sqns with HS-125, *Andover, Pembroke, Devon* ac, *Whirlwind* hel.
Operational conversion units with some 97 combat aircraft, incl 9 *Vulcan*, 11 *Buccaneer*, 7 *Canberra*, 21 *Phantom*, 24 *Jaguar*, 7 *Lightning*, 15 *Harrier*, 3 *Nimrod, Andover, Hercules;* trg units with *Hunter, Hawk, Gnat, Bulldog, Jet Provos t,*

---

* Some nine drawn from BAOR on short tours.

C-130, *Victor, Dominie* ac; *Wessex, Whirlwind, Puma, Gazelle* hel.

8 hel sqns: 5 tac tpt (2 with 24 *Puma* HC-1, 3 with 40 *Wessex* HC-2), 3 SAR with 17 *Whirlwind* HAR-10, 8 *Wessex*.

Sidewinder, Sparrow, Red Top, Firestreak AAM; *Martel,* AS.12, AS.30 ASM.

2 SAM sqns with *Bloodhound* 2.

(24 *Harrier* FGA, 11 *Nimrod* AEW, 9 VC-10 tankers, 175 *Hawk, Bulldog* trg ac, 30 *Chinook* hel; *Bloodhound* SAM; *Super Sidewinder, Sky Flash* AAM on order; 385 *Tornado* MRCA (220 FGA, 165 AD) planned.)

ROYAL AIR FORCE REGIMENT:

7 fd and 5 AD sqns with *Rapier* SAM.

1 flt with *Tigercat* SAM.

DEPLOYMENT:

The Royal Air Force includes an operational home command (Strike Command), responsible for the UK Air Defence Region and the Near and Far East, and 1 overseas command (RAF Germany: 8,600). Sqns are deployed overseas as follows:

Germany: 2 *Phantom* FGR2, 2 *Buccaneer,* 5 *Jaguar,* 2 *Harrier,* 1 *Wessex,* 1 *Bloodhound,* 4 *Rapier,* 1 fd sqn RAF Regt.

Gibraltar: Hunter det.

Cyprus: 1 *Whirlwind* (4 ac with UNFICYP); periodic dets of other ac; 1 sqn RAF Regt.

Malta: 1 *Canberra* PR7 (to be withdrawn 1978).

Hong Kong: 1 *Wessex.*

Belize: Harrier (6 ac), *Puma,* 1 sqn RAF Regt.

RESERVES: 30,300 regular; about 300 volunteer.

CANADA

Population: 23,700,000.
Military service: voluntary.
Total armed forces: 80,000 (4,500 women).
Estimated GNP 1977: $US 197.9 bn.
Defence Expenditure 1978–79: $Can 4.13 bn ($US 3.64 bn).
　$US1 = $Can 1.14 (1978), $Can 1.05 (1977).

Army (Land Forces): 29,300.*
Mobile Command (about 17,700 land and air).†
2 bde gps each comprising:
　3 inf bns.
　1 armd regt.
　1 lt arty regt of 2 close support, 1 AD btys.
　1 engr regt.
　support units.
1 special service force comprising:
　1 armd regt.
　1 inf bn.
　1 AB regt.
　1 arty regt of 2 close support btys.
　support units.

1 sigs regt.
32 *Leopard* A2 med tks;‡ 121 *Ferret* scout cars, 174 *Lynx* AFV; 827 M-113 APC; 58 105mm pack, 159 105mm how, 50 M-109 155mm SP how; 810 *Carl Gustav* 84mm RCL; 150 *TOW* ATGW; CL-89 drones; 57 40mm AA guns; 103 *Blowpipe* SAM. (114 *Leopard* med tks, 177 Mowag armd cars, 241 Mowag APC, *TOW* ATGW on order.)

DEPLOYMENT:

Europe: One mech bde gp of 2,800 with 32 *Leopard* med tks, 375 M-113 APC/recce, 24 M-109 155mm SP how.

Cyprus (UNFICYP): 515.
Egypt (UNEF): 855.
Syria (UNDOF): 161.
Lebanon (UNIFIL): 99.
Other UN: 333.

RESERVES: about 15,200 Militia; 99 combat arms units plus support units (all in Mobile Command).

Navy (Maritime): 14,200.*
Maritime Command (about 9,000).†
3 submarines (*Oberon*-class).
4 ASW hel destroyers each with 2 CH-124 (*Sea King*) hel and 2 *Sea Sparrow* SAM.
19 ASW frigates (8 with 1 CH-124 hel, 4 with *ASROC,* 3 in reserve).
3 support ships with 3 CH-124 hel.
6 coastal patrol trg ships.
6 reserve trg vessels.

DEPLOYMENT:

Atlantic: 3 subs, 13 surface (1 in reserve), 2 spt ships.
Pacific: 10 surface (2 in reserve), 1 spt ship.

RESERVES: about 3,200.

Air Force (Air): 36,500;* some 214 combat aircraft.
Air Command (23,000).†

2 trg sqns: 1 with 16 CF-5A, 19 CF-5D; 1 with 10 CF-104, 10 CF-104D.

Air Defence Group:
　4 main, 17 auxiliary sites of Distant Early Warning (*DEW*) Line.
　24 long-range radar sites (*Pine Tree Line*).
　3 AWX sqns with 36 CF-101 *Voodoo.*

---

* The Canadian Armed Forces were unified in 1968; the strengths shown here for army, naval and air forces are only approximate.

† Mobile Command commands army combat forces, and Maritime Command all naval forces. Air Command commands all air forces but Maritime Command has operational control of maritime air forces, and HQ 4 ATAF in Europe operational control of 1 CAG; Air Defence Group is part of NORAD. There are also a Communications Command and a Canadian Forces Training System.

‡ Leased until tanks on order are delivered.

1 ECM sqn with 8 CF-100, 3 CC-117 (*Falcon* 20), 15 T-33.

Air Transport Group:
4 tpt sqns: 2 with 24 C-130E/H, 1 with 5 CC-137 (Boeing 707), 1 with 7 *Cosmopolitan*, 4 CC-117.
4 tpt/SAR sqns with 14 CC-115 *Buffalo*, 8 CC-138 *Twin Otter* ac, 3 CH-113 *Labrador*, 3 CH-113A *Voyageur*, 3 CH-135 (UH-1N) hel. 1 SAR unit with 3 CH-113 hel.
(2 DHC-7 tpts on order.)

Maritime Air Group:
3 maritime patrol sqns, 1 trg and 1 testing sqn with 26 CP-107 *Argus*.
1 MR sqn with 13 CP-121 (*Tracker*).
2 ASW hel sqns with 26 CH-124 (SH-3A).
2 sqns with 9 T-33, 3 CP-121 ac, 6 CH-124 hel.
(18 CP-140 *Aurora* (*Orion*) on order.)

10 Tactical Air Group (10 TAG):
2 fighter sqns with 20 CF-5, 4 CF-5D.
5 hel sqns with 30 CH-135, 37 CH-136 (*Kiowa*).
1 tpt sqn with 8 CH-147 (*Chinook*) hel.

1 Canadian Air Group (1 CAG):
3 fighter sqns with 54 CF-104 and 6 CF-104D. *Sidewinder*, AIM-4D *Falcon* AAM.

DEPLOYMENT:
Europe: 1 Canadian Air Group (1 CAG). 11 CH-136 (*Kiowa*) hel.

RESERVES: 700. Air Reserve Group: 4 wings with DHC-3, DHC-6 and C-47.

DENMARK

Population: 5,080,000.
Military service: 9 months.
Total armed forces: 34,000 (12,270 conscripts).
Estimated GNP 1977: $43.8 bn.
Defence expenditure 1978–79: kr 7.13 bn ($1.28 bn).
$1 = 5.57 kroner (1978), 5.85 kroner (1977).

Army: 21,000 (9,000 conscripts).
3 mech inf bdes, each with 1 tk, 2 mech, 1 arty bn, 1 recce sqn, 1 engr coy, spt units.
2 mech inf bdes, each with 1 tk, 2 mech, 1 arty bn, 1 engr coy, spt units.
1 indep recce bn.
Some indep mot inf bns.
120 *Leopard* 1, 200 *Centurion* med, 48 M-41 lt tks; 630 M-113, 68 M-106 mortar-armed APC; 24 155mm guns; 144 105mm, 96 155mm, 12 203mm* how; 72 M-109 155mm SP how; 120mm mor; 252 106mm RCL; *TOW* ATGW; 224 L/60 and L/70 40mm AA guns; *Hamlet* (*Redeye*) SAM; 9 Saab T-17 lt ac; 12 Hughes OH-6A hel.

DEPLOYMENT: *Cyprus* (UNFICYP): 360.

RESERVES: 4,500 Augmentation Force, subject to immediate recall; 41,000 Field Army Reserve, comprising 12,000 Covering Force Reserve (to bring units to war strength and add 1 mech bn to each bde) and 29,000 other reserve units to provide combat and log support; 24,000 Regional Defence Force, with 21 inf, 7 arty bns, ATK sqns, support units; 56,100 Army Home Guard.

Navy: 6,100 (1,900 conscripts).
6 coastal submarines.
2 frigates with *Harpoon* SSM, *Sea Sparrow* SAM.
5 fishery-protection frigates, each with 1 hel.
2 coastal escorts (corvettes).
6 FPB, 10 FPBG with *Harpoon* SSM.
6 minelayers (2 coastal).
8 coastal minesweepers.
22 large patrol craft.
8 *Alouette* III hel.
(3 corvettes, 1 coastal minelayer, *Harpoon* SSM, 7 *Lynx* hel on order.)

RESERVES: 4,500; Navy Home Guard 4,800.

Air Force: 6,900 (1,370 conscripts); 114 combat aircraft.
1 FB sqn with 20 F-35XD *Draken*.
2 FB sqns with 38 F-100D/F.
2 interceptor sqns with 40 F-104G.
1 recce sqn with 16 RF-35XD *Draken*.
1 tpt sqn with 8 C-47, 3 C-130H.
1 SAR sqn with 8 S-61A hel.
3 TF-35XD *Draken*, 23 Saab T-17 trainers.
8 SAM sqns: 4 with 36 *Nike Hercules*, 4 with 24 *Improved HAWK*.
Sidewinder AAM; *Bullpup* ASM.
(58 F-16A/B fighters on order.)

RESERVES: 8,000; Air Force Home Guard 12,000.

FRANCE

Population: 53,850,000.
Military service: 12 months.
Total armed forces: 502,800† (266,200 conscripts).
Estimated GNP 1977: $374.8 bn.
Defence expenditure 1978: fr 80.77 bn ($17.52 bn).
$1 = 4.61 francs (1978), 4.98 francs (1977).

Strategic forces:
SLBM: 64 SLBM in 4 SSBN: 1 with 16 M-2, 3 with 16 M-20 msls. (1 with M-4 building.)
IRBM: 2 sqns, each with 9 SSBS S-2 msls (to be replaced by S-3).
Aircraft:
Bombers: 6 sqns with 33 *Mirage* IVA.
Tankers: 3 sqns with 11 KC-135F.
Reserve: 16 *Mirage* IVA (incl 12 recce).

---

* Dual-capable; no nuclear warheads on Danish soil.
† Incl 9,400 on inter-service central staff.

Army: 324,400, incl Army Aviation and 209,000 conscripts.*
2 corps HQ.
4 armd divs.
3 mech divs.
2 inf divs.
1 alpine div.
1 air-portable mot div (Marines).
1 para div of 2 bdes.
7 armd car regts.
2 mot inf regts.
Berlin sector force (1 lt armd regt, 1 mech inf regt).
5 SSM regts with 30 *Pluton.*
4 SAM regts with 54 *HAWK.*
1,060 AMX-30 med, 1,100 AMX-13 lt tks; some 960 AFV, incl 410 Panhard EBR hy, 450 AML lt armd cars; 500 AMX-10 MICV, AMX-VCI, 1,500 AMX-13 VTT, 100 VAB APC; 195 Model 56 105mm pack, 115 155mm how; 168 AMX 105mm, 185 155mm SP how; *Pluton* SSM; 265 120mm mor; 105/6mm RCL; SS-11/-12, *Milan, HOT, ENTAC* ATGW; 40mm towed, 30mm SP AA guns; *HAWK, Roland* SAM. (30 AMX-30 med tks; 40 AMX-10 armd cars, 40 AMX-10 MICV, 330 VAB APC; *HOT, Milan* ATGW; 120 *Vadar* 20mm SP AA guns; 35 *Roland* I, 70 *Roland* II SAM on order.)

ARMY AVIATION (ALAT): 6,450.
2 groups, 6 hel regts and 5 regional commands.
30 *Broussard,* 91 L-19 lt ac.
190 *Alouette* II, 70 *Alouette* III, 135 SA-330 *Puma,* 170 SA-341 *Gazelle* hel (20 *Gazelle* on order).

DEPLOYMENT:
Germany: 34,000; 2 mech divs.
Berlin: 2,000; 1 lt armd regt, 1 mech inf regt.
Djibouti: 4,000; 2 inf regts, 1 arty regt, 2 sqns lt tks.
Senegal: 1,000 (all services).
Ivory Coast: 400.
Gabon: 450.
Lebanon (UNIFIL): 1,244; 1 bn and log units.
Chad: 1,500.
Overseas Commands:
There are four overseas commands (Antilles-Guyana, South Indian Ocean, New Caledonia, Polynesia), and two naval comds (ALINDIEN, ALPACI). Some 19,000 from all services are deployed overseas (numbers can vary according to local circumstances); equipment incl: 130 AFV, 36 hel, 9 frigates, 2 FPB, 1 tender ship, 2 lt tpt ships, 12 combat and 15 tpt ac.

RESERVES: about 300,000.

Navy: 68,200, incl Naval Air and 18,400 conscripts; 46 major surface combat vessels.
21 submarines (3 building).
2 lt attack aircraft carriers (each with 40 ac).
1 helicopter carrier (trg ship).
1 cruiser with *Exocet* SSM, *Masurca* SAM.
5 frigates: 2 with *Masurca* SAM and *Malafon* ASW msls, 3 with *Malafon* and ASW hel.
14 destroyers: 8 with *Malafon,* 4 with *Tartar* SAM, 2 GP (1 with *Exocet* SSM and ASW hel, 3 building).
23 escorts (5 building).
16 large patrol craft (12 in reserve).
5 FPBG with SS-12 SSM: 4 *Trident,* 1 *Combattante-*class.
35 ocean and coastal MCM (8 in reserve).
2 LSD, 5 LST, 2 log spt ships, 12 LCT, 29 med landing craft.

NAVAL AIR FORCE: 13,000; 123 combat aircraft.
2 attack sqns with 24 *Etendard* IVM.
2 interceptor sqns with 20 F-8E(FN) *Crusader.*
2 ASW sqns with 24 *Alizé.*
4 MR sqns with 25 *Atlantic,* 10 SP-2H *Neptune.*
1 recce sqn with 8 *Etendard* IVP.
2 OCU with 12 *Etendard* IVM, 14 *Magister,* 4 Nord 262.
3 ASW hel sqns with 12 *Super Frelon,* 12 SH-34J, 8 *Alouette* III.
1 assault hel sqn with 12 SH-34J.
2 SAR sqns with 20 *Alouette* II/III.
1 hel sqn with 4 *Alouette* II, 7 *Super Frelon,* 18 *Lynx.*
9 comms sqns with DC-6, C-47 ac, *Alouette* II/III, 5 *Super Frelon* hel.
4 trg and liaison sqns with Nord 262, C-47, *Falcon, Paris, Alizé, Rallye* ac, *Alouette* II/III hel.
(29 *Super Etendard* fighters, 8 *Lynx* hel on order.)

MARINES: 1 bn.

RESERVES: about 50,000.

Air Force: 100,800 (38,800 conscripts); 471 combat aircraft.
Air Defence Command (CAFDA): 6,300.
  8 interceptor sqns: 2 with 30 *Mirage* IIIC, 6 with 90 *Mirage* F1C.
  4 liaison and comms flts with 15 *Magister,* 13 T-33A, 8 *Broussard.*
  10 SAM bns with *Crotale.*
  Automatic *STRIDA II* air-defence system.
Tactical Air Force (FATAC): 7,400.
  17 FB sqns: 7 with 105 *Mirage* IIIE, 2 with 30 *Mirage* VF, 8 with 105 *Jaguar* A/E.
  2 lt bbr sqns with 16 *Vautour* IIB/N (being withdrawn).
  3 recce sqns with 45 *Mirage* IIIR/RD.
  2 OCU: 1 with 25 *Mirage* IIIB/BE/C, 1 with 25 *Jaguar* E.

---

* The army is being re-structured; the 4 armd and 2 inf divs now have the new establishment of 8,000 men in 2 tk, 2 mech inf, and 2 arty regts and 6,500 men in 3 mot inf, 1 armd car and 1 arty regt respectively. In 1979 the 3 mech divs will re-organize to form 4 more armd and 2 inf divs. (A fifth inf div is to be formed later.) An additional 14 inf divs will be formed on mobilization.

8 liaison and comms flts with 25 *Magister*, 30 T-33A, 10 *Broussard*, 5 *Paris*, 3 *Frégate*, 7 *Noratlas*, 2 *Mystère* 20 ac, 13 *Alouette* II/III hel.

Air Transport Command (COTAM): 4,600.

7 tac tpt sqns: 3 with 45 Transall C-160, 4 with 60 *Noratlas*.

4 tpt sqns with 4 DC-8F, 21 *Frégate*, 8 *Mystère* 20, 5 *Caravelle*, 30 *Paris*, 31 *Broussard* ac, 70 *Alouette* II/III, 18 *Puma* hel.

Sidewinder, R.503, R.550 *Magic* AAM; AS.20, AS.30, *Martel* ASM.

Training Command (CEAA): Some 400 aircraft, incl *Magister*, T-33, *Mystère* IV, *Falcon*, *Flamant*, *Noratlas*, *Broussard*, *Paris*.

(33 *Mirage* F1 fighters, 200 *AlphaJet* trg ac, 4 Transall tpts on order.)

Para-Military Forces: 76,400 Gendarmerie (4,800 conscripts) with 38 AMX-13 lt tks, 160 AML armd cars, 100 *Alouette* II/III hel. 6,900 Service de Santé (230 conscripts).

GERMANY: FEDERAL REPUBLIC OF

Population: 63,410,000 (incl West Berlin).
Military service: 15 months.
Total armed forces: 489,900 (236,000 conscripts);*
 mobilization strength about 1,250,000.
Estimated GNP 1977: $508.6 bn.
Defence expenditure 1978: DM 35.0 bn ($17.26 bn).
 $1 = 2.03 (1978), DM 2.39 (1977).

Army: 336,200 (187,000 conscripts).†
Field Army:
16 armd bdes (each with 2 tk, 1 armd inf, 1 armd arty bns).
12 armd inf bdes (each with 1 tk, 2 armd inf, 1 armd arty bns).
3 lt inf bdes.
2 mountain bdes.
3 AB bdes.
(Organized in 3 corps: 12 divs (4 armd, 4 armd inf, 2 *Jäger*, 1 mountain, 1 AB)).
15 SSM bns: 11 with *Honest John*, 4 with *Lance*.
3 army aviation comds (each with 1 lt, 1 med tpt regt).
Territorial Army:
3 Territorial Commands, 6 Military Districts, 6 Home Defence groups, 28 mot inf bns, 300 inf coys. In support are 4 service support comds, 1 sig bde, 2 sig, 2 engr regts. The Territorial Army provides defensive, comms, police and service units on mobilization.
1,342 M-48A2, 2,437 *Leopard* 1 med tks; 408 Spä Pz-2 *Luchs*, 1,100 SPz 11–2, 460 SPz 12–3 (HS-30) armd cars; 2,136 *Marder* MICV; 4,020 M-113 APC; 275 105mm, 71 155mm how; 586 M-109 155mm, 149 M-107 175mm, 77 M-110 203mm SP guns/how; 956 120mm mor; 209 *LARS* 110mm multiple RL; 65 *Honest John*, 26 *Lance* SSM; 770 KJPz 4–5 SP ATK guns; 106mm RCL; 316 SS-11, 561 *Milan*, 170 *TOW* ATGW; 316 RJPz-2 SP ATGW; 1,731 20mm, 710 40mm, 70 *Gepard* 35mm SP AA guns; 911 *Redeye* SAM; 190 UH-1D, 225 *Alouette* II/III, 109 CH-53G hel; 5 CL-89 drones. (1,800 *Leopard* 2 tks, 214 FH-70, 114 RJPz-3 SP ATGW, 177 *TOW*, 1,939 *Milan* ATGW, 362 *Gepard* AA guns, 140 *Roland* II SAM, 212 PAH-1, 227 BO-105M hel on order.)

Navy: 36,500, incl Naval Air Arm and 11,000 conscripts.
18 Type 206, 6 Type 205 coastal submarines.
7 GW destroyers: 3 with *Tartar* SSM and *ASROC*, 4 with *Exocet* SSM.
4 destroyers.
6 frigates.
5 corvettes.
11 *Rhein*-class combat spt ships.
59 MCM ships (18 coastal, 22 fast, 19 inshore).
10 Type 143, 20 Type 148 FPBG with *Exocet* SSM.
10 *Zobel*-class FPB.
22 utility landing craft.
(6 Type 122 frigates, 10 Type 143A FPB, 12 mine-hunters, 150 *Exocet* SSM, 28 *Roland*, 96 *Sea Sparrow* SAM on order.)

NAVAL AIR ARM: 6,000; 134 combat aircraft.
3 FB sqns with 85 F-104G.
1 recce sqn with 30 RF-104G.
2 MR sqns with 19 *Atlantic*.
1 SAR hel sqn with 21 *Sea King* Mk 41.
1 utility sqn with 20 Do-28 ac.
Kormoran ASM.
(110 *Tornado* FGA on order.)

Air Force: 106,200 (38,000 conscripts); 484 combat aircraft.
16 FGA sqns: 4 with 60 F-4F, 8 with 144 F-104G; 4 with 84 G-91R-3 (to be replaced by *AlphaJet*).
4 AWX sqns with 60 F-4F.
4 recce sqns with 81 RF-4E.
2 OCU with 18 TF-104G, 37 G-91T.
5 tpt sqns with 88 Transall C-160.
4 hel sqns with 114 UH-1D.
Sidewinder AAM; AS.30 ASM.
8 SSM sqns with 72 *Pershing* 1A.
24 SAM btys with 216 *Nike Hercules*.

* The military divisions of the Ministry of Defence, Central Military Agencies, and the Central Medical Agencies comprise 11,000 military personnel. The overall strength of the armed forces includes 5,000 reserve duty training positions.
† The army is being reorganized to form 15 armd bdes (each with 3 tk, 1 armd inf, 1 armd arty bns), 17 armd inf bdes (each with 2 tk, 2 armd inf, 1 armd arty bns) and 3 AB bdes.

36 SAM btys with 216 *Improved HAWK.*
4 aircraft control and warning regts.
Other ac: 4 Boeing 707, 3 C-140, 9 HFB-320, 3 VFW-614, 3 *Noratlas*, 120 Do-28D, 16 OV-10Z.
(10 F-4F, 210 *Tornado* FGA, 175 *AlphaJet* FGA, *Kormoran* ASM, 175 *Roland* SAM on order.)

Para-Military Forces: 20,000 Federal Border Guard with armd cars, APC, mor, ATK weapons, *Alouette* II, UH-1D and CH-53G hel.

GREECE

Population: 9,280,000.
Military service: 24–30 months.
Total armed forces: 190,100 (149,000 conscripts).
Estimated GNP 1977: $26.3 bn.
Defence expenditure 1978: 55.8 bn drachmas ($1.52 bn).
$1 = 36.6 drachmas (1978), 37.3 drachmas (1977).

Army: 150,000 (123,000 conscripts).
1 armd div.
11 inf divs (some mech).
1 armd bde.
1 para-cdo bde.
1 marine inf bde.
2 SSM bns with 8 *Honest John.*
1 SAM bn with 12 *Improved HAWK.*
12 arty bns.
14 army aviation coys.
300 M-47, 750 M-48, 120 AMX-30 med, 170 M-24 lt tks; 180 M-8 armd cars; 460 M-59, 520 M-113, Mowag APC; AMX-10P MICV; 100 75mm pack, 80 105mm, 240 155mm how; M-52 105mm, M-44 155mm, M-107 175mm, M-110 203mm SP guns/how; 8 *Honest John* SSM; 550 106mm RCL; SS-11, *Cobra*, *TOW*, *Milan* ATGW; 40mm, 75mm, 90mm AA guns; *Improved HAWK*, *Redeye* SAM; 1 *Super King Air*, 2 *Aero Commander*, 20 U-17, 15 L-21 ac; 5 Bell 47G, 20 UH-1D, 42 AB-204/-205 hel. (100 AMX-30 med tks, AMX-10P MICV on order.)

RESERVES: about 250,000.

Navy: 17,500 (11,000 conscripts).
7 submarines (2 ex-US *Guppy*, 1 *Balao*, 4 Type 209).
12 destroyers (5 ex-US *Gearing-*, 6 *Fletcher-*, 1 *Sumner-*class).
4 frigates (ex-US *Cannon-*class), 1 depot ship.
10 FPBG (8 *Combattante* II/III with *Exocet* SSM, 2 with SS-12 SSM).
16 fast torpedo boats.
5 coastal patrol craft.
2 coastal minelayers.
13 coastal minesweepers.
16 landing ships (10 LST, 5 med, 1 dock).
6 utility, 13 med landing craft.

1 sqn with 4 *Alouette* III hel.
(4 Type 209 subs, 6 *Combattante* II FPBG with *Penguin* SSM, *Harpoon* SSM on order.)

RESERVES: about 20,000.

Air Force: 22,600 (15,000 conscripts); 257 combat aircraft.
6 FGA sqns: 2 with 38 F-4E, 8 RF-4E; 3 with 59 A-7H, 1 with 28 F-104G.
5 interceptor sqns: 3 with 45 F-5A/B, 2 with 39 *Mirage* F1CG.
1 recce sqn with 20 RF-84F.
1 MR sqn with 8 HU-16B *Albatross.*
OCU with 8 F-5B, 4 TF-104G.
2 tpt sqns with 25 C-47, 50 *Noratlas*, 12 C-130H, 1 *Gulfstream*, 8 CL-215.
3 hel sqns with 14 AB-205, 2 AB-206, 10 Bell 47G, 10 H-19D, 35 UH-1D.
Trainers incl 50 T-33A, 20 T-41A, 18 T-37B, 40 T-2E, 3 TF-104G, 8 F-5B.
Sparrow, *Sidewinder*, *Falcon*, R.550 *Magic* AAM.
1 SAM bn with *Nike Hercules.*
(18 F-4E FGA, 6 RF-4E recce, 6 TA-7H trainers, 300 *Super Sidewinder* AAM on order.)

RESERVES: about 20,000.

Para-Military Forces: 29,000 Gendarmerie, 100,000 National Guard.

ITALY

Population: 57,070,000.
Military service: Army and Air Force 12 months, Navy 18 months.
Total armed forces: 362,000 (227,000 conscripts).
Estimated GNP 1977: $193.7 bn.
Defence expenditure 1978: 4,313.8 bn lire ($5.06 bn).
$1 = 852 lire (1978), 888 lire (1977).

Army: 251,000 (180,000 conscripts).
3 corps HQ.
1 armd div (of 1 armd, 2 mech bdes).
3 mech divs (each of 1 armd, 1 mech bde).
1 indep mech bde.
5 indep mot bdes.
5 alpine bdes.
1 AB bde.
2 amph bns.
1 msl bde with 1 *Lance* SSM, 4 *HAWK* SAM bns.
650 M-47, 300 M-60A1, 700 *Leopard* med tks; 4,000 M-106, M-113, M-548, M-577 APC; 1,500 guns/how, incl 334 105mm pack, 155mm, 203mm; 108 M-44, 200 M-109 155mm, 36 M-107 175mm, 150 M-55 203mm SP guns/how; 81mm, 107mm, 120mm mor; *Lance* SSM; 57mm, 106mm RCL; *Mosquito*, *Cobra*, SS-11, *TOW* ATGW; 300 40mm AA guns; *Indigo*, 22 *HAWK* SAM. (180 *Leopard*

tks, 600 M-113 APC, 160 FH-70, SP-70, M-109 SP how, *TOW* ATGW, CL-89 drones on order.)

ARMY AVIATION: 20 units with 40 O-1E, 39 L-21, 80 SM-1019 lt ac; hel incl 70 AB-47G/J, 36 AB-204B, 98 AB-205A, 140 AB-206A/A-1, 26 CH-47C, 5 A-109 (60 A-129 on order).

RESERVES: 550,000.

Navy: 42,000, incl 750 Naval Air Arm, 1,700 Marines and 24,000 conscripts.
9 submarines (3 more building).
1 hel cruiser with 9 AB-204B ASW hel, 1 *Terrier/ ASROC*.
2 cruisers with 4 ASW hel, *Terrier* SAM.
4 GW destroyers (2 with 2 ASW hel, *Tartar* SAM; 2 with 1 ASW hel, *Tartar* SAM).
3 destroyers (1 trg).
2 GW frigates (with *Otomat* SSM, *Sea Sparrow/ Aspide* SAM, 1 hel).
10 frigates (2 with 2 hel, 4 with 1 hel).
8 coastal escorts.
4 ocean, 30 coastal, 10 inshore minesweepers.
4 FPB, 1 hydrofoil with *Otomat* SSM.
12 MTB.
2 LST, 57 landing craft.
1 Marine inf bn with M-113A1, LVTP-7 APC, 81mm mor, 106mm RCL.
(1 hel carrier, 6 *Maestrale-* 2 *Lupo*-class frigates, 6 SSM hydrofoils, 4 minehunters on order.)

NAVAL AIR ARM:
5 ASW hel sqns with 3 SH-34, 24 SH-3D, 32 AB-204AS, 12 AB-212.
(15 AB-212, 9 SH-3D on order.)

RESERVES: 115,800.

Air Force: 69,000 (23,000 conscripts); 319 combat aircraft.
6 FGA sqns: 1 with 18 F-104G, 3 with 54 F-104S/G, 2 with 36 G-91Y.
3 lt attack/recce sqns with 54 G-91R/R1/R1A.
6 AWX sqns with 72 F-104S.
2 recce sqns with 36 F/RF-104G.
3 MR sqns: 2 with 18 *Atlantic*, 1 with 8 S-2F *Tracker*.
1 ECM recce sqn with 6 PD-808, 2 EC-119G, EC-47, ·RC-45, RT-33.
3 tpt sqns: 1 with 28 C-119, 1 with 14 G-222, 1 with 13 C-130H.
5 comms sqns with 33 P-166M, 32 SIAI-208M, 8 PD-808, 2 DC-9, 2 DC-6 ac; 2 SH-3D hel.
2 SAR sqns with 11 HU-16 ac; 14 AB-204, 7 AB-47J, 3 HH-3F hel.
1 OCU with 15 TF-104G.
9 trg sqns with 75 G-91T, 100 MB-326, 14 P-166M, 20 SF-260M ac; 65 AB-47, 40 AB-204 hel.
AIM-7E *Sparrow, Sidewinder* AAM.
8 SAM groups with 96 *Nike Hercules*.

(100 *Tornado* FGA, 30 F-104S fighters, 100 MB-339 trg, 30 G-222 tpts; 17 HH-3F hel; *Aspide* AAM on order.)

RESERVES: 28,000.

Para-Military Forces: 83,500 *Carabinieri*, 1 mech bde with 13 bns, 1 AB bn, 2 cav sqns; 140 M-47 tks, 240 M-6, M-8 armd cars, 96 M-113 APC, 30 AB-47, 11 AB-205, 12 AB-206 hel; ·70,000 Public Security Guard, with 16 mot bns, 4 rescue bns (30 Fiat 6616 armd cars on order). 13 P-64B ac, 18 AB-47J, 13 AB-206, 2 AB-212 hel. 42,000 Finance Guards, with 47 AB-47J, 49 NH-500M hel.

LUXEMBOURG

Population: 365,000.
Military service: voluntary.
Total armed forces: 660
Estimated GNP 1977: $2.49 bn.
Defence expenditure 1978: 978 m francs ($31.0 m).
  $1 = 31.5 francs (1978), 36.6 francs (1977).

Army: 660.
1 lt inf bn.
1 indep coy.
TOW ATGW.

Para-Military Forces: 430 Gendarmerie.

NETHERLANDS

Population: 13,950,000.
Military service: Army 14 months, Navy and Air Force 14–17 months.
Total armed forces: 109,700 (49,100 conscripts).
Estimated GNP 1977: $104.1 bn.
Defence expenditure 1978: 9.12 bn guilders ($4.21 bn).
  $1 = 2.17 guilders (1978), 2.49 guilders (1977).

Army: 75,000 (43,000 conscripts).
2 armd bdes.
4 mech inf bdes.
2 SSM bns with *Honest John* (to be replaced by *Lance*).
3 army aviation sqns (Air Force crews).
340 *Centurion*, 460 *Leopard* med, AMX-13 lt tks; 2,000 AMX-VCI, YP-408 and M-113 APC; 105mm, 155mm, 203mm how; AMX 105mm, M-109 155mm, M-107 175mm, M-110 203mm SP guns/how; 107mm, 120mm mor; 8 *Honest John* SSM; *Carl Gustav* 84mm, 106mm RCL; *LAW, TOW* ATGW; L/70 40mm AA guns; 60 *Alouette* III, 30 BO-105 hel. (880 YPR-765 APC, 90 35mm *Gepard* SP AA guns, 350 *Dragon* ATGW, *Lance* SSM on order.)

DEPLOYMENT: *Germany:* 1 armd bde, 1 recce bn.

RESERVES: 145,000; 1 armd, 2 inf bdes and corps troops, incl 1 indep inf bde, would be completed by call-up of reservists. A number of inf bdes could be mobilized for territorial defence.

Navy: 17,000 (2,000 conscripts, 2,900 Marines, 1,900 naval air arm).
6 patrol submarines.
2 GW destroyers with *Tartar/Sea Sparrow* SAM, *Harpoon* SSM, 1 lt ASW hel.
6 frigates with *Seacat* SAM and 1 lt ASW hel.
9 destroyers.
1 GW ocean escort with *Sea Sparrow* SAM, *Harpoon* SSM, 1 lt ASW hel.
6 coastal escorts.
5 large patrol craft.
37 MCM ships (3 spt, 18 coastal, 16 inshore).
2 fast combat spt ships.
(11 frigates, 15 MCM vessels on order.)

MARINES:
2 amph combat gps.
1 mountain/arctic warfare coy.

NAVAL AIR ARM:
2 MR sqns with 8 *Atlantic,* 15 P-2 *Neptune.*
2 ASW hel sqns with 6 *Lynx,* 12 *Wasp.*
(18 *Lynx* ASW hel on order.)

DEPLOYMENT: *Netherlands Antilles:* 1 destroyer, 1 amph combat det, 1 MR det (3 ac).

RESERVES: about 20,000; 9,000 on immediate recall.

Air Force: 17,700 (4,100 conscripts); 162 combat aircraft.
2 FB sqns with 36 F-104G.
3 FB sqns with 54 NF-5A.
1 FB/trg sqn with 18 NF-5B.
2 interceptor sqns with 36 F-104G.
1 recce sqn with 18 RF-104G.
1 tpt sqn with 12 F-27.
Sidewinder AAM.
4 SAM sqns with *Nike Hercules.*
11 SAM sqns with *Improved HAWK.*
(102 F-16 fighters, *Super Sidewinder* AAM on order.)

RESERVES: about 10,000.

Para-Military Forces: 3,800 Gendarmerie; 4,446 Home Guard.

NORWAY

Population: 4,075,000.
Military service: Army 12 months, Navy and Air Force 15 months.
Total armed forces: 39,000 (28,250 conscripts).
Estimated GNP 1977: $36.2 bn.

Defence expenditure 1978: 6.85 bn kroner ($1.30 bn).
$1 = 5.28 kroner (1978), 5.24 kroner (1977).

Army: 20,000 (17,250 conscripts).
1 bde gp of 3 inf bns in North Norway.
Indep armd sqns, inf bns and arty regts.
78 *Leopard,* 38 M-48 med, 70 NM-116 lt tks (M-24/90); M-113 APC; 250 105mm, 155mm how, 130 M-109 155mm SP how; 107mm mor; 75mm, *Carl Gustav* 84mm, 106mm RCL; *ENTAC, TOW* ATGW; Rh-202 20mm, L/60 and L/70 40mm AA guns; 40 O-1E, L-18 lt ac.

DEPLOYMENT: *Lebanon* (UNIFIL): 1 bn and log units (930).

RESERVES: 120,000. 11 Regimental Combat Teams (bdes) of about 5,000 men each, supporting units and territorial forces; 21 days' refresher training each 3rd/4th year. Home Guard (all services) 85,000 (90 days initial service).

Navy: 9,000, incl 1,600 coast artillery, 6,000 conscripts.
15 coastal submarines.
5 frigates with *Sea Sparrow* SAM and *Penguin* SSM.
2 corvettes.
26 FPBG with *Penguin* SSM.
20 FPB.
10 coastal minesweepers.
2 minelayers.
1 spt ship.
7 LST.
6 patrol ships (fishery protection).
36 coastal arty btys.
(14 FPBG on order.)

RESERVES: 22,000. Coastguard will be established as part of navy.

Air Force: 10,000 (5,000 conscripts); 115 combat aircraft.
2 FGA sqns with 32 F-5A.
1 FGA sqn with 22 CF-104G/D.
1 AWX sqn with 27 F-104G, 2 TF-104G.
1 recce sqn with 13 RF-5A.
1 MR sqn with 5 P-3B.
1 OCU with 14 F-5B.
2 tpt sqns: 1 with 6 C-130H, 1 with 5 DHC-6, 2 *Falcon* 20 ECM ac.
1 SAR sqn with 10 *Sea King* Mk 43 hel.
2 hel sqns with 32 UH-1B.
17 Saab *Safir* trainers.
Sidewinder AAM; *Bullpup* ASM.
4 lt AA bns with L/70 40mm guns.
1 SAM bn with *Nike Hercules.*
(72 F-16 fighters, 1 *Sea King* hel, 40 *Roland* II SAM on order.)

RESERVES: 18,000. 7 lt AA bns for airfield defence with L/60 40mm guns.

PORTUGAL

Population: 9,110,000.
Military service: Army 15–24 months, Navy 36 months.
Total armed forces: 63,500.
Estimated GNP 1977: $16.4 bn.
Defence expenditure 1978: 21.79 bn escudos ($533 m).
$1 = 40.85 escudos (1978), 38.7 escudos (1977).

Army: 40,000.
6 regional commands.
1 inf bde.
1 tk regt.
2 cav regts.
16 inf regts.
4 indep inf bns.
3 arty regts, 2 arty gps.
1 coast arty regt, 2 indep AA arty bns.
2 engr regts.
1 sigs regt.
90 M-47, 23 M-48 med, 10 M-24 lt tks; 100 Panhard EBR armd cars; 86 M-113, 60 Chaimite (Commando) APC; 30 5.5-in. guns, 50 105mm guns/how; 107mm mor; 80 120mm RCL; 15 TOW ATGW; coast and 40mm AA arty.

Navy: 14,000 (2,500 Marines).
3 submarines (Daphne-class).
3 destroyer escorts (Almirante P. Silva-class).
10 escorts (4 J. Belo-, 6 J. Coutinho-class).
10 Cacine-class large patrol craft.
4 Sao Roque-class coastal minesweepers.
8 coastal patrol craft, 2 LCT.

Air Force: 9,500 (1,300 para); 18 combat aircraft.
1 FGA sqn with 18 G-91R-3/-4.
2 tpt sqns with 2 C-130H, 24 CASA C-212 Aviocar.
Trainers incl 5 G-91T, 10 T-33A, 18 T-37C, 6 T-38A, 19 Do-27, 25 Chipmunk, 32 Reims-Cessna FTB 337G.
2 hel sqns with 30 Alouette III, 10 SA-330 Puma.
3 para bns.
(4 C-130H tpts on order.)

Para-Military Forces: 9,500 National Republican Guard, 13,700 Public Security Police, 6,200 Fiscal Guard.

TURKEY

Population: 42,110,000.
Military service: 20 months.
Total armed forces: 485,000 (361,000 conscripts).
Estimated GNP 1977: $46.6 bn.
Defence expenditure 1978–79: 42.5 bn liras ($1.7 bn).
$1 = 25 liras (1978), 17.5 liras (1977).

Army: 390,000 (300,000 conscripts).
1 armd div. ⎫
2 mech inf divs. ⎪
14 inf divs. ⎪ About half are
5 armd bdes. ⎬ below strength
4 mech inf bdes. ⎪
5 inf bdes. ⎪
1 para, 1 cdo bde. ⎭
4 SSM bns with Honest John.
2,800 M-47 and M-48 med tks; 1,650 M-113, M-59 and Commando APC; 1,500 75mm, 105mm, 155mm and 203mm how; 265 105mm, 190 155mm, 36 175mm SP guns; 1,750 60mm, 81mm, 4.2-in mor; 18 Honest John SSM; 1,200 57mm, 390 75mm, 800 106mm RCL; 85 Cobra, SS-11, TOW ATGW; 900 40mm AA guns; 2 DHC-2, 18 U-17, 3 Cessna 421, 7 Do-27, 9 Do-28, 20 Beech Baron ac; 100 AB-205/-206, 20 Bell 47G, 48 UH-1D hel. (193 Leopard tks; TOW, Milan ATGW; 56 AB-205 hel on order.)

DEPLOYMENT: Cyprus: 2 inf divs (25,000).

RESERVES: 500,000.

Navy: 45,000 (31,000 conscripts).
11 submarines (2 Type 209, 9 ex-US Guppy-class, 2 on order).
11 destroyers (5 ex-US Gearing-, 5 Fletcher-, 1 Sumner-class).
2 frigates.
13 FPB (14 on order), 8 FPBG with Harpoon SSM.
41 large, 4 coastal patrol craft.
21 coastal, 4 inshore minesweepers.
8 minelayers (7 coastal).
4 LST, 25 LCT, 36 landing craft.
2 ASW sqns with 8 S-2A, 12 S-2E Tracker, 2 TS-2A.
3 AB-204B, 6 AB-212 ASW hel.
(10 AB-212 hel, 33 Harpoon SSM on order.)

RESERVES: 25,000.

Air Force: 50,000 (30,000 conscripts); 339 combat aircraft.
13 FGA sqns: 2 with 49 F-4E, 4 with 100 F-5A and 10 F-5B, 2 with 32 F/TF-104G, 2 with 30 F-104S, 3 with 50 F-100C/D/F.
1 interceptor sqn with 30 F-102A, 3 TF-102A.
2 recce sqns with 31 RF-5A, 4 F-5B.
4 tpt sqns with 7 C-130E, 20 Transall C-160, 30 C-47, 3 C-54, 3 Viscount 794, 2 Islander, 6 Do-28, 3 Cessna 421 ac; 5 UH-19, 6 HH-1H, 10 UH-IH hel.
Sidewinder, Sparrow, Falcon AAM; AS.12, Bullpup, Maverick ASM.
8 SAM sqns with Nike Hercules.
Trainers incl 40 T-33A, 30 T-37, 20 T-34, 25 T-41.
(22 F-4E, 8 RF-4E, 56 AlphaJet trainers on order.)

Para-Military Forces: 110,000 Gendarmerie (incl 3 mobile bdes).

OTHER EUROPEAN COUNTRIES

ALBANIA

Population: 2,710,000.
Military service: Army 2 years; Air Force, Navy and special units 3 years.
Total armed forces: 41,000 (22,500 conscripts).
Estimated GNP 1974: $1.1 bn.
Defence expenditure 1978: 824 m leks ($154 m).
   $1 = 5.36 leks.

Army: 30,000 (20,000 conscripts).
1 tk bde.
8 inf bdes.
2 tk bns.
1 arty regt.
2 AD regts.
8 lt coastal arty bns.
70 T-34, 15 T-54, 15 T-59 med tks; BRDM-1 scout cars; 20 BA-64, BTR-40/-50/-152, K-63 APC; 76mm, 85mm, 122mm, 152mm guns/how; SU-76, SU-100 SP guns; 120mm mor; 107mm RCL; 45mm, 57mm, 85mm ATK guns; 37mm, 57mm, 85mm, 100mm AA guns; SA-2 SAM.

RESERVES: 60,000.

Navy: 3,000 (1,000 conscripts).
3 submarines (ex-Soviet W-class, 1 trg).
4 coastal escorts (ex-Soviet *Kronstadt*-class).
40 MTB (8 ex-Soviet P-4, 32 *Hu Chwan* hydrofoils).
4 *Shanghai* II-class MGB.
8 MCM ships (2 ex-Soviet T-43, 6 T-301).
10 patrol boats (ex-Soviet PO-2, under 100 tons).

Air Force: 8,000 (1,500 conscripts); 101 combat aircraft.
2 AWX sqns with 10 MiG-17/F-4, 13 MiG-19/F-6.
6 interceptor sqns with 24 MiG-15/F-2, 10 MiG-17/F-4, 32 MiG-19/F-6, 12 MiG-21/F-8 (Chinese).
1 tpt sqn with 4 Il-14, 10 An-2.
2 hel sqns with 30 Mi-4.
Trainers incl 10 MiG-15UTI.

RESERVES: 5,000.

Para-Military Forces: 13,000: internal security force 5,000; frontier guard 8,000.

AUSTRIA

Population: 7,900,000.
Military service: 6 months, followed by 60 days reservist training for 12 years.
Total armed forces: 37,000 (20,000 conscripts; total mobilizable strength 150,000).
Estimated GNP 1977: $47.7 bn.

Defence expenditure 1978: 10.47 bn schilling ($718 m).
   $1 = 14.58 schilling (1978), 16.95 schilling (1977).

Army: 33,000 (18,000 conscripts).
1 mech div of 3 mech bdes, each with 1 tk, 2 mech inf (1 trg), 1 armd arty and/or 1 armd ATK bns.
3 inf bdes, each with 3 inf, 1 arty bns.
4 inf regts (to form 4 inf bdes on mobilization).
3 arty bns.
1 cdo bn.
3 engr, 5 sigs bns.
150 M-47, 120 M-60 med tks; 460 Saurer 4K4F APC; 22 SFKM2 155mm guns; 108 M-2 105mm, 24 M-1 155mm how, 38 M-109 155mm SP how; 300 81mm, 100 M-2 107mm, 82 M-30 120mm mor; 18 Steyr 680 M3 130mm multiple RL; 240 M52/M55 85mm towed, 150 *Kuerassier* SP ATK guns; 400 M-40 106mm RCL.

DEPLOYMENT: *Cyprus* (UNFICYP): 1 inf bn (332); *Syria* (UNDOF): 1 bn (523); other Middle East (UNTSO): 12.

RESERVES: 113,000; 4 reserve bdes (each of 3 inf, 1 arty bns), 16 regts and 4 bns *Landwehr* distributed among 8 regional military comds. 800,000 have a reserve commitment.

Air Force: 4,000 (2,000 conscripts); 30 combat aircraft.*
3 FB sqns with 30 Saab 105Ö.
1 tpt sqn with 2 *Skyvan*, 12 *Turbo-Porter*.
6 hel sqns with 23 AB-204B, 13 AB-206A, 24 *Alouette* III, 12 OH-58B, 2 S-65Oe (HH-53).
2 trg sqns with 18 Saab 91D, 7 Saab 105Ö.
Other ac incl 23 Cessna L-19, 3 DHC-2.
4 indep AD bns.
300 20mm Oerlikon, 70 35mm Z/65, Z/75, 60 40mm Bofors AA guns; *Super-Bat* and *Skyguard* AD system.
(12 AB-212 hel on order.)

RESERVES: 700.

Para-Military Forces: 11,250 Gendarmerie.

EIRE

Population: 3,240,000.
Military service: voluntary.
Total armed forces: 14,581.
Estimated GNP 1977: $9.2 bn.

---

* Austrian air units, an integral part of the Army, are listed separately for purposes of comparison.

Defence budget 1978: £102.2 m ($193 m),
$1 = £0.531 (1978), £0.584 (1977).

Army: 13,227.
2 inf bdes (1 with 3 inf bns, 1 with 2 inf bns, each
  with 1 recce sqn, 1 fd arty bty, 1 engr coy).
2 inf bn gps (each with 1 recce sqn, 1 fd arty bty,
  1 engr coy).
4 indep inf bns.
1 AA arty bty.
8 AML H90, 24 AML H60 armd cars; 30 Panhard
  VTT/M3, 10 *Unimog* APC; 48 25-pdr gun/how;
  204 81mm mor; 447 *Carl Gustav* 84mm, 96
  PV-1110 90mm RCL; 26 Bofors 40mm AA guns.
(4 *Scorpion* lt tks, 5 *Timoney* APC on order.)

DEPLOYMENT: *Lebanon* (UNIFIL): 1 bn (665); *Cyprus*
(UNFICYP): 6.

Navy (Naval Service): 680.
2 patrol vessels (1 on order).
3 coastal minesweepers (ex-British *Ton*-class).
1 training/supply vessel.

Air Force (Air Corps): 674; 16 combat aircraft.
1 COIN sqn with 6 *Super Magister*.
1 COIN/trg sqn with 10 SF-260W.
1 liaison sqn with 8 Cessna FR-172H.
1 hel sqn with 8 *Alouette* III hel.
1 flt with 3 *Dove*, 1 *King Air*.

RESERVES (all services): 18,661 (1st line 456, 2nd
line 18,205).

35mm, 40mm, 57mm towed, ZSU-57-2 SP AA
guns.

DEPLOYMENT: *Egypt* (UNEF): 654; *Cyprus* (UNFICYP):
12.

Navy: 2,500 (incl 600 coastguard).
2 *Riga*-class frigates.
2 corvettes.
14 MGB, 4 *Osa*-II-class FPBG with *Styx* SSM.
5 large, 12 coastguard patrol craft.
1 coastal minelayer.
6 inshore minesweepers.
1 HQ and log ship.
14 small landing craft/tpts.
(5 *Osa*-II-class FPBG, 1 minelayer on order.)

Air Force: 3,000; 47 combat aircraft.
2 fighter sqns with 17 MiG-21F, 12 J-35S, 6 J-35F,
  5 J-35B *Draken*.
1 OCU with 1 MiG-15UT1, 3 MiG-21U, 3 J-35C.
Tpts incl 8 C-47, 2 Cessna 402.
Trainers incl 60 *Magister*, 25 Saab *Safir*.
Liaison ac: 5 *Cherokee Arrow*.
1 hel flt with 3 Mi-4, 6 Mi-8, 1 Hughes 500, 1
  AB-206A.
AA-2 *Atoll*, *Falcon* AAM.
(50 *Hawk*, 30 Leko-70 trg ac on order.)

RESERVES (all services): 690,000 (30,000 a year do
training).

Para-Military Forces: 4,000 frontier guards.

FINLAND

Population: 4,770,000.
Military service: 8–11 months (11 months for
  Officers and NCOs).
Total armed forces: 39,900 (32,000 conscripts;
  total mobilizable strength 700,000 within days).
Estimated GNP 1977: $31.7 bn.
Defence expenditure 1978: 1.9 bn markka ($454 m).
  $1 = 4.2 markka (1978), 3.8 markka (1977).

Army: 34,400.
1 armd bde.
6 inf bdes.
8 indep inf bns.
3 fd arty regts.
2 indep fd arty bns.
2 coast arty regts.
3 indep coast arty bns.
1 AA arty regt.
4 indep AA arty bns.
T-54, T-55 med, PT-76 lt tks; BTR-50P/-60 APC;
  76mm, 105mm, 122mm, 130mm, 150mm, 152mm,
  155mm guns/how; 60mm, 81mm, 120mm mor;
  55mm, 95mm RCL; SS-11 ATGW; 23mm, 30mm,

SPAIN

Population: 36,690,000.
Military service: 15 months.
Total armed forces: 315,500 (191,000 conscripts).
Estimated GNP 1977: $123.6 bn.
Defence expenditure 1978: 188.7 bn pesetas
  ($2.36 bn).
  $1 = 79.84 pesetas (1978), 68.6 pesetas (1977).

Army: 240,000 (150,000 conscripts).
1 armd div   ⎫
1 mech inf div   ⎪
1 mot inf div   ⎬ About
2 mountain divs   ⎪ 70 per cent
1 armd cav bde   ⎪ strength
10 indep inf bdes   ⎭
1 mountain bde.
1 airportable bde.
1 para bde.
2 arty bdes.
10 mixed AA/coast arty regts.
3 Foreign Legion regts.
3 *Regulares* regts (local forces in Ceuta/Melilla).
1 SAM bn with *Nike Hercules* and *HAWK*.

200 AMX-30, 480 M-47/-48 med, 180 M-41 lt tks;
88 AML-60, 100 AML-90 armd cars; 375 M-113
APC; 860 105mm, 200 122mm, 80 155mm, 24
203mm towed, 48 M-108 105mm, 70 M-44,
70 M-109 155mm, 12 M-107 175mm, 4 M-110
203mm SP guns/how; 216mm, 300mm, 381mm
multiple RL; 60mm, 800 81mm, 300 120mm mor;
90mm, 106mm RCL; SS-11, Milan, Cobra ATGW;
54 35mm, 280 40mm, 150 90mm AA guns; 200
88mm, 6-in, 12-in, 15-in coast arty guns; Nike
Hercules, Improved HAWK SAM; 10 CH-47C,
3 Puma, 65 UH-1B/H, 5 Alouette III, 1 AB-206A,
15 OH-13, 15 OH-58A hel.
(60 M-60 tks; 102 M-113 APC; Dragon, TOW
ATGW; 38 Skyguard AD systems; 18 OH-58A, 8
UH-1H hel on order.)

DEPLOYMENT: Balearics: 6,000. Canaries: 16,000.
Ceuta/Melilla: 18,000.

RESERVES: 700,000.

Navy: 40,000 (10,000 Marines, 32,000 conscripts).
10 submarines (4 Daphne-class, 4 US, 2 midget).
1 aircraft carrier (capacity 7 AV-8A, 20 hel).
13 destroyers, 7 with 1 hel (10 ex-US Gearing-,
Fletcher-class).
15 frigates/corvettes (5 with Standard SAM and
ASROC, 7 more on order).
12 large patrol craft (10 more on order).
4 ocean, 12 coastal minesweepers.
2 patrol vessels (ex-ocean minesweepers).
2 attack transports, 1 LSD, 3 LST, 8 LCT, 6 med
landing craft.
1 FGA sqn with 5 AV-8A Matador (Harrier), 2
TAV-8A.
1 comms sqn with 4 Commanche.
5 hel sqns with 10 SH-3D, 11 AB-204/212AS, 12
Bell 47G, 12 Hughes 500HM, 6 AH-1G.
4 Marine lt inf regts and 2 indep gps.
(4 Agosta subs, 40 Harpoon SSM, 5 AV-8A FGA; 5
AB-212, 6 SH-3D hel on order.)

RESERVES: 200,000.

Air Force: 35,500 (9,000 conscripts); 214 combat
aircraft.
Air Defence Command.
5 interceptor sqns: 2 with 34 F-4C(S), 2 with 22
Mirage IIIE, 6 IIID, 1 with 14 Mirage F1C.
1 OCU with 35 T-33A.
Tactical Command.
2 FB sqns with 18 F-5A, 2 F-5B, 25 HA-220
Super Saeta.
1 recce sqn with 22 RF-4, RF-5A.
1 MR sqn with 10 HU-16B, 2 P-3A.
5 liaison flts with 12 O-1E, 27 Do-27.
Sparrow, Sidewinder, R.550 Magic AAM (Super
Sidewinder on order).
Transport Command.
7 sqns with 9 C-130H, 3 KC-97, 12 CASA-207

Azor, 30 CASA-212 Aviocar, 12 DHC-4, 5
Aztec, 1 Navajo.
Training Command.
2 OCU with 24 F-5B, 5 sqns with 35 F-33C
Bonanza, 45 HA-200A/B Saeta, 40 T-33, 25
T-34, 70 T-6, 8 King Air, 10 Baron; 34 AB-47
and AB-205 hel.
Other ac incl:
3 SAR sqns with 5 HU-16A, 6 Do-27 ac, 17 AB-205/
-206, 4 Alouette III hel.
1 SAR sqn with 8 CL-215.
(58 Mirage F1, 4 F-4C, 4 RF-4C, 3 F-27 MR, 6
CASA-212, 60 CASA C-101, 17 Hughes 300C
hel on order.)

RESERVES: 100,000.

Para-Military Forces: 65,000 Guardia Civil, 38,000
Policia Armada.

SWEDEN

Population: 8,290,000.
Military service: Army and Navy $7\frac{1}{2}$–15 months,
Air Force 8–12 months.
Total armed forces: 65,680 (46,500 conscripts;*
total mobilizable strength about 750,000 within
72 hours).
Estimated GNP 1977: $83.0 bn.
Defence expenditure 1978–79: Kr. 13.54 bn
($2.95 bn).
$1 = 4.60 kronor (1978), 4.21 kronor (1977).

Army: 40,580 (34,700 conscripts).*
Peace establishment:
47 non-operational armd, cav, inf, arty, AA, engr
and sig trg regts for basic conscript trg.
War establishment:
5 armd bdes.
20 inf bdes.
4 Norrland bdes.
50 indep inf, arty and AA arty bns.
23 Local Defence Districts with 100 indep bns and
400–500 indep coys.
350 Strv 101, 102 (Centurion), 300 103B (S-tank)
med, Ikv 91 lt tks; Pbv 302A APC; 105mm,
150mm, 155mm how; Bk 1A (L/50) 155mm SP
guns; 81mm, 120mm mor; 90mm ATK guns; Carl
Gustav 84mm, Miniman RCL; Bantam ATGW;
20mm, 40mm AA guns; Redeye, RBS-70,
HAWK SAM; 20 Sk-61 (Bulldog), 12 Super Cub
ac; 15 HKP-3 (AB-204B), 19 HKP-6 (JetRanger)
hel. (Ikv 91 lt tanks, FH77 155mm how, TOW
ATGW, Improved HAWK SAM on order.)

---

* There are normally some 120,000 more conscripts
(105,000 army, 10,000 navy, 5,000 air force) plus
15,000 officer and NCO reservists doing 18–40 days
refresher training at some time in the year.

DEPLOYMENT: *Cyprus* (UNFICYP): 427; *Egypt* (UNEF): 687; *Lebanon* (UNIFIL): 216.

Navy: 11,800 (6,950 conscripts).*
17 submarines (3 building).
6 destroyers.
4 frigates.
2 *Hugin*-class FPBG with *Penguin* SSM (14 on order).
23 large torpedo boats (18 *Spica*-, 5 *Plejad*-class).
8 MTB, 16 coastal patrol craft (under 100 tons).
3 2,700-ton, 9 250-ton coastal minelayers.
12 coastal, 10 inshore minesweepers (8 under 100 tons).
70 landing craft (under 100 tons).
25 mobile, 45 static coastal arty btys with 75mm, 105mm, 120mm, 152mm, 210mm guns, Rb08 SSM.
5 HKP-2 (*Alouette* II), 3 HKP-4B (Vertol 107), 7 HKP-4 (KV-107/II), 10 HKP-6 (*JetRanger*) hel.
(1 minelayer on order.)

Air Force: 13,300 (4,850 conscripts);* 450 combat aircraft.†
6 FGA sqns: 5 with 72 AJ-37 *Viggen*, 1 with 18 SK-60C (Saab 105).
15 AWX sqns: 13 with 234 J-35F *Draken*, 2 with 72 J-35D.
4 recce sqns: 2 with 36 S-35E *Draken*, 2 with 18 SH-37 *Viggen*.
2 tpt sqns with 3 C-130E/H, 2 *Caravelle*, 6 C-47.
5 comms sqns with 110 SK-60A/B (Saab 105), 57 SK-61 (*Bulldog*).
Trainers incl 150 SK-60, 78 SK-61, 20 SK-35C *Draken*, 40 SK-50 *Safir*, 17 SK-37 *Viggen*.
5 hel gps (3–4 ac each) with 1 HKP-2 (*Alouette* II), 6 HKP-3 (AB-204B), 10 HKP-4B (Vertol 107).
Sidewinder, Rb27, Rb28 AAM; Rb04E, Rb05A ASM.
A fully computerized, semi-automatic control and air surveillance system, *Stril* 60, co-ordinates all air defence components.
(90 JA-37 interceptors, *Maverick* ASM on order.)

RESERVES: voluntary defence organizations (all services) 500,000.

SWITZERLAND

Population: 6,440,000.
Military service: 17 weeks recruit training followed by reservist refresher training of 3 weeks for 8 out of 12 years for *Auszug* (age 20–32), 2 weeks for 3 years for *Landwehr* (33–42), 1 week for 2 years for *Landsturm* (43–50).
Total armed forces: about 3,500 regular and 15,000 recruits‡ (total mobilizable strength 625,000 within 48 hours).
Estimated GNP 1977: $60.1 bn.

Defence expenditure 1978: fr 2.91 bn ($1.55 bn).
$1 = 1.88 francs (1978), 2.53 francs (1977).

Army: 580,000 on mobilization.
War establishment:
3 fd corps, each of 1 armd, 2 inf divs.
1 mountain corps of 3 mountain inf divs.
Some indep inf and fortress bdes.
320 *Centurion*, 150 Pz-61, 170 Pz-68 med, 200 AMX-13 lt tks; 1,250 M-113 APC; 105mm guns; 105mm, 155mm, 150 M-109U 155mm SP how; 120mm mor; 80mm multiple RL; 75mm, 90mm, 105mm ATK guns; 83mm, 106mm RCL; *Bantam*, *Dragon* ATGW; 10 patrol boats. (150 Pz-68 med tks, *Dragon* ATGW on order.)

Air Force:§ 45,000 on mobilization (maintenance by civilians); 340 combat aircraft.
9 FGA sqns with 142 *Hunter* F58.
9 FGA sqns with 145 *Venom* FB50 (to be replaced by F-5E).
2 interceptor sqns with 35 *Mirage* IIIS.
1 recce sqn with 18 *Mirage* IIIRS.
1 tpt sqn with 3 Ju-52/3m.
7 lt ac sqns with 6 Do-27, 12 *Porter*, 6 *Turbo-Porter*, 3 *Bonanza*.
2 hel sqns with 30 *Alouette* II/III.
Other ac incl 48 Pilatus P-2, 70 P-3, 65 *Vampire* FB6, 35 T55, 3 *Mirage* IIIBS, 23 FFA C-3605; 70 *Alouette* II/III hel.
Sidewinder, AIM-26B *Falcon* AAM; AS.30 ASM.
1 para coy.
3 air-base regts.
1 AD bde with 1 SAM regt of 2 bns, each with 32 *Bloodhound*, and 7 arty regts (22 bns) with 20mm, 35mm and 40mm AA guns.
(66 F-5E, 6 F-5B FGA, 45 *Skyguard* AA systems on order.)

RESERVES: Militia 621,500.

YUGOSLAVIA

Population: 21,950,000.
Military service: Army and Air Force 15 months; Navy 18 months.
Total armed forces: 267,000 (145,000 conscripts).
Estimated GNP 1977: $37.8 bn.
Defence expenditure 1978: 42.68 bn dinars ($2.33 bn).
$1 = 18.30 dinars (1978), 18.28 dinars (1977).

---

* See note on p. 31.
† More ac in store, including 110 A-32A *Lansen*.
‡ There are two recruit intakes per year (Jan/Jun) each of 15,000. A further 300,000 reservists are called up for refresher training at some time during the year.
§ The Aviation Brigade, an integral part of the Army, is listed separately for purposes of comparison.

Army: 200,000 (130,000 conscripts).
9 inf divs.
7 indep tk bdes.
11 indep inf bdes.
3 mountain bdes.
1 AB bn.
12 arty regts.
6 ATK regts.
12 AA arty regts.
1,500 T-34/-54/-55, M-47, about 650 M-4 med, some PT-76 lt tks; M-3, M-8, BRDM-2 scout cars; M-980 MICV; BTR-50/-60P/-152, M-60 APC; 76mm, 105mm, 122mm, 130mm, 152mm, 155mm guns/how; SU-76, SU-100, 105mm SP how; 81mm, 120mm mor; 128mm multiple RL; *FROG*-7 SSM; 57mm, 75mm, 100mm towed, M-18 76mm, M-36 90mm, ASU-57 SP ATK guns; 57mm, 75mm, 82mm, 105mm RCL; *Snapper*, *Sagger* ATGW; 20mm, 30mm, 37mm, 40mm, 57mm, 85mm, 88mm, 90mm, 94mm towed, ZSU-57-2 SP AA guns; SA-6 SAM.

Navy: 27,000, incl Marines (8,000 conscripts).
5 submarines (2 building).
1 destroyer.
3 corvettes.
10 *Osa*-class FPBG with *Styx* SSM.
14 *Shershen*-class MTB.

23 patrol craft (13 *Kraljevica*, 10 Type 131).
20 '101'-class FPB (under 100 tons).
4 coastal, 10 inshore, 14 river minesweepers.
27 LCT.
25 coast arty btys.
Mi-8, Ka-25 ASW, *Gazelle* hel.
1 marine bde.
(1 corvette/trg ship, 2 LST, 10 FPBG with *Styx* SSM on order.)

Air Force: 40,000 (7,000 conscripts); 329 combat aircraft.
15 FGA sqns with 9 F-84G, 12 *Kraguj*, 110 *Galeb/Jastreb*.
6 interceptor sqns with 120 MiG-21F/PF/M.
3 recce sqns with 15 RT-33A, 25 *Galeb/Jastreb*.
OCU with 18 MiG-21U, 20 *Jastreb*.
Tpts incl 15 C-47, 10 Il-14, 2 Il-18, 4 Yak-40, 1 *Caravelle*, 2 An-12, 9 An-26, 4 Li-2, 1 Boeing 727.
60 *Galeb/Jastreb*, 30 T-33 trainers.
14 Mi-1, 20 Mi-4, 48 Mi-8, 12 *Gazelle* hel.
AA-2 *Atoll* AAM.
8 SA-2, 4 SA-3 SAM bns.
(102 *Gazelle* hel on order.)

Para-Military Forces and Reserves: 500,000 Reservists, 16,000 Frontier Guards, 1,000,000 Territorial Defence Force.

The Middle East and the Mediterranean

Bilateral Agreements with External Powers

The Soviet Union has a fifteen-year treaty of friendship and co-operation with Iraq which was signed in April 1972. A similar but more comprehensive treaty with Egypt, signed in May 1971, was abrogated by Egypt in March 1976. Before May 1975 the Soviet Union was a major arms supplier to Egypt, but no significant quantities of arms or spare parts have been delivered since then. The Soviet Union continues to deliver arms to Iraq, Syria and Libya, and military assistance has also been provided from time to time to Algeria, Morocco, Sudan and the People's Democratic Republic of Yemen.

The United States has varying types of security assistance agreements and has been providing military aid on either a grant or credit basis to Greece, Turkey, Spain, Morocco, Tunisia, Lebanon, Jordan, Saudi Arabia, Israel and Egypt. She provides, in addition, a significant amount of military equipment on a cash-sales basis to many countries, notably Greece, Spain, Israel, Iran, Kuwait, Saudi Arabia and Jordan.

There are US military facilities in Greece and Turkey, recently the subject of renegotiation and much affected by the outcome of current political negotiations. A treaty with Spain extending the use of military bases in Spain for five years was signed and ratified in 1976. (There is also an agreement with Portugal for the use of the Azores.) The United States maintains communications facilities in Morocco under informal arrangements due to be terminated in September 1978.

Britain has an agreement with the Republic of Malta, signed on 26 March 1972, which permits her to base forces on the island for British and for NATO purposes. This expires in March 1979, and almost all forces have now been withdrawn. Britain concluded treaties of friendship with Bahrain, Qatar and the United Arab Emirates in August 1971 and is also an arms supplier to Iran, Kuwait, Bahrain, Qatar, the United Arab Emirates, Saudi Arabia, Oman, Jordan and Egypt. Some British troops have aided government forces in Oman and provided training and technical assistance, although the extent of this aid is diminishing.

Britain – a signatory, with Greece and Turkey, of the 1959 Treaty of Guarantee which guarantees the independence, territorial integrity and security of the Republic of Cyprus – maintains a garrison in two Sovereign Base Areas in Cyprus. Greece and Turkey are each entitled to maintain a contingent in the island under an associated Treaty of Alliance with the Republic. Turkish forces in Cyprus were increased in July 1974, some reductions have followed, and the future arrangements are under discussion.

The People's Republic of China has supplied arms to Albania, Sudan and the People's Democratic Republic of Yemen.

France has a military mission in Morocco and supplies arms to a number of countries, including Egypt, Greece, Libya, Morocco, Abu Dhabi, Iraq, Kuwait and Saudi Arabia.

Multilateral Agreements including External Powers

A number of Mediterranean countries are members of NATO (see pp. 16–28).

The members of the Central Treaty Organization (CENTO) are Britain, Iran, Pakistan and Turkey, with the United States as an associate. All sit on the Military, Economic and Counter-Subversion Committees and on the Permanent Military Deputies Group. The Treaty provides for mutual co-operation for security and defence but has no central command structure for forces allocated to it. For the local powers, the economic organization of Regional Co-operation for Development (RCD), which has evolved independently out of CENTO, is a basis for more concrete co-operation.

There are United Nations forces stationed in Cyprus (UNFICYP), Syria (UNDOF), Egypt (UNEF) and Lebanon (UNIFIL).

Arrangements within the Region

Algeria, Bahrain, Iraq, Jordan, Kuwait, Lebanon, Libya, Morocco, Oman, Qatar, Saudi Arabia, Sudan, Syria, Tunisia, the United Arab Emirates, the Yemen Arab Republic and the People's

Democratic Republic of Yemen are members of the League of Arab States. Among its subsidiary bodies are the Arab Defence Council, set up in 1959, and the Unified Arab Command, organized in 1964.

Defence agreements were concluded by Egypt with Syria in November 1966 and Jordan in May 1967, to which Iraq later acceded. These arrangements provided for the establishment of a Defence Council and Joint Command. The loosely associated Eastern Front Command, comprising Iraq, Jordan, the Palestine Liberation Army and Syria, was reorganized in December 1970 into separate Jordanian and Syrian commands. Iraq and Syria concluded defence pacts in May 1968 and July 1969, but friction between the two countries continues to cast some doubt on their application. Jordan and Syria have set up a joint committee to co-ordinate economic and political planning and a Syrian–Jordanian consultative body to co-ordinate military policy. The Federation of Arab Republics, formed by Libya, Syria and Egypt in April 1971, provided for a common defence policy and a Federal Defence Council, and in January 1973 an Egyptian Commander-in-Chief was appointed to command all Federation forces. The present status of this agreement is unclear. Algeria and Libya signed a defence agreement in December 1975, and Egypt signed one with Sudan in January 1977. Mauretania and Morocco signed a defence agreement in May 1977.

Iran has provided military assistance to Oman.

In 1975 the Arab Military Industrial Organization (AMIO) was set up to encourage indigenous Arab arms production. British, French, German and American equipment is to be produced under licence. The Arab states involved include Egypt, Saudi Arabia, Qatar, the United Arab Emirates and Sudan. Production will be in Egypt, at least in the first instance.

ALGERIA

Population: 18,420,000.
Military service: 6 months.
Total armed forces: 78,800.
Estimated GNP 1977: $10.1 bn.
Defence expenditure 1978: 1.84 bn dinars ($456 m).
   $1 = 4.04 dinars (1978), 4.13 dinars (1977).

Army: 70,000.
1 armd bde.
4 mot inf bdes.
3 indep tk bns.
50 indep inf bns.
1 para bn.
12 coys desert troops.
10 indep arty bns.
7 AA arty bns.
3 engr bns.
350 T-54/-55/-62 med tks; AML armd cars; 440
   BTR-40/-50/-60/-152, Walid APC; 600 85mm,
   122mm, 152mm guns and how; 85 SU-100,
   ISU-122/-152 SP guns; 80 120mm, 160mm mor;
   20 140mm, 30 240mm RL; Sagger ATGW; 57mm,
   85mm, 100mm AA guns.

RESERVES: up to 100,000.

Navy: 3,800.
6 ex-Soviet SO-1 submarine chasers.
6 Komar-, 3 Osa-I-, 4 Osa-II-class FPBG with Styx
   SSM.
10 ex-Soviet P-6 torpedo boats (6 coastguard).
2 fleet minesweepers (ex-Soviet T-43-class).
1 LCT (Polnocny-class).
(3 F-28 tpt ac on order.)

Air Force: 5,000; 204 combat aircraft.
1 lt bbr sqn with 24 Il-28.
3 interceptor sqns with 90 MiG-21.
4 FGA sqns: 2 with 20 Su-7BM, 2 with 30 MiG-17.
1 COIN sqn with 20 Magister.
OCU with 20 MiG-15.
2 tpt sqns with 8 An-12, 10 F-27, 4 Il-14, 4 Il-18.
4 hel sqns with 4 Mi-6, 42 Mi-4, 12 Mi-8, 5 Puma,
   6 Hughes 269A.
Other ac incl 1 King Air, 3 Super King Air, 3
   Queen Air, 2 CL-215.
Trainers incl MiG-15/-17/-21U, Su-7U, 19 Yak-11.
AA-2 Atoll AAM.
SA-2 SAM.

Para-Military Forces: 10,000 Gendarmerie.

BAHRAIN

Population: 345,000.
Estimated GNP 1977: $1.7 bn.
Total armed forces: 2,300.
Defence expenditure 1978: 16.7 m dinars
   ($43 m).
   $1 = 0.388 dinars (1978), 0.400 dinars (1977).

Army: 2,300.
1 inf bn.
1 armd car sqn.
8 *Saladin* armd cars; 8 *Ferret* scout cars; 6 81mm mor; 6 120mm RCL.

Coastguard:
20 patrol launches.

Police:
2 *Scout* hel.

CYPRUS

Population: 625,000 (508,000 Greek-Cypriot, 117,000 Turkish-Cypriot).
Estimated GNP 1977: $154m.
$1 = £C 0.38 (1978), £C 0.41 (1977).

1. GREEK-CYPRIOT FORCE
Military service: 26 months.
Total armed forces: 10,050 (reducing to about 8,000).
Defence expenditure 1978: £C 8.6m ($22.6m).

Army: 10,000.*
1 armd bn.
2 recce/mech inf bns.
20 inf bns (under strength).
15 arty and support units.
25 T-34 med tks and BTR-50 APC; 30 Marmon-Harrington armd cars; 120 100mm, 105mm and 25-pdr guns and 75mm how; 40mm, 3.7-in AA guns.

RESERVES: 20,000.

Navy: 50.
2 patrol boats.

Para-Military Forces: 3,000 armed police.

2. TURKISH-CYPRIOT SECURITY FORCE
About 5,000 men, organized in a number of inf bns.
Some T-34 med tks.

EGYPT

Population: 39,760,000.
Military service: 3 years.
Total armed forces: 395,000.
Estimated GNP 1977: $13.3 bn.
Defence expenditure 1978–79: £E 1.11 bn ($2.81 bn).
$1 = £E 0.395 (1978), £E 0.394 (1977).

Army: 350,000, incl Air Defence Command.
2 armd divs (each with 1 armd, 2 mech bdes).
3 mech inf divs.
5 inf divs (each with 2 inf bdes).
1 Republican Guard Brigade (div).
3 indep armd bdes.
7 indep inf bdes.
2 airmobile bdes.
2 para bdes, 6 cdo gps.
6 arty, 2 hy mor bdes.
1 ATGW bde.
2 SSM regts (up to 24 *Scud*).
850 T-54/-55, 750 T-62 med, 80 PT-76 lt tks; 300 BRDM-1/-2 scout cars; 200 BMP-76PB MICV; 2,500 OT-62/-64, BTR-40/-50/-60/-152, *Walid* APC; 1,300 76mm, 100mm, 122mm, 130mm, 152mm and 180mm guns/how; about 200 SU-100 and ISU-152 SP guns; 300 120mm, 160mm and 240mm mor; 300 122mm, 140mm and 240mm RL; 30 *FROG*-4/-7, 24 *Scud* B, *Samlet* SSM; 900 57mm, 85mm and 100mm ATK guns; 900 82mm and 107mm RCL; 1,000 *Sagger, Snapper, Swatter, Milan, Beeswing* ATGW; 350 ZSU-23-4, ZSU-57-2 SP AA guns; SA-7/-9 SAM.†
(M-113 APC, *Swingfire* ATGW on order.)

AIR DEFENCE COMMAND (75,000): 360 SA-2, 200 SA-3, 75 SA-6 SAM; 2,500 20mm, 23mm, 37mm, 40mm, 57mm, 85mm and 100mm AA guns; missile radars incl *Fan Song, Low Blow, Flat Face, Straight Flush* and *Long Track;* gun radars *Fire Can, Fire Wheel* and *Whiff;* EW radars *Knife Rest* and *Spoon Rest.*†
(*Crotale* SAM on order.)

RESERVES: about 500,000.

Navy: 20,000.
12 submarines (ex-Soviet, 6 W-, 6 R-class).
5 destroyers (4 *Skory*-, 1 ex-British Z-class).
2 escorts (ex-British).
12 SO-1 submarine chasers (ex-Soviet).
16 FPBG (6 *Osa*-I-, 10 *Komar*-class with *Styx* SSM).
26 MTB (6 *Shershen*, 20 P-6).
3 SRN-6 hovercraft.
14 ex-Soviet MCM (6 T-43, 4 *Yurka*, 2 T-301, 2 K-8).
3 LCT (*Polnocny*-class), 13 landing craft utility (9 *Vydra*, 4 SMB-1).
6 *Sea King* ASW hel.
(2 *Lupo*-class frigates, 6 Vosper *Ramadan*-class FPBG, 3 SRN-6 hovercraft, *Otomat* SSM on order.)

RESERVES: about 15,000.

Air Force: 25,000; about 612 combat aircraft.‡
23 Tu-16D/G med bbrs.
5 Il-28 lt bbrs.
3 FB regts with 80 MiG-21F/PFM, 90 MiG-15/-17.
5 FGA/strike regts with 70 Su-7, 19 Su-20, 21 MiG-23, 46 *Mirage* VDE/DD.

---

* Greek-Cypriot National Guard, mainly composed of Cypriot conscripts, but with some seconded Greek Army Officers and NCOs.
† There is a shortage of spares for Soviet equipment.
‡ Additional Soviet ac are grounded for lack of spares.

9 interceptor sqns with 108 MiG-21MF.
Tpts incl 3 C-130, 2 EC-130H, 26 Il-14, 19 An-12,
  1 *Falcon*, 1 Boeing 707, 1 Boeing 737.
Hels incl 20 Mi-4, 32 Mi-6, 70 Mi-8, 30 *Commando*,
  54 *Gazelle*.
Trainers incl 150 MiG-15/-21/-23U, Su-7U, L-29,
  45 *Gomhouria*.
AA-2 *Atoll*, R.530 AAM; AS-1 *Kennel*, AS-5 *Kelt*
  ASM.
(42 F-5E, 8 F-5F, 14 *Mirage* V fighters, 14 C-130H
  tpts, 50 *Lynx* hel on order.)

Para-Military Forces: about 50,000; National
  Guard 6,000, Frontier Corps 6,000, Defence and
  Security 30,000, Coast Guard 7,000.

IRAN

Population: 36,365,000.
Military service: 2 years.
Total armed forces: 413,000.
Estimated GNP 1977: $72.6 bn.
Defence expenditure 1978–79: 700.4 bn rials
  ($9.94 bn).
  $1 = 70.45 rials (1978), 71.2 rials (1977).

Army: 285,000.
3 armd divs.
3 inf divs.
4 indep bdes (1 armd, 1 inf, 1 AB, 1 special force).
4 SAM bns with *HAWK*.
Army Aviation Command.
760 *Chieftain*, 400 M-47/-48, 460 M-60A1 med tks;
  250 *Scorpion* lt tks; *Fox*, *Ferret* scout cars; about
  325 M-113, 500 BTR-40/-50/-60/-152 APC; 710
  guns/how, incl 75mm pack, 85mm, 330 105mm,
  130mm, 155mm, 203mm towed, 440 M-109
  155mm, 38 M-107 175mm, 14 M-110 203mm SP;
  72 BM-21 122mm RL; 106mm RCL; *ENTAC*,
  SS-11, SS-12, *Dragon*, *TOW* ATGW; 1,800 23mm,
  35mm, 40mm, 57mm, 85mm towed, 100 ZSU-23-
  4, ZSU-57-2 SP AA guns; *HAWK* SAM; ac incl 40
  Cessna 185, 6 Cessna 310, 10 Cessna O-2, 2 F-27;
  202 AH-1J, 210 Bell 214A, 21 *Huskie*, 88
  AB-205A, 70 AB-206, 30 CH-47C hel. (1,297
  Chieftain/*Shir Iran* med, 110 *Scorpion* lt tks,
  BMP MICV, ASU-85 SP ATK, 100 ZSU-23-4 SP AA
  guns, *Rapier*, *Improved HAWK*, SA-7/-9 SAM,
  163 Bell 214A, 350 Bell 214ST hel on order.)

DEPLOYMENT: *Oman:* 2 coys, 1 hel sqn (400). *Syria*
  (UNDOF): 385. *Lebanon* (UNIFIL): 1 bn (524).

RESERVES: 300,000.

Navy: 28,000.
3 destroyers (1 ex-British *Battle*-class with *Seacat*
  SAM, 2 ex-US *Sumner*-class with 1 hel, all with
  Standard SSM/SAM).
4 frigates with Mk 2 *Seakiller* SSM and *Seacat* SAM.

4 corvettes (ex-US patrol frigates).
7 large patrol craft.
5 *Combattante*-II-class FPBG with *Harpoon* SSM.
5 minesweepers (3 coastal, 2 inshore).
2 landing ships logistic.
2 landing craft utility.
2 log spt ships.
8 SRN-6, 6 *Wellington* BH-7 hovercraft.
(3 *Tang*-class trg, 6 Type 209 submarines, 4
  Spruance-class destroyers, 6 *Lupo*-class frigates,
  7 FPBG with *Harpoon* SSM, 4 log spt ships on
  order.)

NAVAL AIR:
1 MR sqn with 6 P-3F *Orion*.
1 ASW sqn with 12 SH-3D.
1 tpt sqn with 6 *Shrike Commander*, 4 F-27.
Hel incl 5 AB-205A, 7 AB-212, 6 RH-53D, 10
  SH-3D.
3 Marine bns.
(39 P-3C MR ac, 15 SH-3D hel on order.)

Air Force: 100,000; 459 combat aircraft.
10 FB sqns with 32 F-4D, 177 F-4E.
10 FGA sqns with 12 F-5A, 140 F-5E.
3 fighter sqns with 56 F-14A *Tomcat*.
1 recce sqn with 16 RF-4E.
1 tanker sqn with 13 Boeing 707-320L.
4 med tpt sqns with 64 C-130E/H, 6 Boeing 747.
4 lt tpt sqns with 18 F-27, 4 F-28, 3 Aero *Commander* 690, 4 *Falcon* 20.
10 HH-43F, 6 AB-205, 84 AB-206A, 5 AB-212, 39
  Bell 214C SAR, 2 CH-47C, 16 *Super Frelon*, 2
  S-61A hel.
Trainers include 9 T-33, 28 F-5F, 49 *Bonanza*
  F33A/C.
Phoenix, *Sidewinder*, *Sparrow* AAM; AS.12, *Maverick*, *Condor* ASM.
5 SAM sqns with *Rapier* and 25 *Tigercat*.
(5 RF-4E, 24 F-14, 160 F-16A/B fighters; 7 E-3A
  AWACS ac, 3 F-27 tpts; 4 Boeing 747 tpts; 50
  CH-47 hel; *Blindfire* SAM radar on order.)

Para-Military Forces: 74,000 Gendarmerie with
  O-2 lt ac and hel; 32 patrol boats.

IRAQ

Population: 12,470,000.
Military service: 2 years.
Total armed forces: 212,000.
Estimated GNP 1977: $16.3 bn.
Defence expenditure 1977–78: 491.5 m dinars
  ($1.66 bn).
  $1 = 0.290 dinars (1978), 0.296 dinars (1977).

Army: 180,000.
4 armd divs (each with 2 armd, 1 mech bde).
2 mech divs.

'4 inf divs.
1 indep armd bde.
1 Republican Guard mech bde.
1 indep inf bde.
1 special forces bde.
1,700 T-54/-55/-62, 100 T-34, AMX-30 med, 100
    PT-76 lt tks; 120 BMP MICV; about 1,500 AFV,
    incl BTR-50/-60/-152, OT-62, VCR APC; 800
    75mm, 85mm, 122mm, 130mm, 152mm guns/
    how; 90 SU-100, 40 ISU-122 SP guns; 120mm,
    160mm mor; BM-21 122mm RL; 26 *FROG*-7,
    12 *Scud* B SSM; *Sagger*, SS-11 ATGW; 1,200 23mm,
    37mm, 57mm, 85mm, 100mm towed, ZSU-23-4,
    ZSU-57-2 SP AA guns; SA-7 SAM. (T-62 med tks,
    Scud SSM on order.)

RESERVES: 250,000.

Navy: 4,000.
3 SO-1 submarine chasers.
6 *Osa*-I, 8 *Osa*-II FPBG with *Styx* SSM.
10 P-6 torpedo boats.
2 large patrol craft (ex-Soviet *Poluchat*-class).
6 coastal patrol boats (under 100 tons).
5 minesweepers (2 ex-Soviet T-43, 3 inshore).
3 LCT (*Polnocny*-class).

Air Force: 28,000 (10,000 AD personnel); about 339
    combat aircraft.
1 bbr sqn with 12 Tu-22.
1 lt bbr sqn with 10 Il-28.
12 FGA sqns: 4 with 80 MiG-23B, 3 with 60 Su-7B,
    3 with 30 Su-20, 2 with 20 *Hunter* FB59/FR10.
5 interceptor sqns with 115 MiG-21.
1 COIN sqn with 12 *Jet Provost* T52.
2 tpt sqns with 10 An-2, 8 An-12, 8 An-24, 2 An-26,
    2 Tu-124, 13 Il-14, 2 *Heron*.
8 hel sqns with 35 Mi-4, 14 Mi-6, 80 Mi-8, 47
    Alouette III, 8 *Super Frelon*, 40 *Gazelle*, 3 *Puma*.
Trainers incl MiG-15/-21/-23U, Su-7U, *Hunter*
    T69, 10 Yak-11, 12 L-29, 8 L-39.
AA-2 *Atoll* AAM; AS.11/12 ASM (R.550 *Magic*
    AAM, *Exocet* ASM on order).
SA-2, SA-3 and 25 SA-6 SAM.
(32 *Mirage* F-1C fighters, 4 *Mirage* F-1B trainers,
    Il-76 tpts on order.)

Para-Military Forces: 4,800 security troops, 75,000
    People's Army.

ISRAEL

Population: 3,730,000.
Military service: men 36 months, women 24
    months (Jews and Druses only; Muslims and
    Christians may volunteer). Annual training for
    reservists thereafter up to age 54 for men, up to
    25 for women.
Total armed forces: 164,000 (123,000 conscripts);
    mobilization to 400,000 in about 24 hours.

Estimated GNP 1977: $14.2 bn.
Defence expenditure 1978–79: £I 54.4 bn
    ($3.31 bn).
$1 = £I 16.44 (1978), £I 9.42 (1977).

Army: 138,000 (120,000 conscripts, male and
    female), 375,000 on mobilization.
20 armd bdes.*
9 mech bdes.*
9 inf bdes.*
5 para bdes.*
3,000 med tks, incl 1,000 *Centurion*, 650 M-48, 810
    M-60, 400 T-54/-55, 150 T-62, 40 *Merkava*; 65
    PT-76 lt tks; about 4,000 AFV, incl AML-60, 15
    AML-90 armd cars; RBY *Ramta*, BRDM recce
    vehs; M-2/-3/-113, BTR-40/-50P(OT-62)/-60P/
    -152 APC; 500 105mm how; 450 122mm, 130mm
    and 155mm guns/how; 24 M-109 155mm, L-33
    155mm, 60 M-107 175mm, M-110 203mm SP
    guns/how; 900 81mm, 120mm and 160mm mor
    (some SP); 122mm, 135mm, 240mm RL; *Lance*,
    Ze'ev (*Wolf*) SSM; 106mm RCL; *TOW, Cobra,
    Dragon*, SS-11, *Sagger* ATGW; about 900
    Vulcan/Chaparral 20mm msl/gun systems, 30mm
    and 40mm AA guns; *Redeye* SAM.
(125 M-60 med tks, 700 M-113 APC, 94 155mm
    how, 175mm guns, *Lance* SSM, *TOW* ATGW on
    order.)

Navy: 5,000 (1,000 conscripts), 8,000 on mobiliza-
    tion.
3 Type 206 submarines.
6 *Reshef*-class FPBG with *Gabriel* SSM.
12 *Saar*-class FPBG with *Gabriel* SSM.
About 40 small patrol boats (under 100 tons).
3 medium landing ships.
6 LCT.
3 *Westwind* 1124N MR ac.
Naval cdo: 300.
(4 *Reshef*-class FPBG, 2 Qu-9-35 Type corvettes with
    Gabriel SSM, 2 *Flagstaff*-class hydrofoils, 3
    Westwind MR ac on order.)

Air Force: 21,000 (2,000 conscripts, AD only),
    25,000 on mobilization; 543 combat aircraft.
11 FGA/interceptor sqns: 1 with 25 F/TF-15, 5 with
    170 F-4E, 3 with 30 *Mirage* IIICJ/BJ, 2 with 50
    Kfir/Kfir C2.
6 FGA sqns with 250 A-4E/H/M/N *Skyhawk*.
1 recce sqn with 12 RF-4E, 2 OV-1, 4 E-2C AEW ac.
Tpts incl 10 Boeing 707, 24 C-130E/H, 6 C-97, 18
    C-47, 2 KC-130H.
Liaison ac incl 14 *Arava*, 8 *Islander*, 23 Do-27,
    9 Do-28, 25 Cessna U206, 1 *Westwind*, 16 *Queen
    Air*.
Trainers incl 24 TA-4E/H, 70 *Magister*, 30 *Super
    Cub*.

---

* 11 bdes (5 armd, 4 inf, 2 para) normally kept near full
strength; 6 (1 armd, 4 mech, 1 para) between 50 per cent
and full strength; the rest at cadre strength.

Hel incl 8 *Super Frelon*, 28 CH-53G, 6 AH-1G, 40 Bell-205A, 20 Bell-206, 12 Bell-212, 25 UH-1D, 19 *Alouette* II/III.
Sidewinder, AIM-7E/F *Sparrow*, *Shafrir* AAM; *Maverick*, *Shrike*, *Walleye*, *Bullpup* ASM.
15 SAM btys with 90 *HAWK*.
(15 F-15, 75 F-16 fighters, 30 Hughes 500 hel gunships on order.)

RESERVES (all services): 460,000.

Para-Military Forces: 4,500 Border Guards and 5,000 *Nahal* Militia.

JORDAN

Population: 2,970,000.
Military service: 24 months.
Total armed forces: 67,850.
Estimated GNP 1977: $1.3 bn.
Defence expenditure 1978: 95.3 m dinars ($304 m).
$1 = 0.313 dinars (1978), 0.334 dinars (1977).

Army: 61,000.
2 armd divs.
2 mech divs.
3 special forces bns.
2 AA bdes incl 6 btys with *Improved HAWK* SAM.
320 M-47/-48/-60, 180 *Centurion* med tks; 140 *Ferret* scout cars; 600 M-113 and 120 *Saracen* APC; 110 25-pdr, 90 105mm, 16 155mm, 203mm how; 35 M-52 105mm, 20 M-44 155mm SP how; 81mm, 107mm, 120mm mor; 106mm, 120mm RCL; *TOW*, *Dragon* ATGW; *Vulcan* 20mm, 200 M-42 40mm SP AA guns; *Redeye* SAM, *Improved HAWK* SAM.
(100 M-113 APC, M-110 203mm SP how, 100 M-163 *Vulcan* 20mm AA guns, *Improved HAWK* SAM on order.)

Navy: 200.
10 small patrol craft.

Air Force: 6,650; 76 combat aircraft.
1 FGA sqn, 1 OCU with 8 F-5A/B, 24 F-5E/F.
2 interceptor sqns with 20 F-104A/B, 24 F-5E/F.
4 C-130B, 1 *Boeing* 727, 1 *Falcon* 20, 4 CASA C-212A *Aviocar* tpts.
14 *Alouette* III, 2 S-76 hel.
8 T-37C, 12 *Bulldog*, 1 *Dove* trainers.
Sidewinder AAM.
(1 C-130H tpts; 10 AH-1H, 4 S-76 hel on order.)

RESERVES: 30,000.

Para-Military Forces: 10,000; 3,000 Mobile Police Force, 7,000 Civil Militia.

KUWAIT

Population: 1,160,000.
Military service: 18 months.
Total armed forces: 12,000.
Estimated GNP 1977: $12.0 bn.
Defence expenditure 1977: 93 m dinars ($322.2 m).
$1 = 0.277 dinars (1977).

Army: 10,500.
1 armd bde.
2 inf bdes.
24 *Chieftain*, 50 Vickers, 50 *Centurion* med tks; 100 *Saladin* armd, 20 *Ferret* scout cars; 130 *Saracen* APC; 10 25-pdr guns; 20 AMX 155mm SP how; SS-11, *HOT*, *TOW*, *Vigilant*, *Harpon* ATGW.
(129 *Chieftain* med tks; Scorpion lt tks; APC; arty; SA-7 SAM on order.)

Navy: 500 (Coastguard).
5 FPB.
12 inshore patrol craft.
16 patrol launches.
3 landing craft.

Air Force: 1,000;* 49 combat aircraft.
2 FB sqns (forming) with 20 A-4KU.
1 interceptor sqn with 20 *Mirage* F-1B/C.
1 COIN sqn with 9 *Strikemaster* Mk 83.
2 DC-9, 2 L-100-20 tpts.
3 hel sqns with 30 *Gazelle*, 12 *Puma*.
Trainers incl 4 *Hunter* T67, 2 TA-4KU.
Red Top, *Firestreak*, R.550 *Magic*, *Sidewinder* AAM; *Super* 530 ASM.
50 *Improved HAWK* SAM.
(14 A-4KU, 4 TA-4KU FGA on order.)

LEBANON

Population: 3,060,000.
Total armed forces: 7,800.
Estimated GNP 1977: $2.9 bn.
Defence expenditure 1978: £L 491 m ($167 m).
$1 = £L 2.93 (1978), £L 3.03 (1977).

Army: 7,000 (planned to rise to 15,500).
2 armd recce bns.
6 inf bns (some incomplete).
2 arty bns.
Saladin armd cars; *Saracen*, 80 M-113 APC; 10 122mm, 155mm guns.

Navy: 300.
1 large, 3 coastal patrol craft (under 100 tons).

Air Force: 500; 21 combat aircraft.
1 FGA sqn with 9 *Hunter* F70 and 2 T66.
1 interceptor sqn with 10 *Mirage* IIIEL/BL (not in use).

* Excluding expatriate personnel.

1 hel sqn with 12 *Alouette* II/III, 6 AB-212.
6 SA *Bulldog*, 6 *Magister* and 1 *Chipmunk* trainers.
1 *Dove*, 1 *Turbo-Commander* 690A tpts.
R.530 AAM.
Some French EW/ground-control radars.

Para-Military Forces: Internal Security Force
  5,000; small arms, 40 *Saladin* armd cars, 5
  Saracen APC.

LIBYA

Population: 2,760,000.
Military service: conscription.
Total armed forces: 37,000.
Estimated GDP 1977: $18.5 bn.
Defence expenditure 1978: 130 m Libyan dinars
  ($448 m).
  $1 = 0.290 dinars (1978), 0.296 dinars (1977).

Army: 30,000.
1 armd bde.
2 mech inf bdes.
1 National Guard bde.
1 special forces bde.
3 arty, 2 AA arty bns.
2,000 T-54/-55/-62 med tks;* 100 *Saladin*, Panhard,
  200 EE-9 *Cascavel* armd cars; 140 *Ferret* scout
  cars; BMP MICV; 400 BTR-40/-50/-60, 140
  OT-62/-64, 70 *Saracen*, 100 M-113A1 APC; 40
  105mm, 80 130mm how; M-109 155mm SP how;
  300 *Vigilant*, SS-11, *Sagger* ATGW; 25 *Scud* B
  SSM; 180 23mm, L/70 40mm, 57mm, ZSU-23-4 SP
  AA guns; SA-7 SAM; 6 AB-47, 5 AB-206, 4
  Alouette III hel; some Cessna O-1 lt ac. (16
  CH-47C hel on order.)

Navy: 3,000.
3 F-class submarines.
1 frigate (with *Seacat* SAM).
2 corvettes (1 with *Otomat* SSM).
8 FPBG: 3 *Susa*-class with SS-12M SSM, 5 *Osa*-II-class
  with *Styx* SSM.
14 patrol craft.
2 log support ships, 2 LST (1 *Bidassoa*-, 1 *Polnocny*-
  class).
(3 F-class submarines; 3 corvettes with *Otomat*
  SSM, 10 FPBG, 80 *Otomat* SSM on order.)

Air Force: 4,000; 178 combat aircraft.†
1 bbr sqn with 12 Tu-22 *Blinder*.
2 interceptor sqns (1 OCU) with 24 MiG-23 *Flogger*.
4 FGA sqns and OCU with 90 *Mirage* VD/DE, 10
  VDR, 10 VDD.
2 COIN sqns with 32 *Galeb*.
2 tpt sqns with 8 C-130H, 1 Boeing 707, 9 C-47, 2
  Falcon, 1 *Jetstar*.
Trainers incl 2 *Mystère* 20, 5 MiG-23U, 12 *Magister*,
  Falcon ST 2, 20 SF-260, 17 *Galeb*.

4 hel sqns with 13 *Alouette* II/III, 6 AB-47, 9 *Super
  Frelon*, 10 CH-47C.
AA-2 *Atoll*, R.550 *Magic* AAM.
3 SAM regts with 60 *Crotale* and 9 btys with 60 SA-2,
  SA-3 and SA-6 SAM.
(32 *Mirage* F-1AD/ED fighters; 6 *Mirage* F-1BD,
  150 SF-260 trainers; 20 CH-47C, 1 AS-61A hel
  on order.)

MOROCCO

Population: 18,590,000.
Military service: 18 months.
Total armed forces: 89,000.
Estimated GNP 1977: $9.5 bn.
Defence expenditure 1978: 2.89 bn dirham
  ($681 m).
  $1 = 4.25 dirham (1978), 4.51 dirham (1977).

Army: 81,000.
1 lt security bde.
1 para bde.
5 armd bns.
9 mot inf bns.
18 inf bns.
2 Royal Guard bns.
7 camel corps bns.
2 desert cav bns.
7 arty gps.
2 engr bns.
50 M-48, 40 T-54 med, 80 AMX-13 lt tks; 36
  EBR-75, 50 AML and M-8 armd cars; 40 M-3
  half-track, 60 OT-62/-64, 30 UR-416, 100
  M-113 APC; 150 75mm, 105mm, 34 M-114 155mm
  how; 20 AMX-105, 36 155mm SP how; 81mm,
  82mm, 120mm mor; 75mm, 106mm RCL;
  ENTAC, Dragon, TOW ATGW; 50 37mm, 57mm,
  100mm AA guns; SA-7, 10 *Chaparral* SAM.
(60 M-48 med tks; 234 M-113 APC; *Crotale* SAM
  on order.)

DEPLOYMENT: *Mauritania:* 6 bns (8,000). *Zaire:*
  1,700.

Navy: 2,000 (600 Marines).
5 large patrol craft (2 French PR 72 Type, 1 under
  100 tons).
1 coastal minesweeper.
15 coastal patrol craft.
2 *Batral*-class landing ship log.
1 landing craft.
1 naval inf bn.
(4 large patrol craft, 1 landing ship log on order.)

Air Force: 6,000; 61 combat aircraft.‡
2 FB sqns with 34 F/RF-5A, 5 F-5B.
1 COIN sqn with 22 *Magister*.

---

* Many in storage.
† Some may be in storage.
‡ Some ac, incl 2 MiG-15, 12 MiG-17 FGA in storage.

1 tpt sqn with 12 C-130H, 8 C-119G, 8 C-47, 1 *Gulfstream*, 6 *King Air*, 12 *Broussard*.
2 hel sqns with 40 AB-205A, 2 AB-206, 2 AB-212, 40 *Puma*.
12 T-6, 12 T-34C, 10 AS. 201/18 *Bravo* trainers.
Sidewinder AAM.
(50 *Mirage* F-1CH fighters, 24 *AlphaJet* trainers, 6 CH-47 hel, R.550 *Magic* AAM on order.)

Para-Military Forces: 30,000, incl 11,000 *Sureté Nationale*.

OMAN

Population: 837,000.
Military service: voluntary.
Total armed forces: 19,200.*
Estimated GNP 1977: $2.5 bn.
Defence expenditure 1978: 265 m rial omani ($767 m).
  $1 = 0.346 rial (1978), 0.346 rial (1977).

Army: 16,200.
2 bde HQ.
8 inf bns.
1 Royal Guard regt.
1 arty regt.
1 sigs regt.
1 armd car sqn.
1 para sqn.
1 engr sqn.
36 *Saladin* armd cars; 36 105mm guns; 81mm, 120mm mor; *TOW* ATGW.

Navy: 900.
3 patrol vessels (1 Royal Yacht, 2 ex-Dutch MCM).
1 trg ship (500-ton ex-log ship).
7 FPB (3 with *Exocet* SSM).
4 coastal patrol craft (under 100 tons).
3 small landing craft.
(1 log support ship on order.)

Air Force: 2,100;* 32 aircraft.
1 FGA/recce sqn with 12 *Hunter*.
1 FGA sqn with 12 *Jaguar*.
1 COIN/trg sqn with 8 BAC-167.
3 tpt sqns: 1 with 3 BAC-111, 2 with 10 *Defender/ Skyvan*.
Royal flt with 1 VC-10, 1 *Gulfstream*, 2 AS.202 *Bravo* trainers.
1 hel sqn with 20 AB-205, 2 AB-206, 5 AB-214A/B hel.
2 AD sqns with 28 *Rapier* SAM.
(R.550 *Magic* AAM on order.)

Para-Military Forces: 3,300 tribal Home Guard (Firqats). Police Air Wing: 1 *Learjet*, 2 *Turbo-Porter*, 2 *Merlin* 1VA, 4 AB-205, 2 AB-206 hel.

QATAR

Population: 205,000.
Total armed forces: 4,000.†
Estimated GNP 1977: $2.4 bn.
Defence expenditure 1978: 238 m ryal ($61 m).
  $1 = 3.87 ryal (1978), 3.95 ryal (1977).

Army: 3,500.
2 armd car regts.
1 Guards inf bn.
1 mobile regt.
12 AMX-30 med tks; 30 *Saladin*, 20 EE-9 *Cascavel* armd, 10 *Ferret* scout cars; 12 AMX-10P MICV; 8 *Saracen* APC; 4 25-pdr guns; 81 mm mor.
(*HAWK* SAM on order.)

Navy: 200 (Coastguard).
6 large Vosper Type patrol craft.
31 small coastal patrol craft.

Air Force: 300; 4 combat aircraft.
3 *Hunter* FGA, 1 T79.
1 *Islander* tpt.
2 *Whirlwind*, 4 *Commando*, 2 *Gazelle*, 3 *Lynx* hel.
Tigercat SAM.
(30 *Mirage* F-1 fighters, 3 *Lynx* hel on order.)

SAUDI ARABIA

Population: 7,730,000.
Military service: voluntary.
Total armed forces: 58,500.
Estimated GNP 1977: $55.4 bn.
Defence expenditure 1978–79: 33.30 bn Saudi riyals ($9.63 bn).
  $1 = 3.46 riyals (1978), 3.54 riyals (1977).

Army: 45,000.
2 armd bdes.
4 inf bdes.
2 para bns.
1 Royal Guard bn.
3 arty bns.
6 AA arty btys.
10 SAM btys with *HAWK*.
250 AMX-30, 75 M-60 med tks; 200 AML-60/-90 armd, *Ferret*, 50 *Fox* scout cars; 300 AMX-10P MICV; M-113, Panhard M-3, APC; 105mm pack how, 105mm and 155mm SP how; 75mm RCL; *TOW* ATGW; M-42 40mm SP, AMX-30 SP AA guns; *HAWK* SAM.
(175 M-60 med tks; 50 *Fox* scout cars; 200 AMX-10P MICV; *Dragon* ATGW; M-163 *Vulcan* 20mm SP AA guns; *Redeye*, *Shahine* (*Crotale*), 6 btys *Improved HAWK* SAM on order.)

---

* Excluding expatriate personnel.
† All services form part of the Army.

DEPLOYMENT:
Lebanon (Arab Peace-keeping Force): 700.

Navy: 1,500.
3 FPB (*Jaguar*-class).
1 large patrol craft (ex-US coastguard cutter).
4 coastal minesweepers.
2 utility landing craft.
(6 corvettes with *Harpoon* SSM, 4 FPBG, 4 gunboats, 4 landing craft on order.)

Air Force: 12,000; 171 combat aircraft.
3 FB sqns with 60 F-5E.
2 COIN/trg sqns with 35 BAC-167.
1 interceptor sqn with 16 *Lightning* F53, 2 T55.
3 OCU with 24 F-5F, 16 F-5B, 16 *Lightning* F53, 2 T55.
2 tpt sqns with 35 C-130E/H.
2 hel sqns with 16 AB-206 and 24 AB-205.
Other ac incl 4 KC-130 tankers, 1 Boeing 707, 2 *Falcon* 20, 2 *Jetstar* tpts; 22 *Alouette* III, 1 AB-206, 1 Bell-212, 2 AS-61A hel.
Trainers incl 12 T-41A.
Red Top, *Firestreak*, *Sidewinder*, R.530, R.550 *Magic* AAM; *Maverick* ASM.
(45 F-15 fighters; 15 TF-15 trainers; 1 Boeing 747, 4 KC-130H tpt ac; 6 KV-107 hel on order.)

Para-Military Forces: 35,000 National Guard in 20 regular and semi-regular bns with 150 V-150 *Commando* APC. 6,500 Frontier Force and Coastguard with 50 small patrol boats and 8 SRN-6 hovercraft.

SUDAN

Population: 19,120,000.
Military service: conscription.
Total armed forces: 52,100.
Estimated GNP 1977: $4.4 bn.
Defence expenditure 1977–78: £S 82.6 m ($237 m).
$1 = £S 0.348 (1977), £S 0.35 (1975).

Army: 50,000.
2 armd bdes.
7 inf bdes.
1 para bde.
3 arty regts.
3 AD arty regts.
1 engr regt.
70 T-54, 60 T-55 med tks; 30 T-62 lt tks (Chinese); 50 *Saladin* armd cars; 60 *Ferret* scout cars; 100 BTR-40/-50/-152, 60 OT-64, 49 *Saracen*, 45 *Commando* APC; 55 25-pdr, 40 100mm, 20 105mm, 18 122mm guns/how; 30 120mm mor; 30 85mm ATK guns; 80 40mm, 80 37mm, 85mm AA guns.
(50 AMX-10 APC on order.)

DEPLOYMENT:
Lebanon (Arab Peace-keeping Force): 1,000.

Navy: 600.
6 large patrol craft (2 ex-Yugoslav *Kraljevica*-class).
3 patrol craft (ex-Iranian) under 100 tons.
6 FPB (ex-Yugoslav '101'-class).
2 LCT, 1 landing craft utility.

Air Force: 1,500; 22 combat aircraft.
1 interceptor sqn with 10 MiG-21MF.
1 FGA sqn with 12 MiG-17 (ex-Chinese).
5 BAC-145 and 6 *Jet Provost* Mk 55.
1 tpt sqn with 6 C-130H, 6 An-12, 5 An-24, 4 F-27, 1 DHC-6, 2 DHC-5D, 8 *Turbo-Porter*.
1 hel sqn with 10 Mi-8, 10 BO-105.
AA-2 *Atoll* AAM.
(10 F-5E, 2 F-5B, 24 *Mirage* 50 fighters; 6 EMB-111P2, 2 DHC-5D tpts, 10 *Puma* hel on order.)

Para-Military Forces: 3,500: 500 National Guard, 500 Republican Guard, 2,500 Border Guard.

SYRIA

Population: 8,110,000.
Military service: 30 months.
Total armed forces: 227,500.
Estimated GNP 1977: $6.5 bn.
Defence expenditure 1978: £Syr 4.4 bn ($1.12 bn).
$1 = £Syr 3.93 (1978), £Syr 3.68 (1977).

Army: 200,000, incl 15,000 AD Comd.
2 armd divs (each 2 armd, 1 mech bde).
3 mech divs (each 1 armd, 2 mech bdes).
3 armd bdes.
1 mech bde.
3 inf bdes.
2 arty bdes.
6 cdo bns.
4 para bns.
1 SSM bn with *Scud*, 2 btys with *FROG*.
48 SAM btys with SA-2/-3/-6.
200 T-34, 1,500 T-54/-55, 800 T-62 med, 100 PT-76 lt tks; BRDM recce vehs; BMP MICV; 1,600 BTR-40/-50/-60/-152, OT-64 APC; 800 122mm 130mm, 152mm and 180mm guns/how; ISU-122/-152, 75 SU-100 SP guns; 122mm, 140mm, 240mm RL; 30 *FROG*-7, 36 *Scud* SSM; 82mm, 120mm, 160mm mor; 57mm, 85mm, 100mm ATK guns; *Snapper*, *Sagger*, *Swatter* ATGW; 23mm, 37mm, 57mm, 85mm, 100mm towed, ZSU-23-4, ZSU-57-2 SP AA guns; SA-7/-9 SAM; 25 *Gazelle* hel.
(60 T-62 tks, *Milan*, *HOT* ATGW, SA-6/-8/-9 SAM; 24 *Gazelle* hel on order.)

DEPLOYMENT:
Lebanon: (Arab Peace-keeping Force): 30,000.

RESERVES: 100,000.

AIR DEFENCE COMMAND:*
24 SAM btys with SA-2/-3, 14 with SA-6, AA arty, interceptor ac and radar.

Navy: 2,500.
2 *Petya*-I-class frigates.
6 *Osa*-I- and 6 *Komar*-class FPBG with *Styx* SSM.
1 T-43-class, 2 coastal minesweepers.
1 large patrol craft (ex-French CH Type).
8 MTB (ex-Soviet P-4).

RESERVES: 2,500.

Air Force: 25,000; about 392 combat aircraft.†
6 FGA sqns: 3 with 50 MiG-17, 3 with 60 Su-7.
3 fighter sqns with 50 MiG-23, 12 MiG-27.
12 interceptor sqns with 220 MiG-21PF/MF.
Tpts incl 8 Il-14, 6 An-12, 2 An-24, 4 An-26.
Trainers incl Yak-11/-18, 23 L-29, MiG-15UTI, 32 MBB 223 *Flamingo*.
Hel incl 4 Mi-2, 8 Mi-4, 10 Mi-6, 50 Mi-8, 9 Ka-25 ASW, 15 *Super Frelon*, 6 CH-47C.
AA-2 *Atoll* AAM.
(12 MiG-23 fighters, 18 AB-212, 21 *Super Frelon* hel on order.)

Para-Military Forces: 9,500. 8,000 Gendarmerie; 1,500 Desert Guard (Frontier Force).

TUNISIA

Population: 6,250,000.
Military service: 12 months selective.
Total armed forces: 22,200 (13,000 conscripts).
Estimated GNP 1977: $5.0 bn.
Defence expenditure 1978–79: 77 m dinars ($185 m).
  $1 = 0.416 dinars (1978), 0.44 dinars (1977).

Army: 18,000 (12,000 conscripts).
2 combined arms regts.
1 Sahara regt.
1 para-cdo bn.
1 arty bn.
1 engr bn.
30 AMX-13, 20 M-41 lt tks; 20 *Saladin*, 15 EBR-75 armd cars; 40 105mm, 10 155mm how, SS-11 ATGW; 40mm AA guns.
(*Chaparral* SAM, 45 *Kuerassier* SP ATK guns on order.)

Navy: 2,500 (500 conscripts).
1 destroyer escort (ex-US radar picket).
1 coastal minesweeper.
1 large patrol craft (ex-French *Fougeux*-class).
3 P48-class with SS-12 SSM, 2 Vosper patrol craft.
10 coastal patrol boats (less than 100 tons).

Air Force: 1,700 (500 conscripts); 10 combat aircraft.
1 fighter/trg sqn with 10 F-86F.
1 trg sqn with 12 MB-326B/K, 2 MB-326L.
12 SF-260W, 12 T-6 trainers.
8 *Alouette* II, 6 *Alouette* III, 4 UH-1H, 1 *Puma* hel.
(6 SF-260C trainers on order.)

Para-Military Forces: 2,500; 1,500 Gendarmerie (3 bns), 1,000 National Guard.

UNITED ARAB EMIRATES (UAE)

Population: 875,000.
Military service: voluntary.
Total armed forces: 25,900.‡
Estimated GNP 1977: $7.7 bn.
Defence expenditure 1978–79: 2.57 bn dirhams ($661 m).
  $1 = 3.88 dirhams (1978), 3.90 dirhams (1977).

Army: 23,500.
1 Royal Guard 'bde'.
3 armd/armd car bns.
7 inf bns.
3 arty bns.
3 AD bns.
30 *Scorpion* lt tks; 80 *Saladin*, 6 *Shorland*, Panhard armd cars; 60 *Ferret* scout cars; AMX VCI, Panhard M-3, 12 *Saracen* APC; 22 25-pdr, 105mm guns; 16 AMX 155mm SP how; 81mm mor; 120mm RCL; *Vigilant* ATGW; *Rapier*, *Crotale* SAM.
(*Scorpion* lt tks on order.)

DEPLOYMENT:
Lebanon (Arab Peace-keeping Force): 700.

Navy: 600.
6 Vosper Type large patrol craft.
9 coastal patrol craft (under 100 tons).
(4 *Jaguar* II FPB on order.)

Air Force: 1,800; 46 combat aircraft.
2 interceptor sqns with 32 *Mirage* VAD/DAD/RAD.
1 FGA sqn with 7 *Hunter* FGA76, 2 T77.
1 COIN sqn with 4 MB-326KD/LD, 1 SF-260WD.
Tpts incl 2 C-130H, 1 Boeing 720–023B, 1 G-222, 4 *Islander*, 1 *Falcon*, 3 DHC-4, 1 DHC-5D, 1 Cessna 182.
Hel incl 8 AB-205, 6 AB-206, 3 AB-212, 10 *Alouette* III, 10 *Puma*.

---

* Under Army Command, with Army and Air Force manpower.
† Some aircraft believed to be in storage.
‡ The Union Defence Force and the armed forces of Abu Dhabi, Dubai, Ras Al Khaimah and Sharjah were formally merged in May 1976.

R.550 *Magic* AAM; AS.11/12 ASM.
(1 G-222, 3 DHC-5D tpts, *Lynx* hel on order.)

YEMEN ARAB REPUBLIC (NORTH)

Population: 7,270,000.
Military service: 3 years.
Total armed forces: 38,000.
Estimated GNP 1977: $1.2 bn.
Defence expenditure 1977–78: 360 m riyals ($79 m).
$1 = 4.54 riyals (1977), 4.33 riyals (1975).

Army: 36,000.
2 inf divs (10 inf bdes, incl 3 reserve).
2 armd bdes.
1 para bde.
2 cdo bdes.
5 arty bns.
2 AA arty bns.
220 T-34, T-54 med tks; 50 *Saladin* armd, *Ferret*
  scout cars; 350 BTR-40/-152, *Walid* APC; 50
  76mm, 122mm guns; 50 SU-100 SP guns; 82mm,
  120mm mor; 75mm RCL; 20 *Vigilant* ATGW;
  37mm, 57mm AA guns. (How, AA guns on order.)

DEPLOYMENT:
Lebanon (Arab Peace-keeping Force): 1,500.

Navy: 500.
4 large patrol craft (ex-Soviet *Poluchat*-class).
4 MTB (ex-Soviet P-4-class).

Air Force: 1,500; some 26 combat aircraft.*
1 lt bbr sqn with 14 Il-28.
1 fighter sqn with 12 MiG-17.
3 C-47, 2 *Skyvan*, 1 Il-14 tpts.
4 F-5B, 4 MiG-15UTI, 18 Yak-11 trainers.
1 Mi-4, 2 AB-205 hel.
AA-2 *Atoll* AAM.

Para-Military Forces: 20,000 tribal levies.

YEMEN: PEOPLE'S DEMOCRATIC REPUBLIC (SOUTH)

Population: 1,830,000.
Military service: conscription, 18 months.
Total armed forces: 20,900.
Estimated GNP 1977: $224 m.
Defence expenditure 1978: 19 m South Yemeni
  dinars ($56 m).
$1 = 0.34 dinars (1978), 0.35 dinars (1977).

Army: 19,000.
10 inf bdes, each of 3 bns.
2 armd bns.
5 arty bns.
1 sigs unit.
1 trg bn.
260 T-34, T-54 med tks; 10 *Saladin* armd cars; 10
  Ferret scout cars; BTR-40/-152 APC; 25-pdr,
  105mm pack, 122mm, 130mm how; 120mm mor;
  122mm RCL; 37mm, 57mm, 85mm, ZSU-23-4
  SP AA guns; SA-7 SAM.

Navy: 600 (subordinate to Army).
3 large patrol craft (ex-Soviet, 2 SO-1, 1 *Poluchat*).
2 MTB (ex-Soviet P-6-class).
3 minesweepers (ex-British *Ham*-class).
4 small patrol craft (under 100 tons).
2 LCT (ex-Soviet *Polnocny*-class).

Air Force: 1,300; 34 combat aircraft.*
1 lt bbr sqn with 7 Il-28.
1 FGA sqn with 15 MiG-17.
1 interceptor sqn with 12 MiG-21F.
1 tpt sqn with 4 Il-14, 3 An-24.
1 hel sqn with 8 Mi-8, some Mi-4.
3 MiG-15UTI trainers.
AA-2 *Atoll* AAM.

Para-Military Forces: Popular Militia; 15,000
  Public Security Force.

* Some aircraft are believed to be in storage.

Sub-Saharan Africa

Multilateral Agreements

The Organization of African Unity (OAU), constituted in May 1963, includes all internationally recognized independent African states except South Africa. It has a Defence Commission which is responsible for defence and security co-operation and the defence of the sovereignty, territorial integrity and independence of its members; however, this has rarely met.

Bilateral Agreements

The US has security assistance agreements with Ghana, Kenya, Liberia, Senegal and Zaire.

The Soviet Union signed Treaties of Friendship with Somalia in July 1974 (abrogated in November 1977), with Angola in October 1976 and with Mozambique in March 1977. Military aid is given to Angola, Ethiopia, Guinea, Guinea-Bissau, Mali, Mozambique, Nigeria and Uganda.

China has military assistance agreements with Cameroon, Equatorial Guinea, Guinea, Mali and Tanzania and has given aid to Mozambique.

Britain maintains overflying, training and defence arrangements with Kenya.

France has agreements on defence and military co-operation with the Central African Empire, Gabon, Ivory Coast, Niger and Upper Volta. The military agreement with the Malagasy Republic has been terminated but military co-operation between the two countries maintained. Since March 1974 France has had a co-operation agreement for defence with Senegal, and since February 1974 a co-operation agreement including military clauses with Cameroon. The defence agreements between France and Benin, Chad and Togo have been terminated but replaced by agreements on technical military co-operation. Similarly, a defence agreement with the People's Republic of Congo has been terminated and replaced by an agreement on training and equipment for the Congolese armed forces. An agreement has been concluded with Djibouti for the continued stationing of French forces there. Military assistance has been given to Zaire and Mauritania.

Cuba has given military aid to the People's Republic of Congo, Guinea and Ethiopia, and has some 23–25,000 men in Angola, now engaged in training Angola's armed forces and assisting with internal security, and 16–17,000 in Ethiopia. Cuban advisers are present in a number of other African countries (see note on p. 74).

A number of countries have given military assistance to Zaire.

Military links exist between South Africa and Israel.

Arrangements within the Region

Kenya and Ethiopia signed a defence agreement in 1963.

Military links have existed in practice between South Africa and Rhodesia, with South Africa giving certain defence assistance. There is, however, no known formal agreement.

ANGOLA: PEOPLE'S REPUBLIC OF

Population: 6,300,000.
Military service: conscription.
Total armed forces: 33,000.
Defence expenditure 1975: 2.5 bn escudos
($98.0 m).
$1 = 25.5 escudos (1975).

Army: 30,000.
1 armd regt.
9 inf regts.
1 cdo regt.

1 AD regt.
85 T-34, 75 T-54 med, some 50 PT-76 lt tks; 200 BRDM-2 armd cars; 150 BTR-50/-60/-152, OT-62 APC; 120 guns, incl 76mm, 105mm, 122mm; 500 82mm, 120mm mor; 110 BM21 122mm multiple RL; ZIS-3 76mm ATK guns; 75mm, 82mm, 107mm RCL; *Sagger* ATGW; 23mm, 37mm AA guns; SA-7 SAM.*

---

* Eqpt totals uncertain. Some 23–25,000 Cubans serve with the Angolan forces and operate ac and hy eqpt. Some Portuguese also serve; several hundred Soviet advisers and technicians are reported in Angola.

Navy: 1,500.
4 *Argos*-class patrol boats.
1 *Zhuk*-class patrol boat (under 100 tons).
6 small coastal patrol boats.
2 LCT, 5 utility landing craft.

Air Force: 1,500; 31 combat aircraft.
15 MiG-17, 12 MiG-21, 4 G-91 fighters.
Tpts incl 6 *Noratlas*, 2 C-45, 3 C-47, 10 Do-27,
   5 An-26, 2 *Turbo-Porter*, *Islander*.
Some 7 Mi-8, 24 *Alouette* III, 2 Bell 47 hel.
3 MiG-15UTI trainers.
AA-2 *Atoll* AAM.

PEOPLE'S REPUBLIC OF CONGO

Population: 1,470,000.
Military service: voluntary.
Total armed forces: 7,000.
Estimated GNP 1977: $610 m.
Defence expenditure 1976: 8.89 bn CFA francs
   ($37.2 m).
   $1 = 249 CFA francs (1977), 239 CFA francs (1976).

Army: 6,500.
1 armd bn (5 sqns).
1 inf bn.
1 para-cdo bn.
1 arty gp.
1 engr bn.
T-59 med, 14 Chinese T-62, 3 PT-76 lt tks; 10
   BRDM-1 scout cars; 44 BTR-152 APC; 6 75mm,
   10 100mm guns; 8 122mm how; 82mm, 10
   120mm mor; 57mm, 76mm ATK guns; 10
   14.5mm, 37mm, 57mm AA guns.

Navy: 200.
3 patrol boats (ex-Chinese *Shanghai*-class).
4 river patrol craft (under 100 tons).

Air Force: 300; 10 combat aircraft.
10 MiG-15/-17 fighters.
3 C-47, 4 An-24, 1 F-28, 1 *Frégate*, 5 Il-14, 3
   Broussard tpts.
4 *Alouette* II/III hel.

Para-Military Forces: 1,400 Gendarmerie; 2,500
   militia.

ETHIOPIA

Population: 30,010,000.
Military service: conscription.
Total armed forces: 93,500.
Estimated GNP 1976: $2.9 bn.
Defence expenditure 1978: 345 m birr ($165 m).*
   $US 1 = 2.09 birr (1978), 2.08 birr (1976).

Army: 90,000.†
8 inf divs with some 12 tk bns.
3 lt divs.
2 para/cdo bdes.
5 arty, 2 engr bns.
24 M-60, 30 M-47, 50 T-34, 400 T-54/-55 med,
   50 M-41 lt tks; 56 AML-60 armd cars; BRDM-2
   scout cars; BMP-1 MICV; about 70 M-113,
   Commando, 300 BTR-40/-60/-152 APC; 52
   105mm, 150 122mm, 130mm, 152mm, 12 155mm
   towed, 12 M-109 155mm SP how; 82mm, 120mm,
   280 M-2/-30 4.2in mor; BM-21 122mm RL;
   Sagger ATGW; ZU-23, 37mm, ZU-57 AA guns.

Navy: 1,500.
1 coastal minesweeper (ex-Netherlands).
1 training ship (ex-US seaplane tender).
9 large patrol craft (5 ex-US PGM, 4 ex-US
   Sewart-type, 1 ex-Yugoslav *Kraljevica*-class).
2 *Osa*-II class FPBG with *Styx* SSM.
4 *Swift*-class FPB.
4 coastal patrol craft (under 50 tons).
4 landing craft (ex-US, under 100 tons).

Air Force: 2,000; 99 combat aircraft.
1 lt bbr sqn with 2 *Canberra* B2.
6 FGA sqns: 2 with 14 F-5A/E, 1 with 7 F-86F, 2
   with 50 MiG-21, 1 with 20 MiG-23.
1 COIN sqn with 6 T-28A.
1 tpt sqn with 5 C-47, 2 C-54, 7 C-119G, 3 *Dove*,
   1 Il-14, 1 DHC-3, 3 DHC-6, 8 An-12, 4 An-22.
3 trg sqns with 20 *Safir*, T-28A/D, 11 T-33A, 2 F-5B.
Hels incl 10 AB-204, 5 *Alouette* III, 30 Mi-8,
   Mi-6, 10 UH-1H, 1 *Puma*.

Para-Military Forces: 119,000: 9,000 mobile
   emergency police force; 100,000 People's Militia,
   in 8 divs with mor, ATK guns; 10,000 People's
   Protection bdes.

GHANA

Population: 10,680,000.
Military Service: voluntary.
Total armed forces: 17,700.
Estimated GNP 1977: $4.1 bn.
Defence expenditure 1977: 113.5 m cedi
   ($130.5 m).
   $1 = 1.15 cedi (1977).

Army: 15,000.
2 bdes (6 inf bns and support units).
1 recce bn.
1 mor bn.

* Plus 105 m birr ($50 m) for Law and Security.
† Augmented by 100,000 People's Militia, with a further
50,000 under training. Some 16–17,000 Cubans also
serve with the Ethiopian forces and operate ac and hy
equipment.

1 fd engr, 1 sigs bn.
1 AB coy.
9 *Saladin* armd cars; 26 *Ferret* scout cars; 81mm,
10 120mm mor.

DEPLOYMENT: *Egypt* (UNEF): 1 bn, 597 men.

Navy: 1,300.
2 Vosper Mk 1 ASW corvettes.
1 minesweeper (ex-British *Ton*-class).
4 large patrol craft (2 ex-British *Ford*-class).
1 ex-LCT trg vessel.
(4 *Jaguar*-class FPB on order.)

Air Force: 1,400; 12 combat aircraft.
1 COIN sqn with 6 MB-326F, 6 MB-326K.
2 tpt sqns with 8 *Islander*, 6 *Skyvan* 3M.
1 comms and liaison sqn with 6 F-27, 1 F-28.
1 hel sqn with 2 Bell 212, 4 *Alouette* III, 3 Hughes
269.
12 *Bulldog* trainers

Para-Military Forces: 3,000, 3 Border Guard bns.

KENYA

Population: 14,870,000.
Military service: voluntary.
Total armed forces: 9,100.
Estimated GNP 1977: $3.7 bn.
Defence expenditure 1977: 668 m shillings ($80 m).
$1 = 7.81 shillings (1978), 8.35 shillings (1977).

Army: 7,500.
4 inf bns.
1 arty bn.
1 spt gp, 1 engr bn.
3 *Saladin*, 30 AML-60/-90 armd, 14 *Ferret* scout
cars; 15 UR-416, 10 Panhard M3 APC; 8 105mm
lt guns; 20 81mm, 8 120mm mor; 56 84mm *Carl
Gustav* and 120mm RCL. (38 Vickers Mk3 med
tks on order.)

Navy: 400.
7 large patrol craft.

Air Force: 1,200; 13 combat aircraft.
1 FGA sqn with 4 Hunter FGA9, 4 F-5E/F.
1 COIN sqn with 5 BAC-167 *Strikemaster*.
1 trg sqn with 14 *Bulldog*.
2 lt tpt sqns: 1 with 6 DHC-4, 1 with 7 DHC-2, 2
DHC-5, 2 Do-28D.
Other ac incl 1 *Turbo Commander*, 2 *Navajo* ac;
2 *Puma*, 2 Bell 47G hel.
(8 F-5E/F fighters, 12 *Hawk* trainers, 4 DHC-5D,
4 Do-28D tpts on order.)

Para-Military Forces: 1,500 police (General Service
Unit), 9 Cessna lt ac.

MOZAMBIQUE

Population: 9,870,000.
Military service: voluntary.
Total armed forces: 21,200.*
Defence expenditure 1978: 3,650 m escudos
($109 m).
$1 = 33.51 escudos (1978).

Army: 20,000.
1 tk bn.
28 inf bns.
2–3 arty bns.
150 T-34/-54/-55 med, some PT-76 lt tks; BTR-40,
BRDM armd cars; BTR-40/-152 APC; 76mm,
85mm, 100mm, 122mm guns/how; BM-21 multiple RL; 60mm, 82mm, 120mm mor; 82mm,
107mm RCL; *Sagger* ATGW; 23mm, 37mm, 57mm
AA guns; 24 SA-6, SA-7 SAM.

Navy: 700.
1 *Poluchat*-class large patrol craft.
6 patrol craft (ex-Portuguese, 1 *Antares*-, 3 *Jupiter*-,
2 *Bellatrix*-class).
1 *Alfange*-class LCT.

Air Force: 500; 47 combat aircraft.†
47 MiG-21 fighters.
Tpts incl 6 *Noratlas*, 5 C-47, An-24.
Lt ac incl 7 Zlin.
15 *Harvard* trainers.
2 *Alouette* II/III, some Mi-8 hel.
AA-2 *Atoll* AAM.

NIGERIA

Population: 68,290,000.
Military service: voluntary.
Total armed forces: 231,500.‡
Estimated GNP 1977: $34.2 bn.
Defence expenditure 1977–78: 1,718 bn naira
($2.67 bn).
$1 = 0.623 naira (1978), 0.643 naira (1977).

Army: 221,000.
4 inf divs.
4 engr bdes.
4 recce regts.
4 arty regts.
50 *Scorpion* lt tks; 20 *Saladin*, 15 AML-60/-90
armd cars; 25 *Ferret*, 20 *Fox* scout cars; 8
Saracen APC; 105mm, 122mm guns/how; 76mm
ATK guns; 20mm, 40mm AA guns.

DEPLOYMENT: *Lebanon* (UNIFIL): 1 bn (669).

---

* The aim is to have 30,000 trained troops organized
into 4 bdes. Chinese, Cuban, East German, Romanian
and Soviet advisers reported with Mozambique forces.
† Not all the aircraft shown are necessarily airworthy.
‡ Large-scale demobilization has been planned.

Navy: 4,500.
1 ASW frigate.
2 corvettes.
10 large patrol craft (4 under 100 tons).
1 LCT.
(1 GW frigate, 2 corvettes, 6 FPBG with *Otomat* and *Exocet* SSM, *Seacat* SAM on order.)

RESERVES: 2,000.

Air Force: 6,000; 24 combat aircraft.*
2 FGA/interceptor sqns: 1 with 4 MiG-17, 1 with 20 MiG-21J.
2 tpt sqns with 6 C-130H, 2 F-27, 1 F-28, 1 *Gulf-stream* II.
1 hel sqn with 3 *Whirlwind*, 4 BO-105, 10 *Puma*, 10 *Alouette* III.
3 trg/service sqns with 2 MiG-15, 2 Mig-21U, 32 SA *Bulldog*, 19 Do-27/-28, 3 Piper *Navajo*, 15 L-29.
(6 CH-47, 6 BO-105 hel on order.)

RHODESIA

Population: 6,990,000 (250,000 White).
Military service: 18 months (White, Asian and Coloured population; Black doctors and apprentices are liable for conscription).
Total armed forces: 10,800.†
Estimated GNP 1977: $US 3.1 bn.
Defence expenditure 1978–79: $R 149 m‡
    ($US 242 m).
    $US1 = $R 0.668 (1978), $R 0.617 (1977).

Army: 9,500 (3,250 conscripts).†
1 armd car regt.
6 inf bns.§
4 Special Air Service sqns.
Selous Scouts (Special Forces unit).
Grey's Scouts, mounted inf (250).
1 arty regt.
6 engr sqns.
7 signals sqns.
60 AML-90 *Eland* armd cars; *Ferret* scout cars; *Hippo*, *Hyena* and *Leopard* (local-built) lt APC; 25-pdr, 105mm how, 5.5-in guns/how; 105mm RCL; *Tigercat* SAM.

Air Force: 1,300; 84 combat aircraft.
1 lt bbr sqn with 5 *Canberra* B2 and 2 T4.
2 FGA sqns: 1 with 10 *Hunter* FGA9, 1 with 18 *Vampire* FB9.
1 trg/recce sqn with 8 *Provost* T-52, 11 *Vampire* T55.
1 COIN/recce sqn with 12 AL-60C4, 18 Cessna 337 (*Lynx*).
1 tpt sqn with 10 C-47, 1 *Baron* 55, 6 *Islander*.
2 hel sqns with 66 *Alouette* II/III.

RESERVES:
White, Asian and Coloured citizens aged 17–25 undergo 18 months National Service before joining Territorial Army units (8 bns). Thereafter operational duties amount to about 4 months a year in periods of 30 or 56 days at one time. Those aged 26–37 without previous military training usually receive 84 days basic training for the Territorial Army or 56 days for the Police Reserve or Ministry of Internal Affairs. Commitments thereafter are for up to 4 months a year on a periodic basis. Men aged 38–50 undergo 3 weeks basic training before being posted to the Police Reserve, operational duty consists of up to 70 days a year in periods of 2–4 weeks.
Those over 50 are posted to the Rhodesia Defence Regiment (RDR). The RDR includes all Asians and Coloureds and those not fit for more active duty. Some men over 50 join the Special Reserves with police duties.

Para-Military Forces: British South African Police (BSAP): 8,000 active, 35,000 reservists (the White population provides about a third of the active strength but nearly three-quarters of the reservist strength). Guard Force: establishment 1,000.

SENEGAL

Population: 4,750,000.
Military service: 2 years selective.
Total armed forces: 6,550.
Estimated GNP 1977: $1.7 bn.
Defence expenditure 1978: 11.14 bn CFA francs
    ($48 m).
    $1 = 231 CFA francs (1978), 249 CFA francs (1977).

Army: 6,000.
4 inf bns.
1 engr bn.
1 recce sqn.
2 para coys.
2 cdo coys.
1 arty bty.
AML armd cars; 12 VXB-170 APC; 75mm pack how, 6 105mm how; 8 81mm mor; 30mm, 40mm AA guns.

DEPLOYMENT: *Lebanon* (UNIFIL): 1 bn (634).

---

* There are additional unserviceable aircraft.
† Plus about 15,000 Territorial Army and Police Reserve called up for service at any one time.
‡ A further $R 60 m is in the Police vote.
§ 1 White bn (1,200), 4 Black bns (4,000); a fifth Black forming. There is an establishment for 3 bdes, to be brought up to strength by mobilizing Territorials. Black regular soldiers are allocated to White Territorial Army bns to bring them up to strength.

Navy: 350.
3 large patrol craft.
2 ex-French VC Type patrol craft (under 100 tons).
1 coastal patrol craft (under 100 tons).
1 LCT, 6 landing craft.

Air Force: 200; no combat aircraft.
2 *Magister*; 6 C-47, 4 F-27, 4 *Broussard*, 1 Cessna 337 tpts.
2 *Alouette* II, 1 *Gazelle* hel.

Para-Military Forces: 1,600.

SOMALI DEMOCRATIC REPUBLIC

Population: 3,430,000.
Military service: voluntary.
Total armed forces: 51,500.
Estimated GNP 1977: $425 m.
Defence expenditure 1976: 165 m shillings ($25 m).
$1 = 6.30 shillings (1977), 6.6 shillings (1976).

Army: 50,000 (plus 20,000 Militia).*
3 div HQ.
20 bde HQ.
7 tk bns.
8 mech inf bns.
14 mot inf bns.
16 inf bns.
2 cdo bns.
13 fd, 10 AA arty bns.
50 T-34, 30 T-54/-55 med tks; BRDM-2 scout cars: 50 BTR-40/-50/-60, 100 BTR-152 APC; about 100 76mm, 85mm, 80 122mm, 130mm guns/how; 81mm mor; 100mm ATK guns; 106mm RCL; *Milan* ATGW; 150 14.5mm, 37mm, 57mm and 100mm towed, ZSU-23-4 SP AA guns; SA-2/-3 SAM.

Navy: 500.*
4 *Mol*-class patrol craft (2 with torpedo tubes).
3 *Osa*-II-class FPBG with *Styx* SSM.
6 large patrol craft (ex-Soviet *Poluchat*-class).
4 MTB (ex-Soviet P-6-class).
1 LCT (ex-Soviet *Polnocny*-class).
4 medium landing craft (ex-Soviet T-4-class).

Air Force: 1,000; 25 combat aircraft.*
1 lt bbr sqn with 3 Il-28.
2 FGA sqns with 15 MiG-17 and MiG-15UTI.
1 fighter sqn with 7 MiG-21MF.
1 tpt sqn with 3 An-2, 3 An-24/-26.
Other aircraft incl 3 C-47, 1 C-45, 6 P-148, 15 Yak-11, 2 Do-28.
1 hel sqn with 5 Mi-4, 5 Mi-8, 1 AB-204.
AA-2 *Atoll* AAM.

Para-Military Forces: 29,500: 8,000 Police; 1,500 border guards; 20,000 People's Militia.

SOUTH AFRICA

Population: 27,580,000.
Military service: 24 months.
Total armed forces: 65,500 (48,900 conscripts; total mobilizable strength 404,500).
Estimated GNP 1977: $43.8 bn.
Defence expenditure 1978–79: 2.28 bn rand ($2.62 bn).
$1 = 0.87 rand (1978), 0.87 rand (1977).

Army: 50,000 (43,000 conscripts, 2,100 women).
1 corps, 2 div HQ (1 armd, 1 inf).
1 armd bde.†
2 mech bdes.†
4 mot bdes.†
3 para bns.†
11 fd and 1 med arty regts.†
9 lt AA arty regts.†
10 fd engr sqns.†
5 sigs regts.†
Some 150 *Centurion*, 20 *Comet* med, 90 M-41 lt tks; 1,400 *Eland* (AML-60/-90), Mk IV armd cars; 230 scout cars incl *Ferret*, M-3A1; 280 *Saracen*, *Ratel* APC; 500 lt APC incl *Hippo*, *Rhino*; 125 25-pdr, 5.5-in towed, 50 *Sexton* 25-pdr SP guns, 81mm, 120mm mor; 15 17-pdr, 900 90mm ATK guns; SS-11, *ENTAC* ATGW; 204GK 20mm, 55 K-63 twin 35mm, 25 L/70 40mm, 15 3.7-in AA guns; 18 *Cactus* (*Crotale*), *Tigercat* SAM.

RESERVES: 138,000 Active Reserve (Citizen Force). Reservists serve 30 days per year for 8 years. Some Citizen Force units have been deployed on the Angola border for up to 90 days.

Navy: 5,500 (1,400 conscripts).
3 *Daphne*-class submarines.
1 destroyer (ex-British 'W'-class) with 2 *Wasp* ASW hel.
3 ASW frigates (each with 1 *Wasp* hel).
3 *Reshef*-class FPBG with *Gabriel* SSM.
1 escort minesweeper (training ship).
10 coastal minesweepers (ex-British *Ton*-class).
5 large patrol craft (ex-British *Ford*-class).
(3 *Reshef*-class FPBG on order.)

RESERVES: 10,500 Citizen Force.

Air Force: 10,000 (4,500 conscripts); 345 combat aircraft (incl 70 with Citizen Force and operational trainers).
2 lt bbr sqns: 1 with 6 *Canberra* B(I)12, 3 T4; 1 with 9 *Buccaneer* S50.
1 FGA sqn with 32 *Mirage* F-1AZ.
1 fighter/recce sqn with 36 *Mirage* IIICZ/EZ/RZ/R2Z.
1 interceptor sqn with 16 *Mirage* F-1CZ.

---

* Spares are short and not all equipment is serviceable.
† Cadre units, forming 2 divs when brought to full strength on mobilization of Citizen Force.

2 MR sqns with 7 *Shackleton* MR3, 18 Piaggio P166S.

3 tpt sqns with 7 C-130B, 9 Transall C-160Z, 28 C-47, 5 DC-4, 1 *Viscount* 781, 4 HS-125, 7 Swearingen *Merlin* IVA.

4 hel sqns: 2 with 40 *Alouette* III, 1 with 19 SA-330 *Puma*, 1 with 14 SA-321L *Super Frelon*.

1 flt of 11 *Wasp* with AS.11 (naval assigned), 2 *Alouette* II.

Other hels incl 17 *Alouette* III, 40 SA-330 *Puma*.

4 comms and liaison sqns (army assigned) with 20 Cessna 185A/D/E, 36 AM-3C *Bosbok*, 20 C-4M *Kudu*.

Operational trainers incl 16 *Mirage* IIIBZ/DZ/D2Z, 12 F-86, 120 MB-326M/K *Impala* I/II, other trg ac incl 110 *Harvard* (some armed), 5 C-47 ac, 10 *Alouette* III hel.

R.530, R.550 *Magic* AAM; AS.20/30 ASM.

RESERVES: 25,000 Active Citizen Force.
5 COIN/trg sqns with 60 *Impala* I/II, 10 *Harvard*.

Para-Military Forces: 110,000 Commandos (in inf bn-type units grouped in formations of 5 or more with local industrial and rural protection duties). Members do 12 months' initial and 19 days' annual training. There are 13 Air Cdo sqns with private aircraft. 35,500 South African Police (SAP) (19,500 Whites, 16,000 Non-Whites), 20,000 Police Reserves.

TANZANIA

Population: 16,520,000.
Military service: voluntary.
Total armed forces: 26,700.
Estimated GNP 1977: $2.9 bn.
Defence expenditure 1977: 1.17 bn shillings ($140 m).
$1 = 8.35 shillings (1977).

Army: 25,000.
4 bde HQ.
1 tk regt.
13 inf bns.
3 arty bns.
1 engr regt.
20 T-59 med, T-60, 14 T-62 lt tks; BTR-40/-152, K-63 APC; 24 76mm guns, 30 122mm how; 82mm, 50 120mm mor; 14.5mm, 37mm AA guns; SA-3 SAM.

DEPLOYMENT: *Mozambique:* 1 inf bn.

Navy: 700.
1 large patrol craft (ex-Soviet *Poluchat*-class).
7 FPB (*Shanghai*-class).
3 P-6-, 4 P-4-class MTB, 4 *Hu-Chwan* hydrofoils.
8 coastal patrol craft (under 100 tons).

Air Force: 1,000; 29 combat aircraft.
3 fighter sqns with 11 MiG-21/F-8, 3 MiG-17/F-4, 15 MiG-19/F-6.
1 tpt sqn with 1 An-2, 3 HS-748, 12 DHC-4, 6 Cessna 310.
2 MiG-15UTI, 6 *Cherokee* trainers.
2 Bell 47G, 4 AB-206 hel.
(4 DHC-5D tpts on order.)

Para-Military Forces: 1,400 Police Field Force and a police marine unit; 35,000 Citizen's Militia.

UGANDA

Population: 12,700,000.
Military service: voluntary.
Total armed forces: 21,000.
Estimated GDP 1976: $3.2 bn.
Defence expenditure 1976–77: 429 m shillings ($52 m).
$1 = 8.38 shillings (1976).

Army: 20,000.*
2 bdes, each of 4 bns.
1 recce bn.
1 mech inf bn.
1 para/cdo, 1 marine/cdo bn.
1 trg bn.
1 arty regt.
10 T-34, 15 T-54/-55, 10 M-4 med, PT-76 lt tks; BRDM-2, *Saladin* armd, 15 *Ferret* scout cars; 120 BTR-40/-152, OT-64, *Saracen* APC; 76mm, 122mm guns; 82mm, 120mm mor; *Sagger* ATGW; 50 40mm AA guns; SA-7 SAM.

Navy: A small lake patrol service being formed.

Air Force: 1,000;† 37 combat aircraft.*
2 fighter sqns with 25 MiG-21, 10 MiG-17, 2 MiG-15UTI.
1 tpt sqn with 1 L-100-20, 6 C-47, 1 DHC-6.
1 hel sqn with 6 AB-205, 4 AB-206.
Trainers incl 5 L-29, 10 Piper *Super Cub*, 6 AS 202 *Bravo*.
AA-2 *Atoll* AAM.

ZAIRE REPUBLIC

Population: 27,080,000.
Military service: conscription.
Total armed forces: 33,400.
Estimated GNP 1977: $3.5 bn.
Defence expenditure 1976: 142 m zaires ($164 m).
$1 = 0.86 zaires (1977), 0.81 zaires (1976).

* Not all eqpt and ac are likely to be serviceable.
† Excluding expatriate instructors and maintenance personnel.

Army: 30,000.

2 tk bns.

2 armd bns.

1 mech bn.

14 inf bns.

5 para, 2 cdo bns.

4 'Guard' bns.

60 Type-62 lt tks (ex-Chinese); 44 AML-90, 122 AML-60 armd cars; 60 M-3 APC; 75mm pack, 122mm, 130mm guns/how; 82mm, 120mm mor; 107mm RL; 57mm ATK guns; 75mm, 106mm RCL; *Snapper* ATGW; 20mm, 37mm, 40mm AA guns.

(10 M-60 tks, 10 M-113 APC on order.)

Navy: 400.

2 FPB (*Shanghai*-class).

3 P4 torpedo boats (ex-Korean).

21 coastal patrol crafts (6 ex-US *Sewart* Type).

Air Force: 3,000; 49 combat aircraft.

1 fighter sqn with 14 *Mirage* VM, 3 VDM.

2 COIN sqns with 12 MB-326GB, 8 AT-6G, 12 AT-28D.

1 observation sqn with 20 Reims Cessna FTB 337.

1 tpt wing with 7 C-130H, 2 DC-6, 2 DHC-4A, 3 DHC-5, 4 C-54, 8 C-47, 2 Mu-2.

1 hel sqn with 14 *Alouette* III, 8 *Puma*, 1 *Super Frelon*, 7 Bell 47.

Trg ac incl 23 SF-260MC, 15 T-6, 15 Cessna A150, 15 Cessna 310.

(3 DHC-5 tpts on order.)

Para-Military Forces: 35,000: 8 National Guard, 6 Gendarmerie bns.

ZAMBIA

Population: 5,400,000.

Military service: voluntary.

Total armed forces: 14,300.

Estimated GNP 1976: $2.2 bn.

Defence expenditure 1977: 246 m kwacha ($310 m).

$1 = 0.796 kwacha (1977), 0.643 (1976).

Army: 12,800.

1 armd car regt.

8 inf bns.

1 arty bty.

1 AA arty regt.

1 engr sqn.

1 sigs sqn.

10 T-54 tks; 28 *Ferret* scout cars; 8 M-56 105mm pack how; 24 20mm AA guns.

Air Force: 1,500; 30 combat aircraft.

1 FGA sqn with 6 *Galeb*, 6 *Jastreb*.

1 COIN/trg sqn with 18 MB-326G.

2 tpt sqns: 1 with 2 Yak-40, 2 DC-6, 5 DHC-4, 7 DHC-5, 10 C-47, 1 HS-748; 1 with 7 DHC-2, 10 Do-28.

1 liaison sqn with 20 Saab *Supporter*.

Trainers incl 6 *Chipmunk*, 8 SF-260MZ.

1 hel sqn with 3 AB-205, 5 AB-206, 3 AB-212, 21 Bell 47G, 7 Mi-8.

1 SAM unit with 12 *Rapier*.

Para-Military Forces: 1,200; Police Mobile Unit (PMU) 700 (1 bn of 4 coys); Para-Military Police Unit (PMPU) 500 (1 bn of 3 coys). 2 hels.

For the armed forces of smaller states, see table overleaf.

ARMED FORCES OF OTHER AFRICAN STATES*

Country	Estimated population (000)	Estimated GNP 1977 ($m)	Total armed forces	Army Manpower and formations	Army Equipment	Navy Manpower and equipment	Air Force Manpower and equipment	Para-military forces
Benin	3,380	650 (GDP)	2,250	2,100 / 2 inf bns / 1 engr bn / 1 para/cdo coy / 1 arty bty	7 M-8 armd cars; 105mm how; 60mm, 81mm mor	—	150 / 3 med, 5 lt tpts; 1 Bell 47, 1 *Alouette* II hel	1,000
Burundi	4,000	405	4,500†	3 inf bns / 1 'para' bn / 1 'cdo' bn / 1 armd car coy	AML armd cars	—	3 DC-3 tpts; some hel	2,000
Cameroon	7,300	1,700 (1976)	6,100	5,500 / 4 inf bns / 1 armd car sqn / 1 para coy / engr/spt units	M-8 armd, *Ferret* scout cars; 18 *Commando*, M-3 APC; 75mm, 105mm how; 57mm ATK guns; 60mm, 81mm mor; 106mm RCL	300 / 2 *Shanghai* FPB; 2 P-48 patrol craft, 3 small patrol boats; 1 med, 6 small landing craft	300 / 4 *Magister*; 2 C-130, 4 C-47, 2 DHC-4, 2 HS-748 tpts; 9 lt ac; 3 *Alouette* II/III, 1 *Puma* hel	7,000
Central African Empire	1,850	300 (1976)	1,200	1,100 / 1 inf bn / 1 engr coy / 1 sigs coy	*Ferret* scout cars; 81mm mor; 106mm RCL	—	100 / 1 DC-3, 1 DC-4, 3 C-47, 1 *Caravelle*, 1 *Falcon* tpts; 10 AL-60, 6 *Broussard*, 2 *Rallye*; 1 *Alouette* II, 5 H-34 hel	1,400
Chad	4,290	445	5,200	5,000 / 3 inf/para bns	AML armd cars; 81mm, 120mm mor	—	200 / 4 A-1D FGA; 3 C-54, 9 C-47, 1 *Caravelle*, 2 *Turbo-Porter* tpts; 6 lt ac; 11 *Alouette* II/III, 4 *Puma* hel	6,000
Gabon	115	1,810	1,250	950 / 1 inf bn / 2 cdo coys / 1 engr coy / 1 service coy	AML-90 armd cars; 12 VXB APC; 81mm mor; 106mm RCL (6 *Commando* APC on order)	100 / 1 FPBG with SS-12 SSM; 3 patrol boats	200 / 3 *Mirage* VG, 2 VRG, 4 A-1D FGA; 3 C-130, 2 DC-6, 3 C-47, 3 Nord 262, 1 *Falcon*, 1 *Gulfstream* tpts; 7 lt ac; 4 *Alouette* III, 3 *Puma* hel	1,600

Guinea	4,740	740	8,850	**8,000** 1 armd bn 4 inf bns 1 engr bn	30 T-34/-54 med, 10 PT-76 lt tks; 40 BTR-40/-152 APC; 76mm, 85mm, 105mm, 122mm guns/how; 57mm ATK, 37mm, 57mm, 100mm AA guns	**350** 6 *Shanghai* FPB, 2 *Polu-chat*, 4 P-6, 2 coastal patrol boats, 2 small landing craft	**500** 5 MiG-17 FGA, 4 Il-14, 2 Il-18, 4 An-4 tpts; 2 MiG-15, 7 Yak-18, 3 L-29, trainers; 2 Bell 47 hel	8,000
Ivory Coast	5,270	5,980 (GDP)	4,950	**4,500** 3 inf bns 1 tk sqn 1 para coy 2 arty btys 1 AA arty bty 1 engr coy	5 AMX-13 lt tks; 16 AML-60/-90 armd cars; 4 105mm how; 81mm, 120mm mor; 10 40mm AA guns	**250** 2 patrol boats with SS-12 SSM; 1 80-ton, 5 river patrol boats, 1 landing ship log, 1 trg and supply ship, 2 small landing craft (2 FPB on order)	**200** 3 C-47, 2 F-27, 2 F-28 tpts; 3 Cessna F-337, 2 Cessna 150; 5 *Alouette* II/III, 3 *Puma* hel (12 *AlphaJet* trainers on order)	3,000
Liberia	1,830	910	5,250†	**5,250** 5 inf bns 1 Guard bn 1 arty bn 1 engr bn 1 service bn 1 recce coy	12 M-3A1 scout cars; 75mm, 105mm how; 60mm, 10 81mm mor; 106mm RCL	1 MGB, 5 small patrol boats	2 C-47, 6 Cessna 172/185/207	21,300
Malagasy Republic	8,090	1,795	10,500	**9,550** 2 inf regts 1 engr regt 1 sigs regt 1 service bn	M-8 armd, *Ferret* scout cars; M-3 APC; 81mm mor; 106mm RCL	**600** 1 large patrol craft, 1 landing ship (tpt), 1 trg ship, 1 marine coy	**350** 5 C-47, 1 C-53, 1 *Defender*, 1 *Aztec*, 7 lt ac; 1 Bell 47, 3 *Alouette* II/III, 2 Mi-8 hel	7,000
Malawi	5,450	925	2,400†	**2,400** 2 inf bns 1 recce coy	10 *Ferret* scout cars; 81mm mor	4 small lake patrol boats	4 C-47, 1 *Defender*, 2 Do-28 tpts (4 Do-28 on order)	460
Mali	6,140	615	4,200†	**4,200** 5 inf bns 1 tk coy 1 para coy 1 arty bn 1 engr coy	20 T-34, 6 Type 62 lt tks; 20 BRDM-2 armd cars; BTR-152 APC; 85mm, 100mm guns; 81mm, 120mm mor; 37mm, 57mm AA guns	3 river patrol craft	**5** 5 MiG-17; 2 C-47, 2 An-2, 1 An-24 tpts; 2 MiG-15, Yak trainers, 2 Mi-4 hel	5,700

For notes, see p. 54.

Armed Forces of Other African States (cont.)

Country	Estimated population (000)	Estimated GNP 1977 ($m)	Total armed forces	Army — Manpower and formations	Army — Equipment	Navy — Manpower and equipment	Air Force — Manpower and equipment	Para-military forces
Mauritania	1,430	210 (1976)	12,450	12,000 / 30 mot inf sqns / 3 recce sqns / 1 AB coy / 1 para/cdo coy	15 EBR-75, AML-60/-90 armd cars; APC; 60mm, 81mm mor; 57mm, 75mm, 106mm RCL	300 / 4 patrol boats, 2 small patrol craft (2 FPB on order)	150 / 8 *Defender*, 1 C-54 3 C-47, 2 DHC-5D, 1 *Caravelle*, 2 *Skvvan*, tpts; 4 Cessna F-337, 1 AL-60B (4 IA-58 *Pucará* COIN on order)	6,000
Niger	5,020	825 (1976)	2,050	2,000 / 1 recce sqn / 5 inf coys / 1 para coy / 1 engr coy	10 M-8, M-20 armd cars; 60mm, 81mm mor; 57mm, 75mm RCL	—	50 / 2 C-47, 1 C-54, 3 *Noratlas* tpts; 1 Aero Commander, 2 Cessna 337	1,800
Rwanda	4,520	515 (1976)	3,750†	3,750 / 1 recce sqn / 8 inf coys / 1 cdo coy	12 AML-60/-90 armd cars; 6 57mm guns; 8 81mm mor	—	2 C-47, 2 *Islander* tpts; 3 AM-3C liaison; 1 *Magister* trg ac; 2 *Alouette* III hel	1,200
Sierra Leone	2,820	720	2,200†	2,000 / 2 inf bns	10 Mowag armd cars; 60mm, 81mm mor	3 *Shanghai*-class FPB	2 Saab MFI-15 trainers; 3 Hughes 300/500 hel	2,500
Togo	2,400	565	2,950†	2,950 / 1 mot inf bn / 2 inf bns / 2 para/cdo bns	5 M-8 armd cars; 5 M-3, 30 UR-416 APC	2 coastal patrol craft	5 *Magister*, 3 EMB-326GB COIN; 2 C-47, 2 DHC-5D, 1 F-28 tpts; 4 lt ac; 1 *Puma* hel (3 EMB-326GB COIN, 5 *Alpha-Jet* trg ac on order)	1,400
Upper Volta	6,460	795	8,070†	8,070 / 11 inf bns / 1 armd sqn / 1 para coy / 1 arty bty	AML-60/-90, M-8 armd, *Ferret* scout cars; 105mm how; 60mm, 81mm mor; 75mm RCL	—	2 C-47, 2 Nord 262, 1 HS-748 tpts; 5 lt ac	1,850

* For many developing nations, particularly the smaller ones, maintenance facilities and skills pose problems, and spare parts may not be readily available. The amounts of equipment shown may not necessarily be those which can be used. Logistic and maintenance support may be by civilians or expatriate personnel.

† All services form part of the Army.

Asia and Australasia

CHINA

Chinese defence policy has for many years maintained a balance, at times uneasy, between the two extremes of nuclear deterrence and People's War. The former aims to deter strategic attack, the latter, by mass mobilization of the population, to deter or repel conventional land invasion. With Mao's death in September 1976 and the attack on the 'Gang of Four' thereafter, the strongest adherents of the strategic concept that men are more important than weapons were removed. There is now some indication of an effort to develop more modern general-purpose forces in order to meet more limited military contingencies than the extremes of nuclear deterrence or mass war.

The People's Liberation Army (PLA) was probably the key factor in the accession to power of Hua Kuo-feng, despite some division within its leadership. The PLA can therefore be expected to have increased influence over military policy, and it has not hidden its desire for more modern weapons and for increased spending. Military conferences have covered air defence, aircraft and missiles, and planning, research and production. While this foreshadows efforts at modernization, there is continuing debate about its pace and nature. It is too early yet to see whether, or how soon, the money for it will be forthcoming (but see the note on defence expenditure on p. 57). It is also too early to foresee the effect of Teng Hsiao-ping's reappointment at the end of July 1977 to his three major positions, including Chief of the PLA General Staff. The picture that can be drawn of Chinese forces accordingly is not dissimilar from that of last year.

Nuclear Weapons

The testing programme continued, with two 20KT atmospheric tests in the year: one in September 1977, the other in March 1978, bringing the total to twenty-three since testing started in 1964. A theatre nuclear force is operational, capable of reaching large parts of the Soviet Union and Asia. The stockpile of weapons, both fission and fusion, probably amounts to several hundreds and could continue to grow rapidly. Fighter aircraft could be used for tactical delivery, and for longer ranges there is the Tu-16 medium bomber, with a radius of action up to 2,000 miles. MRBM with a range of some 600–700 miles are operational but may be phased out and replaced by IRBM, also operational now, with a range of 1,500–1,750 miles. The missile force seems to be controlled by the Second Artillery, apparently the missile arm of the PLA.

A multi-stage ICBM with a limited range of 3,000–3,500 miles was first tested in 1976 and some may have been deployed. An ICBM thought to have a range of 8,000 miles has also been under development but is unlikely to become operational for some years yet. Full-range testing, which would require impact areas in the Indian or Pacific Oceans, has not yet been carried out, but the missile has been successfully used (and thus tested) as a launcher for satellites. China has one G-class submarine with missile launching tubes, but does not appear to have missiles for it. All the present missiles are liquid-fuelled, but solid propellants are being developed.

Conventional Forces

The PLA is organized in 11 Military Regions and divided into Main and Local Forces. Main Force (MF) divisions, administered by the Military Regions in which they are stationed but commanded by the Ministry of National Defence, are available for operations in any region and are better equipped. Local Forces (LF), which include Border Defence and Internal Defence units, are predominantly infantry and concentrate on the defence of their own localities in co-operation with para-military units.

The PLA is generally equipped and trained for the environment of People's War, but new efforts are being made to arm a proportion of the formations with modern weapons. Infantry units account for most of the manpower and 121 of the 136 Main Force divisions; there are only 12 armoured divisions. The naval and air elements of the PLA have only about one-seventh of the total manpower, compared with about a third for their counterparts in the Soviet Union, but naval strength is increasing, and the equipment for both arms is steadily being modernized. The PLA, essentially a defensive force, lacks facilities and logistic support for protracted large-scale operations outside China.

Major weapons systems produced include MiG-19 and F-9 fighters (the last Chinese-designed), SA-2 SAM, Type 59 medium and Type 60 amphibious tanks, and a Chinese-designed Type 62 light tank and APC. R- and W-class medium-range diesel submarines are being built in some numbers, together with SSM destroyers and fast patrol boats; a nuclear-powered attack submarine (armed with conventional torpedoes) has been under test for some years. Most military equipment is 10–20 years out of date, but China has shown increasing interest in acquiring Western military technology.

Bilateral Agreements

China has a 30-year Treaty of Alliance and Friendship with the Soviet Union, signed in 1950, which contains mutual defence obligations, but it is highly unlikely that this remains in force. There is a mutual defence agreement with North Korea, dating from 1961, and an agreement to provide free military aid. There are non-aggression pacts with Afghanistan, Burma and Cambodia. Chinese military equipment and logistic support has been offered to a number of countries. Major recipents of arms in the past have been Albania, Pakistan and Tanzania.

CHINA

Population: 960–975,000,000.

Military service: Army 2–4 years, Air Force 4 years, Navy 5 years.

Total regular forces: 4,325,000.

GNP and defence expenditure – see note on p. 57.

Strategic Forces
IRBM: 30–40 CSS-2.
MRBM: 30–40 CSS-1.
Aircraft: about 80 Tu-16 med bbrs.

Army: 3,625,000.

Main Forces:
  11 armd divs.
  121 inf divs.
  3 AB divs.
  40 arty divs (incl AA divs).
  15 railway and construction engr divs.
  150 indep regts.

Local Forces:
  70 inf divs.
  130 indep regts.
10,000 Soviet IS-2 hy, T-34 and Chinese-produced Type-59/-63 med, Type-60 (PT-76) amph and Type-62 lt tks; 3,500 M-1967, K-63 APC; 18,000 122mm, 130mm, 152mm guns/how, incl SU-76, SU-85, SU-100 and ISU-122 SP arty; 20,000 82mm, 90mm, 120mm, 160mm mor; 132mm, 140mm RL; 57mm, 75mm, 82mm RCL; 57mm, 85mm, 100mm ATK guns; 37mm, 57mm, 85mm, 100mm AA guns.

DEPLOYMENT:

China is divided into 11 Military Regions (MR), in turn divided into Military Districts (MD), with usually two or three Districts to a Region. Divs are grouped into some 40 armies, generally of 3 inf divs, 3 arty regts and, in some cases, 3 armd regts. Main Force (MF) divs are administered by Regions but are under central comd.

The distribution of divs, excluding arty and engrs, is believed to be:

North and North-East China (Shenyang and Peking MR*): 55 MF, 25 LF divs.

North and North-West China (Lanchow and Sinkiang MR): 15 MF, 8 LF divs.

East and South-East China (Tsinan, Nanking, Foochow and Canton† MR): 32 MF, 22 LF divs.

Central China (Wuhan MR): 15 MF (incl 3 AB), 7 LF divs.

West and South-West China (Chengtu and Kunming MR*): 18 MF, 8 LF divs.

Navy: 300,000, incl 30,000 Naval Air Force and 38,000 Marines; 23 major surface combat ships.
1 *Han*-class nuclear-powered submarine.
1 G-class submarine (with SLBM tubes).‡
73 fleet submarines (incl 50 Soviet R-, 21 W-, 2 *Ming*-class).§
7 *Luta*-class destroyers with *Styx* SSM (more building).
4 ex-Soviet *Gordy*-class destroyers with *Styx* SSM.
12 frigates (4 *Riga*-type with *Styx* SSM).
14 patrol escorts.

---

* Figures include the equivalent of 2–3 divs of border troops in each of these MR.
† Includes Hainan island.
‡ China is not known to have any missiles for this boat.
§ Incl trg vessels.

39 sub chasers (20 *Kronstadt-*, 19 *Hainan*-class).

70 *Osa-* and 70 *Hoku/Komar*-type FPBG with *Styx* SSM (more building).

140 P-4/-6-class MTB (under 100 tons).

105 *Hu Chwan* hydrofoils (under 100 tons).

440 MGB (*Shanghai-*, *Swatow-*, *Whampoa*-classes).

30 minesweepers (18 Soviet T-43-type).

15 LST, 14 LSM, 15 inf landing ships, some 450 landing craft.

300 coast and river defence vessels (most under 100 tons).

DEPLOYMENT:

North Sea Fleet: about 300 vessels deployed from the mouth of the Yalu river to south of Lienyunkang; major bases at Tsingtao, Lushun, Luta.

East Sea Fleet: about 450 vessels; deployed from south of Lienyunkang to Tangshan; major bases at Shanghai, Chou Shan, Ta Hsiehtao.

South Sea Fleet: about 300 vessels; deployed from Tanshan to the Vietnamese frontier; major bases at Huangpu, Chanchiang, Yulin.

NAVAL AIR FORCE: 30,000; about 700 shore-based combat aircraft, organized into 4 bbr and 5 fighter divs, incl about 130 Il-28 torpedo-carrying, Tu-16 med and Tu-2 lt bbrs and some 500 fighters, incl MiG-17, MiG-19/F-6 and some F-9; a few Be-6 *Madge* MR ac; 50 Mi-4 *Hound* hel and some lt tpt ac. Naval fighters are integrated into the AD system.

Air Force: 400,000, incl strategic forces and 120,000 AD personnel; about 5,000 combat aircraft.

About 80 Tu-16 *Badger* and a few Tu-4 *Bull* med bbrs.

About 300 Il-28 *Beagle* and 100 Tu-2 *Bat* lt bbrs.

About 500 MiG-15 and F-9 *Fantan* FB.

About 4,000 MiG-17/-19, 80 MiG-21 and some F-9 fighters organized into air divs and regts.

About 450 fixed-wing tpt ac, incl some 300 An-2, about 100 Li-2, 50 Il-14 and Il-18, some An-12/-24/-26 and *Trident*. 350 hel, incl Mi-4, Mi-8 and 16 *Super Frelon*. These could be supplemented by about 500 ac from the Civil Aviation Administration, of which about 150 are major tpts.

There is an AD system, capable of providing a limited defence of key urban and industrial areas, military installations and weapon complexes. Up to 4,000 naval and air force fighters are assigned to this role, also about 100 CSA-1 (SA-2) SAM and over 10,000 AA guns.

Para-Military Forces: Public security force and a civilian militia with various elements: the Armed Militia, up to 7 million, organized into about 75 divs and an unknown number of regts; the Urban Militia, of several million; the Civilian Production and Construction Corps, about 4 million; and the Ordinary and Basic Militia, 75–100 million, who receive some basic training but are generally unarmed.

GROSS NATIONAL PRODUCT AND DEFENCE EXPENDITURE

Gross National Product

There are no official Chinese figures for GNP or National Income. Western estimates have varied greatly, and it is difficult to choose from a range of figures, variously defined and calculated. The United States Arms Control and Disarmament Agency (ACDA) has estimated GNP for 1975 to be $299 bn, while a recent British estimate for 1976 was $350 bn.

Defence Expenditure

China has not made public any budget figures since 1960, and there is no general agreement on the volume of resources devoted to defence. Such estimates as there are have been speculative. Western estimates place Chinese defence spending at roughly 10 per cent of GNP, or about $35 bn. The National Defence, Scientific and Technological Commission of China would like to see the defence budget increased, principally for the development and deployment of modern weapons, and there has been much talk of buying technologically advanced weapons in Europe and Japan. This suggests that defence expenditure will be significantly increased, but probably not before the 1980s. Even then, China will wish to build under licence rather than buy outright from others.

OTHER ASIAN COUNTRIES AND AUSTRALASIA

Bilateral Agreements

The United States has bilateral defence treaties with Japan, the Republic of China (Taiwan) and the Republic of Korea, and one (being renegotiated) with the Philippines. Under several other arrangements in the region, she provides military aid on either grant or credit basis to Taiwan, Indonesia, the Republic of Korea, Malaysia, the Philippines and Thailand, and sells military equipment to many countries, notably Australia, Japan, Korea and Taiwan. There are military facilities agreements with Australia, Japan, the Republic of Korea, the Philippines and Taiwan. There are major bases in the Philippines and on Guam. The 1973 Diego Garcia Agreement between the British and American governments provides for the development of the present limited US naval communications facility on Diego Garcia into a US naval support facility.

The Soviet Union has treaties of friendship, co-operation and mutual assistance with India, Bangladesh, Mongolia and the Democratic People's Republic of Korea. Military assistance agreements exist with Sri Lanka (Ceylon) and the Socialist Republic of Vietnam. Important Soviet military aid is also given to Afghanistan.

Australia has supplied a small amount of defence equipment to Malaysia and Singapore and is giving defence equipment and assistance to Indonesia, including the provision of training facilities.

Vietnam and Laos signed in July 1977 a series of agreements which contained military provisions and a border pact and may have covered the stationing of Vietnamese troops in Laos.

Multilateral Agreements

In 1954 the United States, Australia, Britain, France, New Zealand, Pakistan, the Philippines and Thailand signed the South-East Asia Collective Defence Treaty, which came into force in 1955 and brought the Treaty Organization, SEATO, into being. Pakistan left SEATO in 1973. The SEATO Council decided in 1975 that the Organization should be phased out, and it was formally closed down on 30 June 1977.

Australia, New Zealand and the United States are members of a tripartite treaty known as ANZUS, which was signed in 1951 and is of indefinite duration. Under this treaty each agrees to 'act to meet the common danger' in the event of attack on either metropolitan or island territory of any one of them, or on armed forces, public vessels or aircraft in the Pacific.

Five-Power defence arrangements, relating to the defence of Malaysia and Singapore and involving Australia, Malaysia, New Zealand, Singapore and Britain, came into effect on 1 November 1971. These stated that, in the event of any externally organized or supported armed attack or threat of attack against Malaysia or Singapore, the five governments would consult together for the purpose of deciding what measures should be taken, jointly or separately. Britain withdrew her forces from Singapore, except for a small contribution to the integrated air-defence system, by 31 March 1976. New Zealand troops remained, as did Australian air forces in Malaysia.

AFGHANISTAN

Population: 20,470,000.
Military service: 2 years.
Total armed forces: 110,000.
Estimated GNP 1977: $2.3 bn.
Defence expenditure 1977–78: 2.73 bn afghanis ($60.7 m).
$1 = 45 afghanis (1977).

Army: 100,000.
3 armd divs.
10 inf divs.
3 mountain inf bdes.

1 arty bde, 3 arty regts.
2 cdo regts.
200 T-34, 500 T-54/-55, T-62 med, 40 PT-76 lt tks; BMP MICV; 400 BTR-40/-50/-60/-152 APC; 900 76mm, 100mm, 122mm and 152mm guns/how; 100 120mm mor; 50 132mm multiple RL; 350 37mm, 85mm, 100mm towed, 20 ZSU-23-4 SP AA guns; *Sagger, Snapper* ATGW; SA-7 SAM.

RESERVES: 150,000.

Air Force: 10,000; 144 combat aircraft.
3 lt bbr sqns with 30 Il-28.
6 FGA sqns: 4 with 50 MiG-17, 2 with 24 Su-7BM.

3 interceptor sqns with 40 MiG-21.
2 tpt sqns with 10 An-2, 10 Il-14, 2 Il-18.
3 hel sqns with 18 Mi-4, 13 Mi-8.
Trainers incl 20 MiG-15/-17UTI/-21U, 2 Il-28U.
AA-2 *Atoll* AAM.
1 AD div: 1 SAM bde (3 bns with 48 SA-2), SA-3, 1
   AA bde (2 bns with 37mm, 85mm, 100mm guns),
   1 radar bde (3 bns).

RESERVES: 12,000.

Para-Military Forces: 30,000 Gendarmerie.

AUSTRALIA

Population: 14,200,000.
Military service: voluntary.
Total armed forces: 70,057.
Estimated GNP 1977: $US 92 bn.
Defence expenditure 1977–78: $A 2.43 bn
   ($US 2.68 bn).
   $1 = $A 0.875 (1978), $A 0.908 (1977).

Army: 32,084.
1 inf div HQ and 3 task force HQ.
1 armd regt.
1 recce regt.
1 APC regt.
6 inf bns.
1 Special Air Service regt.
4 arty regts (1 med, 2 fd, 1 lt AA).
1 aviation regt.
3 fd engr, 1 fd survey regt.
2 sigs regts.
87 *Leopard* med tks; 778 M-113 APC; 34 5.5-in
   guns; 254 105mm how; 72 M-40 106mm RCL;
   Redeye SAM; 17 Pilatus *Porter*, 9 *Nomad* ac;
   50 Bell 206B-1 hel; 32 watercraft. (16 *Leopard*
   med tks, 13 M-113 APC, 20 *Rapier* SAM, 10
   Blindfire AD radar on order.)

DEPLOYMENT: *Egypt* (UNEF/UNTSO): 10.

RESERVES: 22,900 (with trg obligations) in combat,
   support, log and trg units.

Navy: 16,342 (incl Fleet Air Arm).
6 *Oberon*-class submarines.
1 aircraft carrier (carries 8 A-4, 6 S-2, 10 hel).
3 *Perth*-class ASW destroyers with *Tartar* SAM, *Ikara*
   ASW msls.
2 modified *Daring*-class destroyers.
6 *River*-class destroyers with *Seacat* SAM/SSM, *Ikara*
   ASW msls.
1 trg ship.
1 coastal minesweeper, 2 coastal minehunters
   (modified British *Ton*-class).
12 *Attack*-class patrol boats.
1 oiler, 1 destroyer tender, 6 landing craft.
(3 frigates, 1 amph hy lift ship, 15 patrol craft on
   order.)

FLEET AIR ARM: 22 combat aircraft.
1 FB sqn with 8 A-4G *Skyhawk*.
2 ASW sqns with 3 S-2E, 11 S-2G *Tracker* (5 in
   reserve).
1 ASW/SAR hel sqn with 7 *Sea King*, 2 *Wessex* 31B.
1 hel sqn with 5 Bell UH-1H, 2 Bell 206B, 4 *Wessex*
   31B.
1 trg sqn with 8 MB-326H, 3 TA-4G, 5 A-4G.
2 HS-748 ECM trg ac.

RESERVES: 925 (with trg obligations).

Air Force: 21,631; 117 combat aircraft.
2 strike/recce sqns with 22 F-111C.
3 interceptor/FGA sqns with 48 *Mirage* IIIO.
1 recce sqn with 13 *Canberra* B20.
2 MR sqns: 1 with 10 P-3B *Orion*; 1 with 10 P-3C
   (being delivered).
5 tpt sqns: 2 with 24 C-130A/E; 2 with 22 DHC-4;
   1 with 2 BAC-111, 2 HS-748, 3 *Mystère* 20.
Tpt flts with 17 C-47.
1 Forward Air Controller flight with 6 CA-25.
1 OCU with 14 *Mirage* IIIO/D.
1 hel tpt sqn with 6 CH-47 *Chinook* (6 more in
   reserve).
3 utility hel sqns with 47 UH-1H *Iroquois*.
Trainers incl 80 MB-326, 8 HS-748T2, 37 CT-4
   Airtrainer.
Sidewinder, R.530 AAM.
(12 C-130H tpts on order.)

DEPLOYMENT: *Malaysia/Singapore:* 2 sqns with
   Mirage IIIO.

RESERVES: 475 (with trg obligations) in 5 Citizens
   Air Force sqns.

BANGLADESH

Population: 82,450,000.
Military service: voluntary.
Total armed forces: 73,500.
Estimated GDP 1977: $6.9 bn.
Defence expenditure 1977–78: 2.35 bn taka
   ($151 m).
   $1 = 14.78 taka (1978), 15.55 taka (1977).

Army: 65,000.
5 inf div HQ.
11 inf bdes (33 inf bns).
1 tk regt.
7 arty regts.
3 engr bns.
30 T-54 med tks; 30 105mm, 5 25-pdr guns/how;
   81mm, 50 120mm mor; 106mm RCL.*

Navy: 3,500.
2 frigates (ex-British, 1 Type 61, 1 Type 41).
4 patrol craft (2 *Kraljevica*-class).

---

* Spares are short; some equipment is unserviceable.

5 armed river patrol boats.
1 trg ship.

Air Force: 5,000; 9 combat aircraft.*
1 FB sqn with 9 MiG-21MF.
1 tpt sqn with 1 An-24, 2 An-26.
1 hel sqn with 4 *Alouette* III, 2 *Wessex* HC2, 6 Bell 212, 8 Mi-8.
Trainers incl 2 MiG-21U, 6 *Magister*.
AA-2 *Atoll* AAM.

Para-Military Forces: 20,000 Bangladesh Rifles, 36,000 Armed Police Reserve.

BRUNEI

Population: 190,000.
Military service: voluntary.
Total armed forces: 2,750.†
Estimated GNP 1976: $381.7m.
Defence expenditure 1978: $B 297.2 m ($US 128.7 m).
$1 US = $B 2.31 (1978), $B 2.62 (1976).

Army: 2,750.
2 inf bns.
1 armd recce sqn.
16 *Scorpion* lt tks; 24 Sankey APC, 16 81mm mor.

Navy
3 FPBG
3 coastal, 3 river patrol craft } All under 100 tons.
2 landing craft

Air Force
1 HS-748 tpt, 2 *Cherokee* trg ac.
3 Bell 205, 3 Bell 206, 4 Bell 212 hel.

Para-Military Forces: 1,700 Royal Brunei Police.

BURMA

Population: 33,260,000.
Military service: voluntary.
Total armed forces: 169,500.
Estimated GNP 1977: $4.2 bn.
Defence expenditure 1977: 1.09 bn kyat ($164 m).
$1 = 6.64 kyat (1977).

Army: 153,000.
3 inf divs, each with 10 bns.
2 armd bns.
84 indep inf bns (in regional comds).
5 arty bns.
Comet med tks; 40 Humber armd cars; 45 *Ferret* scout cars; 50 25-pdr, 5.5-in guns/how; 120 76mm, 80 105mm how; 120mm mor; 50 6-pdr and 17-pdr ATK guns; 10 40mm, 3.7-in AA guns.*

Navy: 9,000 (800 marines).*
2 frigates (ex-British, 1 *River-*, 1 *Algerine-*class).
4 coastal escorts.
37 gunboats (17 under 100 tons).
35 river patrol craft (under 100 tons).
1 support ship.
9 landing craft (1 utility, 8 med).

Air Force: 7,500; 16 combat aircraft.*
2 COIN sqns with 6 AT-33, 10 SF-260M.
Tpts incl 4 C-47, 4 F-27, 7 Pilatus PC-6/-6A, 6 Cessna 180.
Hel incl 10 KB-47G, 2 KV-107/II, 7 HH-43B, 10 *Alouette* III, 14 UH-1.
Trainers incl 10 T-37C (18 PC-7 *Turbo-Trainers* on order).

Para-Military Forces: 38,000 People's Police Force, 35,000 People's Militia.

CHINA: REPUBLIC OF (TAIWAN)

Population: 17,630,000.
Military service: 2 years.
Total armed forces: 474,000.
Estimated GNP 1977: $20.1 bn.
Defence expenditure 1977: $NT 63.47 bn ($US 1.67 bn).
$US 1 = $NT 37.97 (1977).

Army: 330,000.
2 armd divs.
12 hy inf divs.
6 lt inf divs.
2 armd cav regts.
2 AB bdes.
4 special forces gps.
1 SSM bn with *Honest John*.
3 SAM bns: 2 with 80 *Nike Hercules*, 1 with 24 *HAWK*.
150 M-47/-48 med, 625 M-41 lt tks; 300 M-113 APC; 550 105mm, 300 155mm guns/how; 350 75mm M-116 pack, 90 203mm, 10 240mm how; 225 105mm SP how; 81mm mor; *Honest John* SSM; 150 M-18 76mm SP ATK guns; 500 106mm RCL; 300 40mm AA guns (some SP); *Nike Hercules*, 20 *Chaparral* SAM; 80 UH-1H, 2 KH-4, 7 CH-34 hel. (*TOW* ATGW, 24 *Improved HAWK* SAM, 118 UH-1H hel on order.)

DEPLOYMENT: *Quemoy:* 60,000; *Matsu:* 20,000.

RESERVES: 1,000,000.

Navy: 35,000.
2 submarines (ex-US *Guppy-*II-class).
22 destroyers (ex-US: 8 *Gearing-*class, 2 with *Gabriel*

---

* Spares are short; some equipment is unserviceable.
† All services form part of the Army.

7 SSM, 3 with *ASROC*; 8 *Sumner*-class, 3 with *Gabriel*; 4 *Fletcher*-class with *Chaparral* SAM).
11 frigates (10 ex-US armed transports).
3 corvettes (ex-US *Auk*-class).
6 MTB (under 100 tons).
14 coastal minesweepers.
51 landing vessels: 2 LSD, 1 comd, 22 LST, 4 LSM, 22 utility.
(2 FPBG with *Otomat* SSM, *Harpoon*, *Gabriel* SSM on order.)

RESERVES: 45,000.

Marines: 39,000.
2 divs.
M-47 med tks; LVT-4 APC; 105mm, 155mm how; 106mm RCL.

RESERVES: 35,000.

Air Force: 70,000; 316 combat aircraft.
12 fighter sqns with 90 F-100A/F, 165 F-5A/E.
3 interceptor sqns with 44 F-104G.
1 recce sqn with 8 RF-104G.
1 MR sqn with 9 S-2A *Tracker*.
1 SAR sqn with 8 HU-16A ac.
Tpts incl 25 C-46, 40 C-47, 30 C-119, 10 C-123, 1 Boeing 720B.
160 trainers, incl 55 PL-1B *Chien Shou*, 32 T-33, 30 T-38, F-5B/F, 3 TF-104G, 6 F-104D, F-100F.
Hels incl 95 UH-IH, 7 UH-19, 10 Bell 47G.
Sidewinder AAM, *Bullpup* ASM.
(25 F-5E fighters, 21 F-5F trg ac, *Shafrir* AAM on order.)

RESERVES: 90,000.

Para-Military Forces: 100,000 militia.

INDIA

Population: 635,440,000.
Military service: voluntary.
Total armed forces: 1,096,000.
Estimated GNP 1977: $101 bn.
Defence expenditure 1978: 29.45 bn rupees ($3.57 bn).
　$1 = 8.25 rupees (1978), 8.83 rupees (1977).

Army: 950,000.
2 armd divs.
17 inf divs (1 more forming).
10 mountain divs.
5 indep armd bdes.
1 indep inf bde.
1 para bde.
14 indep arty bdes, incl about 20 AA arty regts, 4 arty observation sqns and indep flts.
100 *Centurion* Mk 5/7, 900 T-54/-55, some 700 *Vijayanta* med, 150 PT-76, AMX-13 lt tks; 700 BTR-50/-152, OT-62/-64(2A) APC; about 2,000 75mm, 25-pdr (mostly towed), about 300 100mm, 105mm (incl pack how) and *Abbot* 105mm SP, 550 130mm, 5.5-in, 155mm, 203mm guns/how; 500 120mm, 160mm mor; 106mm RCL; SS-11, *ENTAC* ATGW; 57mm, 100mm ATK guns; ZSU-23-4 SP, 30mm, 40mm AA guns; 40 *Tigercat* SAM; 40 *Krishak*, 20 *Auster* AOP9 lt ac; some *Alouette* III, 38 *Cheetah* hel. (70 T-72 med tks, 75 *Cheetah* hel on order.)

RESERVES: 200,000. Territorial Army 40,000.

Navy: 46,000, incl Naval Air Force.
8 submarines (Soviet F-class).
1 aircraft carrier (capacity 25 ac, incl 12 *Sea Hawk*, 4 *Alizé*, 2 *Alouette* III).
1 cruiser.
25 frigates (4 *Leander*-class with 2 *Seacat* SAM, 1 hel; 2 *Whitby*-class with *Styx* SSM, 12 *Petya*-II-class, 5 GP, 2 trg).
3 *Nanuchka*-class corvettes with SSM, SAM.
16 *Osa*-I/-II-class FPBG with *Styx* SSM.
4 large patrol craft.
7 coastal patrol craft (incl 5 *Poluchat*-class).
8 minesweepers (4 inshore).
1 LST, 6 LCT (*Polnocny*-class).
(2 *Kashin*-class destroyers, 2 *Leander*-class frigates, 5 *Nanuchka*-class corvettes, 3 landing craft on order.)

NAVAL AIR FORCE: 2,000.
1 attack sqn with 25 *Sea Hawk* (12 in carrier).
1 MR sqn with 12 *Alizé* (4 in carrier).
3 MR sqns with 5 *Super Constellation*, 3 Il-38, 5 *Defender*, 2 *Devon*.
1 hel sqn with 10 *Alouette* III.
3 ASW sqns with 12 *Sea King*, 8 *Alouette* III hel.
7 HJT-16 *Kiran*, 4 *Vampire* T55, 4 *Sea Hawk* ac, 4 Hughes 300 hel.
(8 *Sea Harrier*, 3 Il-38 MR ac, 3 *Sea King* ASW, 5 Ka-25 hel on order.)

Air Force: 100,000; about 661 combat aircraft.
3 lt bbr sqns with 50 *Canberra* B(I)58, B(I)12.
13 FGA sqns: 5 with 100 Su-7B, 4 with 80 HF-24 *Marut* 1A, 4 with 65 *Hunter* F56.
11 interceptor sqns with 200 Mig-21F/PFMA/FL/MF/bis.
8 interceptor sqns with 160 *Gnat* F1.
1 recce sqn with 6 *Canberra* PR57.
10 tpt sqns: 1 with 16 HS-748, 2 with 32 C-119G; 2 with 30 An-12; 1 with 29 DHC-3; 3 with 50 C-47; 1 with 20 DHC-4.
12 hel sqns: 6 with 100 Mi-4; 3 with 35 Mi-8; 3 with 120 *Chetak* (*Alouette* III); 12 AB-47, 2 S-62.
Comms flts with 1 Tu-124, 6 HS-748, C-47, *Devon*.
OCU with MiG-21U, 5 Su-7U, *Hunter* T66, *Mystère* IVA, *Canberra* T13.

Trainers incl 110 *Kiran*, 70 HT-2, 32 HS-748, C-47, 45 *Iskra*, 15 *Marut* ac, *Alouette* III hel.
AA-2 *Atoll* AAM; AS.30 ASM.
20 SAM sites with 120 SA-2/-3.
(110 MiG-21MF, 100 *Ajeet* (*Gnat*), 20 HS-748M, 45 *Marut* Mk 1T, 40 *Iskra* ac, 45 *Chetak* hel on order.)

Para-Military Forces: About 200,000 Border Security Force, 100,000 in other organizations.

INDONESIA

Population: 139,300,000.
Military service: selective.
Total armed forces: 247,000.
Estimated GNP 1977: $43.1 bn.
Defence expenditure 1978–79: 701.8 bn rupiahs ($1.69 bn).
$1 = 415 rupiahs (1977 and 1978).

Army: 180,000.*
1 armd cav bde (1 tk bn, support units).†
14 inf bdes (90 inf, 14 arty, 13 AA, 10 engr bns, 1 in KOSTRAD).
2 AB bdes (6 bns).†
5 fd arty regts.
4 AA arty regts.
Stuart, 150 AMX-13, 75 PT-76 lt tks; 75 *Saladin* armd, 55 *Ferret* scout cars; AMX-VCI MICV; *Saracen*, 130 BTR-40/-152 APC; 50 76mm, 40 105mm, 122mm guns/how; 200 120mm mor; 106mm RCL; *ENTAC* ATGW; 20mm, 40mm, 200 57mm AA guns; 2 C-47, 2 Aero *Commander* 680, 1 Beech 18, Cessna 185, 18 *Gelatik* ac; 16 Bell-205, 7 *Alouette* III hel.‡

DEPLOYMENT: *Egypt* (UNEF): 1 bn (510),

Navy: 39,000, incl Naval Air and 12,000 Marines.‡
3 submarines (ex-Soviet W-class).
11 frigates (3 ex-Soviet *Riga*-, 4 ex-US *Jones*-class).
22 large patrol craft (6 ex-Soviet *Kronstadt*-, 2 ex-Australian *Attack*-, 5 ex-Yugoslav *Kraljevica*-class).
9 *Komar*-class FPBG with *Styx* SSM.
5 MTB (Lurssen TNC-45-class).
8 coastal patrol craft (under 100 tons).
5 ex-Soviet T-43 ocean, 2 R-class coastal mine-sweepers.
3 comd/spt ships.
9 LST, 2 landing craft utility.
1 marine bde.
(2 Type 206 submarines, 3 corvettes, 5 mine-sweepers, 4 FPBG, 6 patrol boats, *Exocet* SSM on order.)

NAVAL AIR: 1,000.
5 HU-16, 6 C-47, 6 *Nomad* MR ac; 4 Bell 47G, 6 *Alouette* II/III hel. (6 *Nomad* on order.)

Air Force: 28,000; 32 combat aircraft.§
2 FGA sqns with 16 CA-27 *Avon-Sabre*.
1 COIN sqn with 16 OV-10F.
Tpts incl 11 C-130B, 1 C-140 *Jetstar*, 12 C-47, 3 *Skyvan*, 8 F-27, 6 CASA C-212, 5 *Nomad*, 12 Cessna 207/401/402, 7 DHC-3, 18 *Gelatik*.
2 hel sqns with 12 UH-34D, 5 Bell 204B, 4 *Alouette* III, 1 S-61A, 46 BO-105, 19 *Puma*, 16 Bell 47.
Trainers incl 4 T-6, 10 T-33, 31 T-34, *Airtourer*.
(12 F-5E, 4 F-5F fighters, 16 CASA C-212, 4 F-27, 6 *Nomad* tpts, 8 *Hawk* trg ac; 6 *Puma* hel on order.)

Para-Military Forces: 12,000 Police Mobile bde; about 100,000 Militia.

JAPAN

Population: 115,120,000.
Military service: voluntary.
Total armed forces: 240,000.
Estimated GNP 1977: $677 bn.
Defence expenditure 1978–79: 1,901 bn yen ($8.57 bn).
$1 = 221.9 yen (1978), 277.6 yen (1977).

Army: 155,000.
1 mech div.
12 inf divs (7–9,000 men each).
1 tk bde.
1 AB bde.
1 composite bde.
1 arty bde.
5 engr bdes.
1 sigs bde.
8 SAM gps (each of 4 btys) with *HAWK*.
1 hel wing and 34 aviation sqns.
690 Type 61 and Type 74 med, 100 M-41 lt tks; 640 Type 60 and Type 73 APC; 900 75mm, 105mm, 155mm, 203mm guns/how; 470 105mm, 155mm SP how; 1,900 81mm and 107mm mor (some SP); 4 Type 75 130mm SP RL; 1,100 57mm, 75mm, 106mm, 106mm SP RCL; Type 30 SSM; Type 64, KAM-9 ATGW; 260 35mm twin, 37mm, 40mm and 75mm AA guns; *HAWK* SAM; 90 L-19, 20 LM-1/2, 7 LR-1 ac; 50 KV-107, 40 UH-1H, 80 UH-1B, 70 OH-6J, 50 H-13 hel.
(48 Type 74 tks; *Carl Gustav* 84mm RL; *Hawk* SAM; 2 LR-1 ac, 3 KV-107, 13 UH-1H, 10 OH-6D, 1 AH-1S hel on order.)

RESERVES: 39,000.

---

* About one-third of the army is engaged in civil and administrative duties.
† In KOSTRAD (Strategic Reserve Command).
‡ Some equipment and ships non-operational for lack of spares.
§ Some aircraft non-operational for lack of spares. In addition to the aircraft shown above, some 22 Tu-16, 10 Il-28, 40 MiG-15/-17, 35 MiG-19, 15 MiG-21, 10 Il-14, 10 An-12 ac, 20 Mi-4, 9 Mi-6 hel are in store.

Navy: 41,000 (including Naval Air).
14 submarines.
31 destroyers (2 with 3 hel and *ASROC*; 2 with *Tartar* SAM, *ASROC*; 4 with 2 hel, *ASROC*; 9 with *ASROC*; 12 GP, 2 trg).
15 frigates (11 with *ASROC*, 4 GP).
12 coastal escorts.
5 MTB.
9 coastal patrol craft (under 100 tons).
39 MCM (3 spt ships, 30 coastal, 6 inshore).
6 LST.
(5 destroyers, 1 frigate, 2 submarines, 4 MCM, *Harpoon* SSM on order.)

NAVAL AIR: 12,000.
11 MR sqns with 110 P-2J, P2V-7, S2F-1, 18 PS-1.
7 hel sqns with 7 KV-107, 61 HSS-2.
1 tpt sqn with 4 YS-11M, 1 S2F-C.
5 SAR flts with 3 US-1 ac, 1 S-61A, 8 S-62A hel.
Trainers incl 6 YS-11T, 5 TC-90, 30 B-65; 8 T-34, 30 KM-2 ac; S-61A, 7 Bell 47, 4 OH-6J hel.
(8 P-3C MR, 5 PS-1, 18 KM-2, 2 US-1, 11 P-2J, 1 TC-90 ac, 14 HSS-2, 4 SH-3, 2 S-61A hel on order; 1 P2V-7, 6 S2F-1 in store.)

RESERVES: 600.

Air Force: 44,000; 358 combat aircraft.
3 FGA sqns with 87 F-86F, 9 F-1.
10 interceptor sqns: 6 with 150 F-104J, 4 with 98 F-4EJ.
1 recce sqn with 14 RF-4E.
3 tpt sqns with 13 YS-11, 22 C-1A.
1 SAR wing with 20 MU-2 ac, 22 KV-107, 26 S-62 hel.
Trainers incl 57 T-1A/B, 40 T-2A, 18 T-3, 185 T-33, 82 T-34, F-104DJ, 4 C-46, YS-11E, MU-2J.
AAM-1, *Sparrow*, *Falcon*, *Sidewinder* AAM.
5 SAM gps with *Nike-J* (6th forming).
A Base Defence Ground Environment with 28 control and warning units.
(23 F-15, 14 TF-15, 50 F-4EJ, 59 F-1, 10 T-2, 14 T-3, 7 C-1, 2 MU-2, 2 MU-2J ac, 3 KV-107 hel on order.)

KAMPUCHEA (CAMBODIA)

Population: 7,300,000.
Total armed forces: 70,000.

Army: The former Khmer Liberation Army, which was organized into some 4 divs and 3 indep regts, appears still to have the same strength it had at the end of hostilities in 1975, and none of the former regime's troops seem to have been incorporated into the structure. Equipment, a mixture of Soviet, Chinese and American arms, includes AMX-13 lt tks; 10 BTR-152, 200 M-113 APC;

300 105mm, 122mm, 130mm, 20 155mm guns/how; 107mm, 120mm mor; 57mm, 75mm, 82mm, 107mm RCL, 40mm AA guns.

Navy:* Some 150 small patrol, river and 6 landing craft.

Air Force:* Aircraft are thought to include some 10 AU-24 COIN, 9 C-47 and C-123 tpts, 15 T-41, 20 T-28 trainers, 25 UH-1H hel gunships. However, their condition is not known.

KOREA: DEMOCRATIC PEOPLE'S REPUBLIC (NORTH)

Population: 17,170,000.
Military service: Army, Navy 5 years, Air Force 3–4 years.
Total armed forces: 512,000.
Estimated GNP 1977: $9.8 bn.
Defence expenditure 1977: 2.12 bn won ($1.03 bn).†
$1 = 2.05 won.

Army: 440,000.
2 tk divs.
3 mot inf divs.
20 inf divs.
4 inf bdes.
3 recce bdes.
8 lt inf bdes.
3 AA arty divs.
5 indep tk regts.
5 AB bns.
3 SSM bns with *FROG*.
20 arty regts.
10 AA arty regts.
350 T-34, 1,600 T-54/-55 and Type 59 med, 100 PT-76, 50 T-62 lt tks; 800 BTR-40/-60/-152, M-1967 APC; 3,000 guns and how up to 152mm; 1,300 RL; 9,000 82mm, 120mm and 160mm mor; 1,500 82mm RCL; 57mm to 100mm ATK guns; 9 *FROG*-5 SSM; 5,000 AA guns, incl 37mm, 57mm, 85mm, 100mm, ZSU-57-2 SP.

Navy: 27,000.
15 submarines (4 ex-Soviet W-, 11 ex-Chinese R-class).
3 frigates (1 building).
21 large patrol craft (15 ex-Soviet SO-1-class).
10 *Komar*-I-, 8 *Osa*-I-class FPBG with *Styx* SSM.
100 MGB (incl 8 ex-Chinese *Shanghai*- and 8 *Swatow*-class; 28 under 100 tons).

---

* May be part of the Army.
† It is uncertain whether this covers all defence expenditure, and there is no consensus on a suitable exchange rate for the dollar conversion.

157 MTB (incl 4 ex-Soviet *Shershen*-, 12 P-4-, 60 P-6-class).
90 landing craft.

Air Force: 45,000; 655 combat aircraft.
3 lt bbr sqns with 85 Il-28.
13 FGA sqns with 20 Su-7, 320 MiG-15/-17.
10 interceptor sqns with 120 MiG-21 and 110 MiG-19.
250 tpts, incl 200 An-2, An-24, 10 Il-14/-18, 1 Tu-154.
Hel incl 50 Mi-4, 10 Mi-8.
Trainers incl 50 Yak-18, 60 MiG-15UTI/-21U, Il-28.
AA-2 *Atoll* AAM.
3 SAM bdes with 250 SA-2.

Para-Military Forces: 40,000 security forces and border guards; civilian militia of 1,000,000 to 2,000,000 with small arms, some AA arty.

KOREA: REPUBLIC OF (SOUTH)

Population: 35,940,000.
Military service: Army and Marines 2½ years, Navy and Air Force 3 years.
Total armed forces: 642,000.
Estimated GNP 1977: $31.5 bn.
Defence expenditure 1978: 1.26 bn won ($2.60 bn).
   $1 = 484 won.

Army: 560,000.
1 mech div.
19 inf divs.
2 armd bdes.
5 special forces bdes.
2 AD bdes.
7 tk bns.
30 arty bns.
1 SSM bn with *Honest John*.
2 SAM bdes with *Improved HAWK* and *Nike Hercules*.
M-60, 880 M-47/-48 med tks; 500 M-113/-577, 20 Fiat 6614 APC; 2,000 105mm, 155mm, 203mm towed, M-107 175mm and M-110 203mm SP guns/how; 5,300 81mm and 107mm mor; *Honest John* SSM; M-18 76mm SP ATK guns; 57mm, 75mm, 106mm RCL; *TOW, LAW* ATGW; *Vulcan* 20mm, 40mm AA guns; 80 *HAWK*, 45 *Nike Hercules* SAM; 14 O-2A ac; 44 OH-6A, 5 KH-4 hel. (150 Fiat 6614 APC; *TOW* ATGW, 56 OH-6A hel on order.)

RESERVES: 1,100,000.

Navy: 32,000.
9 destroyers (4 *Gearing*, 2 *Sumner*-, 3 *Fletcher*-class).
9 destroyer escorts.

10 coastal escorts.
10 large, 23 coastal patrol craft (31 under 100 tons).
8 FPBG with *Standard* SSM (7 PSMM, 1 *Asheville*-class).
5 FPB.
11 coastal minesweepers.
22 landing ships (8 LST, 1 LSD, 12 LSM, 1 utility).
(120 *Harpoon* SSM on order.)

RESERVES: 25,000.

Marines: 20,000; 1 div, 2 bdes with LVTP-7 APC.

RESERVES: 60,000.

Air Force: 30,000; 276 combat aircraft.
15 FB sqns: 4 with 37 F-4D/E; 9 with 35 F-5A, 126 F-5E; 2 with 48 F-86F.
1 recce sqn with 10 RF-5A.
1 ASW sqn with 20 S-2F.
1 SAR sqn with 2 UH-19, 5 UH-1D, 6 Bell 212 hel.
Tpts incl 12 C-46, 10 C-54, 10 C-123, 2 HS-748, Aero *Commander*.
Trainers incl 20 T-28D, 30 T-33A, 20 T-41D, 30 F-5B, 3 F-5F.
4 UH-19, 50 Hughes 500MD hel.
Sidewinder, Sparrow AAM.
(18 F-4E, 9 F-5F fighters, 24 OV-10G COIN, 6 C-130H tpts, 6 CH-47C, 50 Hughes 500MD hel, AIM-9L *Super Sidewinder* AAM, *Maverick* ASM on order.)

RESERVES: 55,000.

Para-Military Forces: A local defence militia, 1,000,000 Homeland Defence Reserve Force.

LAOS

Population: 3,530,000.
Military service: conscription, term unknown.
Total armed forces: 48,550.
Estimated GNP 1977: $256 m.
Defence expenditure 1977: 8.4 bn kip ($42 m).
   $1 = 200 kip Pot Poi (1977).

Army: (Lao People's Liberation Army): 46,000.*
100 inf bns (under Military Regions).
Supporting arms and services.
M-24, PT-76 lt tks; BTR-40, M-113 APC; 75mm, 85mm, 105mm, 155mm how; 81mm, 82mm, 4.2-in mor; 107mm RCL; 37mm AA guns; 4 U-17A lt ac.

Navy: About 550.
20 river patrol craft.
14 landing craft/tpts (all under 100 tons).

---

* The Royal Lao Army has been disbanded; some men may have been absorbed into the Liberation Army.

Air Force: 2,000; 55 combat aircraft.*
1 sqn with 10 MiG-21.
40 T-28A/D COIN ac.
5 AC-47 gunships.
Tpts incl 1 Yak-40, 10 C-47, 10 C-123, 6 An-24,
  1 Aero *Commander*, 1 *Beaver*.
6 T-41D trainers.
4 *Alouette* III, 42 UH-34, 6 Mi-8 hel.
AA-2 *Atoll* AAM.

MALAYSIA

Population: 12,995,000.
Military service: voluntary.
Total armed forces: 64,500.
Estimated GNP 1977: $US 12.3 bn.
Defence expenditure 1978: $M 1.65 bn
  ($US 699 m).
  $1 = $M 2.36 (1978), $M 2.49 (1977).

Army: 52,500.
2 div HQ.
9 inf bdes, consisting of:
  29 inf bns.
  3 recce regts.
  3 arty regts.
  2 AD btys.
  1 special service unit.
  5 engr, 4 sigs regts.
  Administrative units.
140 Panhard, M-3 armd, 60 *Ferret* scout cars; 200
  V-150 *Commando*, M-3 APC; 80 105mm how;
  81mm mor; 120mm RCL; 35 40mm AA guns.
(AT-105 APC; 12 105mm how on order.)

RESERVES: About 26,000.

Navy: 6,000.
2 frigates (1 ASW with *Seacat* SAM).
4 FPBG (*Combattante*-II-class with *Exocet* SSM).
4 FPB.
22 large patrol craft.
6 coastal minesweepers (ex-British *Ton*-class).
3 LST.
(4 *Spica*-class FPB, *Exocet* SSM on order.)

RESERVES: 1,000.

Air Force: 6,000; 36 combat aircraft.
2 FB sqns with 16 F-5E/B.
2 COIN/trg sqns with 20 CL-41G *Tebuan*.
4 tpt, 1 liaison sqns with 6 C-130H, 3 *Heron*,
  2 HS-125, 2 F-28, 16 DHC-4A, 2 *Dove*.
4 hel sqns with 36 S-61A-4, 28 *Alouette* III, 5 Bell
  206B, 3 AB-212.
1 trg sqn with 15 *Bulldog* 102, 12 Cessna 402B ac,
  6 Bell 47G, 3 *Sioux* hel.
Sidewinder AAM.
(20 *Gazelle* hel, *Super Sidewinder* AAM on order.)

Para-Military Forces: Police Field Force of 13,000:
  17 bns, 200 V-150 *Commando* APC, 40 patrol
  boats. People's Volunteer Corps over 200,000.

MONGOLIA

Population: 1,580,000.
Military service: 2 years.
Total armed forces: 30,000.
Estimated GNP 1974: $2.8 bn.
Defence expenditure 1978: 405 m tugrik ($120 m).
  $1 = 3.36 tugrik (1978), 4.00 tugrik (1974).

Army: 28,000.
2 inf bdes.
1 construction bde.
30 T-34, 100 T-54/-55 med tks; 40 BTR-60, 50
  BTR-152 APC; 76mm, 100mm, 130mm, 152mm
  guns/how; 10 SU-100 SP guns; *Snapper* ATGW;
  37mm, 57mm AA guns.

RESERVES: 30,000.

Air Force: 2,000;† 10 combat aircraft.
1 FGA sqn with 10 MiG-15.
20 An-2, 6 Il-14, 4 An-24 tpts.
10 Mi-1 and Mi-4 hel.
Yak-11/-18 trainers.

Para-Military Forces: about 18,000 frontier guards
  and security police.

NEPAL

Population: 13,480,000.
Military service: voluntary.
Total armed forces: 20,000.
Estimated GNP 1976: $1.6 bn.
Defence expenditure 1977: 173 m rupees ($13.8 m).
  $1 = 12.53 rupees (1977), 12.50 rupees (1976).

Army: 20,000.‡
5 inf bdes (1 Palace Guard).
1 para bn.
1 arty regt.
1 engr regt.
1 sigs regt.
AMX-13 lt tks; 4 3.7-in pack how; 4 4.2-in, 18
  120mm mor; 2 40mm AA guns; 3 *Skyvan*, 1
  HS-748 tpts; 5 *Alouette* III, 2 *Puma* hel.

DEPLOYMENT: *Lebanon* (UNIFIL): 1 bn (642).

Para-Military Forces: 12,000 Police Force.

---

* Most aircraft inherited from the Royal Lao Air
Force; degree of serviceability unknown.
† Excluding expatriate personnel.
‡ There is no Air Force: the 70-man Army Air Flight
Department operates the aircraft.

NEW ZEALAND

Population: 3,200,000.
Military service: voluntary, supplemented by Territorial service of 12 weeks for the Army.
Total armed forces: 12,623.
Estimated GNP 1977: $US 13.6 bn.
Defence expenditure 1977–78: $NZ 254 m ($US 242 m).
$1 = $NZ 0.97 (1978), $NZ 1.05 (1977).

Army: 5,730.
2 inf bns.
1 arty bty.
Regular troops also form the nucleus of 2 bde gps and a log gp; these would be completed by mobilization of Territorials.
7 M-41 lt tks; 9 Ferret scout cars; 66 M-113 APC; 15 5.5-in guns; 44 105mm how; 24 106mm RCL.

DEPLOYMENT: *Singapore:* 1 inf bn with log support.

RESERVES: 1,571 Regular, 5,812 Territorial.

Navy: 2,734.
4 frigates with Seacat SAM (2 Type 12, 2 Leander-class with Wasp hel).
4 large patrol craft.
1 survey ship.

DEPLOYMENT: 1–2 frigates in Pacific area.

RESERVES: 2,898 Regular, 304 Territorial.

Air Force: 4,159; 34 combat aircraft.
1 FB sqn with 10 A-4K, 3 TA-4K Skyhawk.
1 FB/trg sqn with 16 BAC-167.
1 MR sqn with 5 P-3B Orion.
2 med tpt sqns with 5 C-130H, 6 Andover.
1 tpt hel sqn with 7 Sioux, 3 Wasp, 10 UH-1D/H.
1 comms sqn with 4 Andover, 2 Devon.
Trainers: 8 Devon, 13 Airtrainer, 4 Airtourer ac, 3 Sioux hel. (6 Airtrainer on order.)

DEPLOYMENT: *Singapore:* 1 hel flt (3 UH-1).

RESERVES: 713 Regular, 160 Territorial.

PAKISTAN

Population: 76,780,000.
Military service: voluntary.
Total armed forces: 429,000.
Estimated GNP 1977: $17.6 bn.
Defence expenditure 1978–79: 9.15 bn rupees ($938 m).
$1 = 9.75 rupees (1978), 9.89 rupees (1977).

Army: 400,000 (incl 29,000 Azad Kashmir troops).
2 armd divs.
16 inf divs.
3 indep armd bdes.

3 indep inf bdes.
6 arty, 2 AD bdes.
5 army aviation sqns.
M-4, 250 M-47/-48, 50 T-54/-55, 700 T-59 med, 15 PT-76, T-60, 50 M-24 lt tks; 550 M-113 APC; about 1,000 75mm pack, 25-pdr, 100mm, 105mm, 130mm and 155mm guns/how; M-7 105mm SP guns; 270 107mm, 120mm mor; 57mm, M-36 90mm SP ATK guns; 75mm, 106mm RCL; Cobra ATGW; ZU-23, 30mm, 37mm, 40mm, 57mm, 90mm, 3.7-in AA guns; 9 Crotale SAM; 40 O-1E lt ac; 12 Mi-8, 6 Puma, 20 Alouette III, 12 UH-1, 15 Bell 47G hel. (TOW ATGW, 29 Puma hel on order.)

RESERVES: 500,000.

Navy: 11,000.
4 submarines (Daphne-class).
5 SX-404 midget submarines.
1 lt cruiser (trg ship).
6 destroyers (1 ex-British Battle-, 1 CH-, 2 CR-, 2 ex-US Gearing-class).
1 frigate (ex-British Type 16).
3 large patrol craft (2 ex-Chinese Hainan-class).
12 FPB (ex-Chinese Shanghai-class), 4 Hu Chwan hydrofoils.
7 coastal minesweepers.
4 Alouette III, 6 Sea King SAR hel.
(3 Hainan-class patrol craft on order.)

RESERVES: 5,000.

Air Force: 18,000; 257 combat aircraft.
1 lt bbr sqn with 11 B-57B (Canberra).
4 fighter sqns with 21 Mirage IIIEP/DP, 28 VPA.
9 FGA sqns; 7 with 135 MiG-19/F-6, 2 with 40 F-86.
1 recce sqn with 13 Mirage IIIRP, 4 RT-33A.
1 MR sqn with 3 Atlantic, 2 HU-16B.
Tpts incl 12 C-130B/E, 1 L-100, 1 Falcon 20, 1 F-27, 1 Super King Air, 1 Bonanza.
10 HH-43B, 4 Super Frelon, 12 Alouette III, 1 Puma, 12 Bell 47 hel.
Trainers incl MiG-15UTI, 45 Saab Supporter, 12 T-33A, 30 T-37, F-86.
Sidewinder, R.530, R.550 Magic AAM.

RESERVES: 8,000.

Para-Military Forces: 109,100. 22,000 National Guard, 65,000 Frontier Corps, 15,000 Pakistan Rangers, 2,000 Coastguard, 5,100 Frontier Constabulary.

PHILIPPINES

Population: 46,600,000.
Military service: selective.
Total armed forces: 99,000.

Estimated GNP 1977: $20.0 bn.
Defence expenditure 1978–79: 5.85 bn pesos
 ($793 m).
 $1 = 7.37 pesos (1978), 7.35 pesos (1977).

Army: 63,000.
4 lt inf divs.
1 indep inf bde.
21 *Scorpion*, 7 M-41 lt tks; 60 M-113, 20 V-150
 Commando APC; 120 105mm, 5 155mm how;
 81mm, 40 107mm mor; 75mm, 106mm RCL;
 HAWK SAM.

RESERVES: 17,000.

Navy: 20,000 (7,000 Marines and naval engrs).
8 frigates.
11 corvettes.
76 patrol craft: 15 large, 61 coastal (under 100 tons).
2 coastal minesweepers.
2 command ships.
39 landing ships (27 LST, 4 med, 8 spt), 71 landing
 craft.
1 SAR sqn with 10 *Islander*.
3 BO-105 hel.
6 marine bns.

RESERVES: 12,000.

Air Force: 16,000; 111 combat aircraft.
2 FB sqns with 20 F-5A/B, 20 F-86.
1 fighter/trg sqn with 17 T-34A.
3 COIN sqns with 18 SF-260WP, 24 T-28.
1 gunship sqn with 12 AC-47.
1 SAR sqn with 8 HU-16 ac, UH-19, 3 SH-34G, 12
 UH-1H, H-13, Hughes 300 hel.
1 hel sqn with 18 UH-1H.
6 tpt sqns with 6 C-130H, 3 L-100-20, 1 Boeing 707,
 1 BAC-111, 30 C-47, 10 F-27, 4 YS-11, 15
 C-123K, 12 *Nomad*.
1 liaison sqn with O-1E, Cessna 180, 6 U-17A/B,
 Cessna 310K, 21 DHC-2.
3 trg sqns with 10 T/RT-33A, 12 T-41A, 8 F-86F,
 32 SF-260MP.
Other hel incl 12 UH-1D, 8 FH-1100, 5 UH-19, 2
 H-34, 2 S-62A.
Sidewinder AAM.
(11 F-5E, 25 F-8H fighters; 38 BO-105, 17 UH-1
 hel on order.)

RESERVES: 16,000.

Para-Military Forces: 65,000: 40,000 Philippine
 Constabulary, 25,000 Local Self-Defence Force.

SINGAPORE

Population: 2,375,000.
Military service: 24–36 months.
Total armed forces: 36,000.
Estimated GNP 1977: $US 6.5 bn.

Defence expenditure 1977–78: $S 1.01 bn
 ($US 410 m).
 $US1 = $2.46 (1977).

Army: 30,000.
1 armd bde (1 tk, 2 APC bns).
4 inf bdes (9 inf, 5 arty, 3 engr, 3 sigs bns).
75 AMX-13 tks; 250 M-113, 30 V-100, 250 V-200
 Commando APC; 60 155mm how; 50 120mm
 mor; 90 106mm RCL. (294 M-113 APC on order.)

RESERVES: 45,000, 18 reserve battalions.

Navy: 3,000.
6 FPBG (*Jaguar*-class with *Gabriel* SSM).
6 FPB (Vosper).
2 large patrol craft.
2 coastal minesweepers.
6 ex-US LST and 6 landing craft.

Air Force: 3,000; 103 combat aircraft.
2 FGA/recce sqns with 31 *Hunter* FGA74, 4 FR74,
 7 T75.
2 FGA sqns with 40 A-4S, 6 TA-4S.
1 COIN/trg sqn with 15 BAC-167.
1 tpt sqn with 2 C-130B, 6 *Skyvan*.
1 SAR hel sqn with 7 *Alouette* III, 3 AB-212.
Hel incl 15 UH-1H.
Trainers incl 14 SF-260MS.
2 SAM sqns: 1 with 28 *Bloodhound*, 1 with 10 *Rapier*.
(21 F-5E/F FGA, AIM-9L *Super Sidewinder* AAM on
 order.)

Para-Military Forces: 7,500 police/marine police;
 Gurkha guard units; 30,000 Home Guard.

SRI LANKA (CEYLON)

Population: 14,900,000.
Military service: voluntary.
Total armed forces: 13,300.
Estimated GNP 1977: $4.0 bn.
Defence expenditure 1978: 211 m rupees ($14.3 m).
 $1 = 14.7 rupees (1978), 7.27 rupees (1977).

Army: 8,900.
1 bde of 3 bns.
1 recce regt.
1 arty regt.
1 engr regt.
1 sigs regt.
6 *Saladin* armd cars, 30 *Ferret* scout cars; 10 BTR-
 152 APC; 76mm, 85mm guns.

RESERVES: 12,000; 7 bns, supporting services and a
 Pioneer Corps.

Navy: 2,400.
6 fast gunboats (5 *Shanghai*-, 1 ex-Soviet *Mol*-class).
5 FPB.
20 coastal patrol craft (under 100 tons).

Air Force: 2,000; 8 combat aircraft.
1 FGA sqn with 4 MiG-17F, 1 MiG-15UTI, 3 *Jet Provost* Mk 51.
1 tpt sqn with 1 CV-440, 2 DC-3, 2 Riley *Heron*, 1 HS *Heron*.
1 comms sqn with 3 Cessna 337.
1 hel sqn with 7 AB-206, 6 Bell 47G, 2 SA-365 *Dauphin* 2.
4 Cessna 150, 7 *Chipmunk*, 5 *Dove* trainers.

RESERVES: 1,000; 4 sqns Air Force Regt, 1 sqn Airfield Construction Regt.

Para-Military Forces: 14,500 Police Force, 4,500 Volunteer Force.

THAILAND

Population: 46,390,000.
Military service: 2 years.
Total armed forces: 212,000.
Estimated GNP 1977: $18.1 bn.
Defence expenditure 1977–78: 15.21 bn baht ($746 m).
$1 = 20.40 baht (1977).

Army: 141,000.
1 cav div.
6 inf divs (incl 4 tk bns).
3 indep regimental combat teams.
4 AB and special forces bns.
1 SAM bn with 40 *HAWK*.
5 aviation coys and some flts.
150 M-41 lt tks; 20 *Saracen* armd cars; 32 *Shorland* Mk 3 recce; 250 M-113, LVTP-7 APC; 300 105mm, 50 155mm how; 81mm mor; 57mm RCL; 40mm AA guns; 90 O-1 lt ac; 90 UH-1B/D, 4 CH-47, 24 OH-13, 16 FH-1100, 3 Bell 206, 2 Bell 212, 6 OH-23F, 28 KH-4 hel. (*Scorpion* lt tks, 80 APC and armd cars, 24 how, 3 *Merlin* IVA tpt ac, 2 Bell 214B hel on order.)

RESERVES: 500,000.

Navy: 28,000 (8,000 Marines).
3 frigates (1 with *Seacat* SAM).
26 large patrol craft.
3 FPBG with *Gabriel* SSM.
20 coastal patrol craft (under 100 tons).
2 coastal minelayers.
4 coastal minesweepers.
1 MCM spt ship.
30 coastal gunboats (29 under 100 tons).
9 landing ships (5 LST, 3 LSM, 1 inf), 32 landing craft (26 med, 6 utility).
3 trg ships.
1 MR sqn with 10 S-2F *Tracker*, 2 HU-16B *Albatross*.
1 Marine bde (3 inf, 1 arty bns).
(3 FPBG, *Exocet* SSM, 2 CL-215 tpt ac on order.)

Air Force: 43,000; 149 combat aircraft.
1 FGA/recce sqn with 12 F-5A, 2 F-5B, 4 RF-5A.
7 COIN sqns with 45 T-28D, 32 OV-10C, 16 A-37B, 31 AU-23A *Peacemaker*.
1 recce sqn with 4 T-33, 3 RT-33A.
1 utility sqn with 35 O-1 lt ac.
3 tpt sqns with 15 C-47, 30 C-123B, 2 HS-748, 1 *Islander*, 3 *Skyvan*, 15 AC-47, 2 *Merlin* IVA, 10 *Turbo-Porter*.
2 hel sqns with 18 S-58T, 30 UH-1H, 40 CH-34C, 13 UH-19, 3 HH-43B.
Trainers incl 10 *Chipmunk*, 14 T-37B, 15 T-41D, 12 SF-260, 15 CT-4.
Sidewinder AAM.
4 bns of airfield defence troops.
(20 F-5E/F FGA, 6 OV-10C COIN, 4 CASA C-212 tpts, 18 S-58T, 13 UH-IH hel on order.)

Para-Military Forces: 52,000 Volunteer Defence Corps, 14,000 Border Police, 20 V-150 *Commando* APC, 16 lt ac, 27 hel.

VIETNAM: SOCIALIST REPUBLIC OF*

Population: 48,090,000.
Military service: 2 years minimum.
Total armed forces: 615,000.
Estimated GNP 1977: $7.1 bn.

Army: 600,000.
25 inf divs,† 2 trg divs.
1 arty comd (of 10 regts).
1 engr comd.
About 15 indep inf regts.
35 arty regts.
40 AA arty regts.
20 SAM regts (each with 18 SA-2 launchers).
15 indep engr regts.
900 T-34, T-54 and T-59 med, PT-76, Type 60 lt tks; BTR-40/-50/-60 APC; 75mm, 76mm, 85mm, 100mm, 105mm, 122mm, 130mm, 152mm, 155mm guns/how; SU-76, ISU-122 SP guns; 82mm, 100mm, 107mm, 120mm, 160mm mor; 107mm, 122mm, 140mm RL; *Sagger* ATGW; 23mm, 37mm, 57mm, 85mm, 100mm, 130mm towed, ZSU-57-2 SP AA guns; SA-2/-3/-6/-7 SAM.

DEPLOYMENT: 40,000 in Laos (numbers fluctuate).

---

* Equipment of the former forces of South Vietnam are not included here. It is estimated to have included up to 550 M-48 med and M-41 lt tks; 1,200 M-113 APC; 1,330 105mm and 155mm guns/how (some SP); 2 frigates; 2 patrol vessels; 42 patrol gunboats; 13 landing ships; 17 landing craft; 800 riverine craft; 11 support vessels; 1,000 ac of all types, incl 75 F-5A, 113 A-37B, 10 C-130, 25 A-1H/J, 37 AC-119C/K, 10 AC-47, 114 O-1, 33 DHC-2, 13 C-47; 36 CH-47, 430 UH-1 hel.
† Inf divs, normally totalling 8–10,000 men, include 1 tk bn, 3 inf, 1 arty regts and support elements.

Navy: 3,000.
3 coastal escorts (ex-Soviet SO-1-class).
2 *Komar*-class FPBG with *Styx* SSM.
22 MGB (8 *Shanghai*-, 14 *Swatow*-class).
4 MTB (ex-Soviet P-4-, P-6-class).
About 30 small patrol boats (under 100 tons).
Some 20 landing craft.
10 Mi-4 SAR hel.

Air Force: 12,000; 300 combat aircraft.
1 lt bbr sqn with 10 Il-28.
8 FGA sqns with 120 MiG-17, 30 Su-7.

6 interceptor sqns with 70 MiG-19/F-6, 70 MiG-21F/PF.
Tpts incl 20 An-2, 4 An-24, 12 Il-14, 4 Il-18, 23 Li-2.
Hels incl 20 Mi-4, 10 Mi-6, 9 Mi-8.
AA-2 *Atoll* AAM.
About 30 trainers incl Yak-11/-18, MiG-15UTI/-21U.

Para-Military Forces: 70,000 Frontier, Coast Security and People's Armed Security Forces; Armed Militia of about 1,500,000.

Latin America

Continental Treaties and Agreements

In March and April 1945 the Act of Chapultepec was signed by Argentina, Bolivia, Brazil, Chile, Colombia, Costa Rica, Cuba, the Dominican Republic, Ecuador, Guatemala, Haiti, Honduras, Mexico, Nicaragua, Panama, Paraguay, Peru, the United States, Uruguay and Venezuela. This Act declared that any attack upon a member party would be considered an attack upon all and provided for the collective use of armed force to prevent or repel such aggression.

In September 1947 all the parties to the Chapultepec Act – except Ecuador and Nicaragua – signed the Inter-American Treaty of Reciprocal Assistance, otherwise known as the Rio Defence Treaty (Cuba withdrew from the Treaty in March 1960). This Treaty constrained signatories to the peaceful settlement of disputes among themselves and provided for collective self-defence should any member party be subject to external attack.

The Charter of the Organization of American States (OAS), drawn up in 1948, embraced declarations based upon the Rio Defence Treaty. The member parties – the signatories to the Act of Chapultepec plus Barbados, El Salvador, Jamaica and Trinidad and Tobago – are bound to peaceful settlement of internal disputes and to collective action in the event of external attack upon one or more signatory states.*

The Act of Havana (1940), signed by representatives of all the then 21 American Republics, provides for the collective trusteeship by American nations of European colonies and possessions in the Americas, should any attempt be made to transfer the sovereignty of these colonies from one non-American power to another. The Havana Convention (1940) which makes the Act of Havana legally binding, was signed by the same states, although not ratified by Bolivia, Chile, Cuba and Paraguay.

A Treaty for the Prohibition of Nuclear Weapons in Latin America (The Tlatelolco Treaty) was signed in February 1967 by 22 Latin American countries; 20 countries have now ratified it (Argentina has signed but not ratified, and Brazil has ratified but reserved her position on peaceful nuclear explosions). Britain and the Netherlands have ratified it for the territories within the Treaty area for which they are internationally responsible. Britain and the Netherlands have signed Protocol I (which commits states outside the region to accept, for their territories within it, the Treaty restrictions regarding the emplacement or storage of nuclear weapons); France has not; the United States has announced her intention of doing so. The United States, Britain, France and China have signed Protocol II to the Treaty (an undertaking not to use or threaten to use nuclear weapons against the parties to the Treaty); the Soviet Union has not. An Agency has been set up by the contracting parties to ensure compliance with the Treaty.

Other Agreements

In July 1965, El Salvador, Guatemala, Honduras and Nicaragua agreed to form a military bloc for the co-ordination of all resistance against possible Communist aggression.

The United States has bilateral military assistance agreements or representation with Argentina, Bolivia, Brazil, Chile, Colombia, the Dominican Republic, El Salvador, Guatemala, Honduras, Mexico, Nicaragua, Panama, Paraguay, Peru, Uruguay and Venezuela. She has a bilateral agreement with Cuba for jurisdiction and control over Guantanamo Bay.† She also had a treaty with the Republic of Panama granting the United States, in perpetuity, virtual sovereign rights over the Canal Zone. This has been superseded by two new treaties: the first, the so-called 'Neutrality Treaty' (ensuring the perpetual neutrality of the zone), was ratified by the Senate on 16 March 1978; the second, the 'Basic Treaty' (covering arrangements for the canal's transfer to Panama by the year 2000), on 18 April 1978.

The Soviet Union has no defence agreements with any of the states in this area, although she has supplied military equipment to Cuba and Peru.

---

* Legally, Cuba is a member of the OAS but has been excluded – by a decision of OAS Foreign Ministers – since January 1962. Barbados and Trinidad and Tobago signed the Charter in 1967.
† This agreement was confirmed in 1934. In 1960 the United States stated that it could be modified or abrogated only by agreement between the parties, and that she had no intention of agreeing to modification or abrogation.

ARGENTINA

Population: 26,390,000.
Military service: Army and Air Force 1 year, Navy 14 months.
Total armed forces: 132,900.
Estimated GNP 1977: $76.4 bn.*
Defence expenditure 1978: 1,186 bn pesos ($1.66 bn).*
$1 = 715 pesos (1978), 329 pesos (1977).

Army: 80,000.
2 armd bdes.
4 inf bdes.
2 mountain bdes.
1 airmobile bde.
5 AD bns.
1 aviation bn.
100 M-4 *Sherman* med, 80 AMX-13 lt tks; *Shorland* armd cars; 140 M-113, 60 Mowag, AMX-VCI, M-3 APC; 155mm towed, M-7 155mm SP guns; 105mm (incl pack), 155mm towed, 24 Mk F3 155mm SP how; 81mm, 120mm mor; 75mm, 90mm, 105mm RCL; SS-11/-12, *Bantam, Cobra* ATGW; 30mm, 35mm, 40mm, 90mm AA guns; *Tigercat* SAM; 5 *Turbo Commander* 690A, 2 DHC-6, 3 G-222, 4 Swearingen *Metro* IIIA, 4 *Queen Air*, 1 *Sabreliner*, 5 Cessna 207, 15 Cessna 182, 20 U-17A/B, 5 T-41 ac; 7 Bell 206, 4 FH-1100, 20 UH-IH, 4 Bell 47G, 2 Bell 212 hel. (5 *Turbo Commander* ac; 3 CH-47C hel on order.)

RESERVES: 250,000: 200,000 National Guard, 50,000 Territorial Guard.

Navy: 32,900 (12,000 conscripts), incl Naval Air Force and Marines.
4 submarines (2 Type 209, 2 ex-US *Guppy*-class).
1 aircraft carrier (15 A-4Q, 6 S-2A/E, 4 S-61D).
2 cruisers (ex-US *Brooklyn*-class) with *Seacat* SAM, 2 hel.
9 destroyers (1 Type 42 with *Sea Dart* SAM, 5 *Fletcher*-, 2 *Sumner*-, 1 *Gearing*-class).
12 patrol vessels (2 trg, 1 coastguard).
5 large patrol craft (3 in coastguard).
6 coastal minesweepers/minehunters.
2 *Combattante* II-class FPB.
1 LSD, 5 LST, 28 landing craft (1 LCT).
(2 Type 209 subs, 1 Type 42 destroyer, 2 Type 148 FPBG on order.)

NAVAL AIR FORCE: 4,000; 34 combat aircraft.
1 FB sqn with 15 A-4Q.
1 MR sqn with 6 S-2A/E, 10 SP-2H, 3 HU-16B, PBY-5A.
Tpts incl 3 *Electra*, 2 C-54, 2 DC-4, 8 C-47, 1 HS-125, 1 *Guarani* II, 1 *Sabreliner*.
Other ac incl 2 DHC-2, 1 DHC-6, 2 *Super King Air*, 4 *Queen Air*, 4 Piper *Navajo*, 4 *Turbo-Porter*.
Hel incl 4 S-61D, 6 *Alouette* III, 3 UH-19, 5 S-55, 3 Bell 47G.

Trainers incl 12 MB-326GB, 12 T-6/-28, 2 AT-11, 3 T-34C.
(12 T-34C trg ac, 3 *Lynx* hel on order.)

MARINES: 7,000.
5 bns.
1 cdo bn.
1 fd arty bn.
1 AD regt.
1 engr bn, 1 sigs bn.
7 indep inf coys.
20 LVTP-7, 15 LARC-5 APC; 105mm how; 106mm, 120mm mor; 75mm, 105mm RCL; *Bantam* ATGW; 88mm AA guns; 10 *Tigercat* SAM.

Air Force: 20,000; 184 combat aircraft.
1 bbr sqn with 9 *Canberra* B62, 2 T64.
4 FB sqns with 70 A-4P *Skyhawk*.
1 FB sqn with 20 F-86F.
3 FGA sqns with 48 MS-760A *Paris* I.
1 interceptor sqn with 16 *Mirage* IIIEA, 2 IIIDA.
1 COIN sqn with 17 IA-58 *Pucará*.
1 assault hel sqn with 14 Hughes 500M, 6 UH-1H.
1 SAR sqn with 3 HU-16B ac, 12 *Lama*, 2 S-58T, 2 S-61N/R hel.
5 tpt sqns with 1 Boeing 707-320B, 7 C-130E/H, 1 *Sabreliner*, 2 *Learjet* 35A, 3 G-222, 13 C-47, 10 F-27, 6 F-28, 6 DHC-6, 22 IA-50 *Guarani* II, 2 *Merlin* IVA.
1 Antarctic sqn with 2 DHC-2, 3 DHC-3, 1 LC-47 ac, 1 S-61R hel.
1 comms sqn with 4 *Commander*, 14 *Shrike Commander, Paris*, T-34, IA-35 *Huanquero*.
Hel incl 4 UH-1D, 3 UH-19, 3 Bell 47G.
Trainers incl 35 T-34, 12 *Paris*, 37 Cessna 182.
R.530 AAM, AS.11/12 ASM.
(7 *Mirage* IIIEA, 33 IA-58 *Pucará*, 16 *Turbo Commander* ac; 3 CH-47, 8 Bell 212 hel on order.)

Para-Military Forces: 42,000. Gendarmerie: 11,000; M-113 APC, 20 lt ac, 10 hel under Army command, mainly for frontier duties. National Maritime Prefecture: 9,000. *Policía Federal:* 22,000; APC, 4 BO-105 hel.

BOLIVIA

Population: 6,100,000.
Military service: 12 months selective.
Total armed forces: 22,500.
Estimated GNP 1977: $2.5 bn.
Defence expenditure 1978: 1.82 bn pesos ($90 m).
$1 = 20.2 pesos (1978), 20.2 pesos (1977).

Army: 17,000.
4 cav regts.
1 mech regt.

---

* Rapid inflation makes defence expenditure and GNP figures in local currency and dollar terms unreliable.

1 mot regt.
13 inf regts (1 Palace Guard).
2 ranger regts.
1 para bn.
3 arty regts.
6 engr bns.
18 M-113, 10 V-200 *Commando*, 20 Mowag APC;
  6 75mm guns; 25 75mm pack, 20 FH-18, 25
  M-101 105mm how.

Navy: 1,500.
16 small patrol craft.
1 river transport.

Air Force: 4,000; 42 combat aircraft.
1 fighter/trg sqn with 10 T-33A/N.
2 COIN sqns with 18 EMB-326GB, 10 T-6D, 4
  T-28A/D.
Tpts incl 3 C-130H, 1 *Electra*, 2 C-54, 1 *Sabreliner*,
  1 *Learjet*, 5 *Arava*, 4 CV-440, 10 C-47, 1 C-46, 2
  Cessna 402, 1 *Turbo-Porter*, 2 *Turbo Centurion*,
  11 Cessna 185, 1 *Super King Air*, 1 Cessna 421.
1 hel sqn with 9 Hughes 500M, 3 Hiller OH-23C/D.
Trainers incl Cessna 310, 6 T-41D, 12 T-23
  Uirapuru, 5 Fokker S-11, 6 SF-260M.
(1 *Arava*, 16 PC-7 *Turbo-Trainer* on order.)

BRAZIL

Population: 115,850,000.
Military service: 1 year.
Total armed forces: 273,800 (113,000 conscripts).
Estimated GNP 1977: $177 bn.
Defence expenditure 1978: 34.4 bn cruzeiros
  ($2.04 bn).
  $1 = 16.90 cruzeiros (1978), 13.0 cruzeiros (1977).

Army: 182,000 (110,000 conscripts).
8 divs: each up to 4 armd, mech or mot inf bdes.
2 indep inf bdes.
1 indep para bde.
5 lt 'jungle' inf bns.
60 M-4 med, 220 M-3A1, 250 M-41, 25 X-1 lt tks;
  120 *Cascavel*, M-8 armd cars; *Urutu*, M-59, 600
  M-113 APC; 500 75mm pack, 450 105mm (some
  M-7, M-108 SP), 90 155mm how; 81mm mor;
  108-R, 114mm RL; 106mm RCL; *Cobra* ATGW;
  40mm, 90mm AA guns; 20 *Roland* SAM; 40 L-42
  Regente, O-1E lt ac; 10 AB-206A hel.

Navy: 49,000 (3,000 conscripts, 13,500 Naval Air
  Force, Marines and Auxiliary Corps).
10 submarines (3 *Oberon*-, 7 ex-US *Guppy* II/III-
  class).
1 aircraft carrier (20 ac, incl 7 S-2A, 4 *Sea King* hel).
15 destroyers (1 with *Exocet* SSM, *Seacat* SAM, 1 hel;
  2 with *Ikara* ASW, *Seacat* SAM, 1 hel; 2 with
  Seacat SAM).
10 corvettes (fleet tugs).

5 river patrol ships.
1 river monitor.
6 large, 10 river patrol craft.
6 coastal minesweepers.
4 coastal auxiliaries, 2 LST, 25 small landing craft.
(3 destroyers on order.)

NAVAL AIR FORCE:
1 ASW sqn with 5 SH-3D *Sea King* hel.
1 utility sqn with 5 *Whirlwind*, 6 *Wasp*, 1 FH-1100,
  2 Bell 47G, 18 AB-206B, 2 *Lynx* hel.
1 trg sqn with 10 Hughes 269/300 hel.
(7 *Lynx* hel on order.)

Air Force: 42,800; 135 combat aircraft.
1 interceptor sqn with 11 *Mirage* IIIEBR, 4 DBR.
2 FGA sqns with 34 F-5E, 5 F-5B.
8 COIN/recce sqns with 39 AT-26 *Xavante*, 20 T-25
  Universal ac, 6 UH-1D, 4 Bell 206, 4 OH-6A hel.
1 ASW sqn with 8 S-2E, 8 S-2A (7 in carrier).
1 MR sqn with 6 EMB-111M.
4 SAR sqns with 11 SA-16 *Albatross*, 3 RC-130E,
  6 PBY-5A ac, 5 SH-1D, UH-1H, Bell 47G hel.
12 tpt sqns with 2 Boeing 737, 10 C-130E/H,
  2 KC-130H, 9 HS-125, 1 *Viscount*, 12 HS-748,
  21 DHC-5, 74 EMB-110 *Bandeirante* (56 C-95, 6
  R-95, 4 EC-95, 8 C-95A), 5 EMB-121 *Xingu* ac,
  6 AB-206 hel.
3 liaison sqns with L-42, T-25, O-1E, 10 EMB-810C
  (*Seneca* II) ac, UH-1H hel.
Trainers incl 100 T-23 *Uirapuru*, 130 T-25, 10 T-33,
  50 AT-26.
R.530 AAM.
(4 *Mirage* IIIEBR interceptors, 50 AT-26 trg,
  12 EMB-110 (C-95A) tpts, 6 EMB-111M MR ac
  on order.)

Para-Military Forces: Public security forces about
  200,000; state militias in addition.

CHILE

Population: 11,100,000.
Military Service: 1 year.
Total armed forces: 85,000 (21,600 conscripts).
Estimated GNP 1977: $9.8 bn.*
Defence expenditure 1978: 22.6 bn pesos
  ($750 m).*
  $1 = 30.14 pesos (1978), 17.8 pesos (1977).

Army: 50,000 (20,000 conscripts).
6 divs, incl 7 cav regts (3 armd, 3 horsed, 1 hel-
  borne), 20 inf regts (incl 9 mot, 3 mountain), 6
  arty groups, some AA arty spt dets.
M-4 med, 10 M-3, 60 M-41, 47 AMX-13 lt tks;
  M-113, Mowag MR-8 APC; 105mm, M-56
  105mm pack how; Mk F3 155mm SP how; 81mm,

---

* Rapid inflation makes defence expenditure and GNP
figures in local currency and dollar terms unreliable.

120mm mor; 106mm RCL; 20mm, 40mm AA guns; 4 O-1, 5 T-25 trg ac, 9 *Puma*, 3 UH-1H, 2 AB-206 hel.

RESERVES: 160,000.

Navy: 24,000 (1,600 conscripts), incl Naval Air and Marines.
3 submarines (2 *Oberon-*, 1 ex-US *Balao*-class).
3 cruisers (2 ex-US *Brooklyn-*, 1 ex-Swedish *Tre Kroner*-class).
6 destroyers (2 *Almirante*-class with *Exocet* SSM and *Seacat* SAM, 2 ex-US *Sumner-*, 2 *Fletcher*-class).
2 frigates (*Leander*-class with *Exocet* SSM, *Seacat* SAM, 1 hel).
3 destroyer escorts (ex-US fast transports).
4 corvettes.
2 large patrol craft (under 100 tons).
4 MTB.
7 landing ships/craft (4 ex-US LST, 3 medium).

NAVAL AIR FORCE: 500.
1 ASW/SAR sqn with 6 EMB-111, 2 PBY-5A, 3 PBY-6A, 4 SP-2E, 5 Beech D18S, 1 Piper *Navajo*, 1 F-27 ac, 4 UH-19, 2 UH-1D hel.
Tpts incl 4 C-47, 6 EMB-110C *Bandeirante*.
Hel incl 4 AB-206, 3 UH-19, 2 UH-1D, 12 Bell 47G, 6 *Alouette* III.
5 T-34 trainers.
(5 EMB-111N on order.)

MARINES: 3,800.
1 bde; coast-defence units.

Air Force: 11,000; 97 combat aircraft.
3 FB sqns with 20 *Hunter* F71, 18 F-5E/F.
1 fighter/trg sqn with 9 F-80C, 8 T-33A.
2 COIN sqns with 34 A-37B.
1 SAR/ASW sqn with 8 HU-16B *Albatross*.
Tpts incl 2 C-130H, 5 C-118, 6 DC-6B, 12 C-47.
2 utility sqns with 11 DHC-6, 10 C-45, 1 *King Air*, 5 *Twin Bonanza*, 10 Cessna 180.
Hel incl 6 S-55T, 6 SL-4, 2 UH-1H, 6 UH-12E, 6 *Lama*.
Trainers incl 30 T-34, 30 T-37B, 8 T-41, 11 *Vampire* T22/55, 4 *Hunter* T77, 5 T-6, 9 Beech 99, 5 T-25, 1 F-27.
Sidewinder AAM.
1 AA arty regt.
(*Shafrir* AAM on order.)

Para-Military Forces: 30,000 *Carabineros*, with 15 Mowag MR-8 APC, 25 lt ac.

COLOMBIA

Population: 27,000,000.
Military service: 2 years.
Total armed forces: 75,500.
Estimated GNP 1977: $12.9 bn.

Defence expenditure 1978: 6.58 bn pesos ($173 m)
$1 = 38.1 pesos (1978), 36.5 pesos (1977).

Army: 60,000.
11 inf bdes ('Regional Bdes').
1 Presidential Guard.
1 ranger bn.
4 AB bns.
1 AA arty bn.
7 mech cav, 25 inf, 7 arty, 7 engr units.
M-4A3 med, M-3A1 lt tks; M-8, M-20 armd cars; M-101 105mm how; mor; 40mm AA guns.

RESERVES: 425,000.

Navy: 9,000 (2,800 Marines).
4 submarines (2 midget, 2 Type 209).
3 destroyers (2 Swedish *Halland*-class, 1 ex-US *Sumner*-class).
9 frigates (1 ex-US *Courtney*-class, 1 former fast transport, 3 *Cherokee-*, 4 ex-Port *J. Coutinho*-class).
21 coastal patrol craft (13 under 100 tons).
2 marine bns.

Air Force: 6,500; 18 combat aircraft.
1 fighter/recce sqn with 14 *Mirage* VCOA, 4 VCOR/D.
Tpts incl 2 C-130B, 8 C-54, C-45, 29 C-47, 3 HS-748, 1 F-28, 9 DHC-2, 4 DHC-3.
Hel incl 13 AH-1H, 3 UH-1B, 6 UH-1H, 1 UH-1N, 20 OH-6A, 8 OH-13.
Trainers incl 10 T-37, 6 T-38, 30 T-41D, 31 AT-33, 30 T-34.
R.530 ASM.

Para-Military Forces: 50,000 National Police Force.

CUBA

Population: 9,750,000.
Military service: 3 years.
Total armed forces: 159,000.
Estimated GNP 1970: $4.5 bn.
Estimated defence expenditure 1977: 784 m pesos ($784 m).
$1 = 1 peso.

Army: 130,000.
15 inf 'divs' (bdes).
3 armd regts.
Some indep 'regts' (bn gps).
Over 600 tks, incl 60 IS-2 hy, T-34/-54/-55, 50 T-62 med, PT-76 lt; BRDM-1 armd cars; 400 BTR-40/-60/-152 APC; 75mm pack, 122mm, 130mm, 152mm guns/how; 100 SU-100 SP guns; 45 *FROG*-4 SSM; 57mm, 76mm, 85mm ATK guns; 57mm RCL; *Snapper* ATGW; ZU-23, 37mm, 57mm, 85mm, 100mm, ZSU-23-4 SP AA guns; SA-7 SAM.

DEPLOYMENT: *Angola:* 23–25,000; *Ethiopia:* 16–17,000.*

RESERVES: 90,000.

Navy: 9,000.
18 submarine chasers (12 ex-Soviet SO-1, 6 *Kronstadt*).
5 *Osa*-I-, 3 *Osa*-II-, 18 *Komar*-class FPBG with *Styx* SSM.
24 MTB (ex-Soviet P-4 and P-6).
30 armed patrol boats (under 100 tons).
7 med landing craft.
Some 50 *Samlet* coast-defence SSM.

Air Force: 20,000, incl Air Defence Forces; 163 combat aircraft.
2 FB sqns with 30 MiG-17.
7 interceptor sqns: 3 with 48 MiG-21F, 2 with 30 MiG-21MF, 2 with 40 MiG-19.
1 trg sqn with 15 MiG-15.
Tpts incl 50 I1-14, An-24 and An-2.
Hel incl 30 Mi-1, 24 Mi-4.
Trainers incl MiG-15UTI, 60 Zlin 326.
AA-2 *Atoll* AAM.
24 SAM bns with 144 SA-2 *Guideline* and SA-3 *Goa*.

Para-Military Forces: 10,000 State security troops; 3,000 border guards; 100,000 People's Militia.

DOMINICAN REPUBLIC

Population: 5,130,000.
Military service: voluntary.
Total armed forces: 18,500.
Estimated GNP 1977: $4.3 bn.
Defence expenditure 1978: 49.6 m pesos ($49.6 m).
$1 = 1 peso.

Army: 11,000.
3 inf bdes.
1 mixed armd bn.
1 mountain inf bn.
1 para 'bn'.
1 Presidential Guard bn.
1 arty regt.
1 AA arty regt.
1 engr bn.
1 armd recce sqn.
20 AMX-13 lt tks; AML armd cars; M-3 APC; 105mm how.

Navy: 4,000.
3 patrol frigates (2 ex-US *Tacoma*-class, 1 ex-Canadian *River*-class trg ship).
2 corvettes (ex-Canadian *Flower*-class).
2 fleet minesweepers.
14 patrol craft (12 under 100 tons).
1 LCT, 1 med landing craft.
1 cdo bn.

Air Force: 3,500; 43 combat aircraft.
1 bbr sqn with 7 B-26K.
1 fighter sqn with 10 *Vampire* F1/FB50.
1 fighter/trg sqn with 20 F-51D.
1 COIN/trg sqn with 6 T-28D.
2 PBY-5A SAR ac.
1 tpt sqn with 6 C-46, 6 C-47, 3 DHC-2.
Hel incl 3 *Alouette* II/III, 2 H-19, 2 UH-12E, 7 OH-6A.
Trainers incl 4 Cessna 172, T-6, T-11.

Para-Military Forces: 10,000 Gendarmerie.

ECUADOR

Population: 7,790,000.
Military service: 2 years, selective.
Total armed forces: 25,300.
Estimated GNP 1977: $5.9 bn.
Defence expenditure 1977: 2.86 bn sucres ($114 m).
$1 = 25 sucres (1977).

Army: 17,500.
11 inf bns (2 mot).
1 para bn.
3 recce, 4 horsed cav sqns.
1 Presidential Guard sqn.
10 indep inf coys.
3 arty gps, 1 AA arty bn.
2 engr bns.
30 M-3, 80 AMX-13 lt tks; 27 AML-60/-90 armd cars; M-113, AMX-VCI APC; 105mm, 6 Mk F3 155mm SP how; 40mm AA guns; 1 *Skyvan*, 6 *Arava*, 3 *Porter* tpts, 7 lt ac, 2 hel.
(VAB APC on order.)

Navy: 3,800 (700 Marines).
1 Type 209 submarine.
3 frigates (1 ex-US fast transport, 2 ex-British *Hunt*-class).
2 coastal escorts (ex-US).
3 FPBG with *Exocet* SSM, 3 FPB.
2 large, 5 coastal patrol craft (5 under 100 tons).
2 LST, 2 LSM.
3 *Arava*, 2 T-37, 2 T-41, 1 Cessna 320, 1 Cessna 177 ac, 2 *Alouette* III hel.
(3 Type 209 submarines, 1 *Lupo*-class frigate, 4 corvettes on order.)

Air Force: 4,000; 46 combat aircraft.
1 lt bbr sqn with 5 *Canberra* B6.
1 FB sqn with 12 *Jaguar* A/B.
1 COIN sqn with 10 A-37B.
1 recce sqn with 6 *Meteor* FR9.
1 FGA/trg sqn with 12 BAC-167 *Strikemaster*.

---

* Cuban advisers and technicians are also reported in Algeria, Benin, Congo, Guinea, Libya, Mozambique, Sierra Leone, Tanzania, Uganda, South Yemen, Zambia.

1 PBY-5A *Catalina* MR aircraft.
Tpts incl 4 *Electra*, 2 C-130H, 4 DC-6B, 2 *Learjet*,
    4 HS-748, 12 C-47, 5 C-45, 2 DHC-5, 3 DHC-6.
Hel incl 2 *Puma*, 4 *Alouette* III, 4 *Lama*, 3 Bell 47G.
Trainers incl 20 T-34C, 12 SF-260, 24 Cessna 150A.
R.550 *Magic* AAM.
(18 *Mirage* F1C fighters, 2 F1B trainers, 12 *Super
    Mystère* B2 FB, 2 DHC-5 tpts on order.)

Para-Military Forces: 5,800.

GUATEMALA

Population: 6,320,000.
Total armed forces: 14,270.
Estimated GNP 1977: $4.6 bn.
Defence expenditure 1978: 58.5m quetzal ($58.5m).
    $1 = 1 quetzal.

Army: 13,500.
3 bde HQ.
10 inf bns.
1 Presidential Guard bn.
1 para bn.
1 engr bn.
1 armd car coy.
9 arty btys.
8 AMX-13 lt tks; 8 M-8 armd cars; 6 M-3A1, 10
    M-113, 10 RBY-1, 7 *Commando* APC; 12 75mm,
    12 105mm how; 81mm, 12 4.2in mor, 10 40mm
    SP AA guns.

Navy: 400, incl 200 Marines.
11 small coastal patrol craft (under 100 tons).
1 med landing craft.

Air Force: 370; 11 combat aircraft.
1 FGA sqn with 11 A-37B.
1 tpt sqn with 1 DC-6, 9 C-47, 10 *Arava*.
1 comms sqn with 6 Cessna 172, 3 Cessna 180,
    2 Cessna U-206C ac, 9 Bell UH-1D hel.
2 T-33A trainers.

Para-Military Forces: 3,000.

HONDURAS

Population: 3,400,000.
Military service: voluntary.
Total armed forces: 14,200.
Estimated GNP 1977: $1.3 bn.
Defence expenditure 1978: 62.8 m lempira ($31m).
    $1 = 2 lempira (1978), 2 lempira (1977).

Army: 13,000.
10 inf bns.
1 Presidential Guard bn.
3 arty btys.
1 engr, 1 sigs bn.

12 75mm pack, 8 105mm how; 81mm, 120mm mor;
    57mm RCL.
(*Scorpion* lt tks on order.)

Air Force: 1,200; 18 combat aircraft.
1 FB sqn with 12 *Super Mystère* B2.
1 COIN sqn with 6 A-37B.
Tpts incl 1 C-54, C-45, 1 C-47, 3 *Arava*, 1 *Westwind*,
    4 Cessna 180/185.
Trainers incl 6 T-6, 4 T-28E, 5 T-41A, 3 RT-33A.

Para-Military Forces: 3,000.

MEXICO

Population: 66,770,000.
Military service: voluntary, with part-time conscript
    militia.
Total armed forces: 97,000 regular, 250,000 part-
    time conscripts.
Estimated GNP 1977: $83.8 bn.
Defence expenditure 1978: 12.66 bn pesos ($557 m).
    $1 = 22.7 pesos (1978), 22.6 pesos (1977).

Army: 72,000 regular, 250,000 conscripts.
1 mech bde gp (Presidential Guard).
1 inf bde gp.
1 para bde.
Zonal Garrisons incl:
    23 indep cav regts, 64 indep inf bns, 1 arty regt.
AA, engr and support units.
M-3, M-5 lt tks; 100 M-3A1, M-8 armd cars;
    HWK-11 APC; 75mm, 105mm how (incl M-8
    75mm, M-7 105mm SP).

Navy: 19,000, incl Naval Air Force and Marines.
2 destroyers (ex-US *Fletcher*-class).
1 frigate (ex-US *Edsall*-class trg ship).
18 ex-US *Auk*-class (coastguard) corvettes.
6 transports (4 ex-US).
16 ex-US fleet minesweepers.
22 *Azteca*-class patrol craft.
9 river, 6 coastal patrol boats (under 100 tons).
2 LST.
(9 *Azteca*-class patrol craft on order.)

NAVAL AIR FORCE: 350.
10 HU-16 *Albatross* MR ac.
Other ac incl 1 *Learjet* 24D, 4 C-45, 3 DC-3,
    1 Beech *Baron*, 3 *Bonanza*, 4 *Cessna* 150.
4 *Alouette* II, 3 Bell 47, 5 Hughes 269A hel.

MARINES: 2,000; 19 security companies.

Air Force: 6,000; 80 combat aircraft.
1 COIN sqn with 15 AT-33A.
5 COIN/trg sqns with 20 T-6, 45 T-28A.
1 SAR sqn with 18 LASA-60 ac, 9 *Alouette* III,
    1 Hiller 12E hel.

4 tpt sqns with 2 Boeing 727, 1 DC-7, 1 DC-6, 5 C-118, 5 C-54, 1 *Jetstar*, 1 BAC-111, 20 C-47, 3 *Skyvan*, 12 *Islander*, 10 *Arava*, Aero Commander.
Hel incl 5 Bell 206B, 3 Bell 212, 10 Bell 205.
Trainers incl 20 T-6, 30 T-28, 20 Beech F33-19, 20 *Musketeer*.
1 para bn.
(12 PC-7 *Turbo-Trainer* on order.)

PARAGUAY

Population: 2,870,000.
Military service: 18 months.
Total armed forces: 17,000.
Estimated GNP 1977: $2.0 bn.
Defence expenditure 1978: 5.19 bn guaranies ($41 m).
$1 = 126 guaranies (1978), 126 guaranies (1977).

Army: 12,500.
1 cav 'div' (bde) with 2 mech cav regts, 1 inf bn, 1 arty bty.
6 inf 'divs' (bn gps).
2 indep horsed cav regts.
2 indep inf bns.
1 Presidential Guard bn.
1 arty regt.
5 engr, 1 sigs bns.
9 M-4 med, 6 M-3 lt tks; APC; 75mm pack, 105mm how; 2 Bell 47, 3 UH-12E hel.

Navy: 2,000 (500 Marines and Naval Air).
2 river defence vessels.
3 patrol boats (ex-Argentinian minesweepers).
8 coastal patrol craft (under 20 tons).
1 LSM, 2 landing craft, utility.
1 marine 'regt' (bn).
4 Cessna U206, 2 Cessna 150 ac, 2 Bell 47G hel.

Air Force: 2,500; 12 combat aircraft.
1 COIN sqn with 12 T-6 *Texan*.
Tpts incl 5 DC-6B, 2 C-54, 3 CV-240, 10 C-47, 1 DHC-6, 1 *Dove*, 1 DHC-3.
14 Bell UH-13A hel.
Trainers incl 8 Fokker S-11, 8 T-23 *Uirapuru*, 10 T-6, 1 MS-760, 5 Cessna 185.
1 para 'regt' (bn).
(10 AT-26 *Xavante* COIN, 10 EMB-110 tpts on order.)

Para-Military Forces: 4,000 security forces.

PERU

Population: 17,070,000.
Military service: 2 years, selective.
Total armed forces: 89,000 (49,000 conscripts).
Estimated GNP 1977: $13 bn.*
Defence expenditure 1977: 30.04 bn soles ($406 m).*
$1 = 74 soles (1977).

Army: 65,000 (49,000 conscripts).
2 armd 'divs' (bdes).
2 armd, 2 horsed regts (cav 'div').
8 inf and mech 'divs' (bdes).
1 para-cdo 'AB div' (bde).
1 jungle 'div' (bde).
3 armd recce sqns.
Arty and engr bns.
250 T-54/-55, 60 M-4 med, 110 AMX-13 lt tks; M-8 armd cars; 50 M-3A1 scout cars; 300 M-113, V-200 *Chaimite*, UR-416, Mowag APC; 105mm, 122mm, 130mm, 155mm how; 120mm mor; 28 40mm, 76mm towed, ZSU-23-4 SP AA guns; SA-3 SAM; 5 U-10B, 5 Cessna 185 lt ac; 42 Mi-8 (36 in store), 4 *Alouette* III, 5 *Lama* hel.
(200 T-55 tks, 122mm, 130mm guns, SA-3/-7 SAM, 2 *Nomad* lt tpt ac on order.)

Navy: 14,000 (incl Naval Air, 1,000 Marines).
8 submarines (2 ex-US *Guppy* I-, 4 ex-US *Mackerel*-class, 2 Type 209).
4 cruisers (2 ex-Dutch *De Ruyter*-, 2 ex-British *Ceylon*-class).
4 destroyers (2 ex-British *Daring*-class with *Exocet* SSM, 2 ex-US *Fletcher*-class).
3 frigates (1 *Lupo*-class, 2 ex-US *Cannon*-class).
6 river gunboats, 3 river patrol craft (under 100 tons).
4 landing ships/craft (2 LST, 2 med).
9 S-2A *Tracker* ASW, 6 C-47, 2 F-27, 1 *Aztec* tpt ac.
6 AB-212 ASW, 5 Bell 47G, 10 Bell 206, 6 UH-1D/H, 2 *Alouette* III hel.
8 T-34 trainers.
(2 Type 209 submarines, 3 *Lupo*-class frigates with *Otomat* SSM and *Albatros* SAM, 6 *Combattante*-class FPBG on order.)
1 marine bn.

Air Force: 10,000; 163 combat aircraft.
2 lt bbr sqns with 32 *Canberra* B2, B(I)8/56, 2 T4.
4 FB sqns: 2 with 35 *Mirage* VP, 2 with 32 Su-22, 4 Su-22UTI.
2 fighter sqns: 1 with 8 F-86F, 1 with 10 *Hunter* F52.
1 trg sqn with 12 MiG-21 (on loan from Cuba).
2 COIN sqns with 24 A-37B.
1 MR sqn with 4 HU-16B *Albatross*.
Tpts incl 3 L-100-20, 4 C-130E, 5 DC-6, 4 C-54, 2 *Learjet*, 16 An-26, 2 F-27, 4 F-28, 7 DHC-6, 16 DHC-5, 18 *Queen Air*, 3 *King Air*, 2 Beech 99, 12 *Turbo-Porter*, 5 Cessna 185.
Hel incl 12 *Alouette* III, 6 UH-1D, 20 Bell 47G, 14 Bell 212, 6 Mi-6, 6 Mi-8.
Trainers incl 15 T-6, 6 T-34, 8 T-33A, 19 T-41, 26 T-37B/C, 4 Cessna 150.
AS.30 ASM.

Para-Military Forces: 20,000 *Guardia Civil*.

---

* Rapid inflation makes defence expenditure and GNP figures in local currency and dollars unreliable.

URUGUAY

Population: 3,170,000.
Military service: voluntary.
Total armed forces: 27,000.
Estimated GNP 1977: $3.6 bn.*
Defence expenditure 1977: 304 bn pesos
  ($72 m).*
  $1 = 4.22 pesos (1977).

Army: 20,000.
4 regional 'Armies' (divs) comprising:
  3 armd regts, 13 inf bns, 6 cav regts, 4 arty 'bns'
  (btys), 1 AD bn, 5 engr bns.
17 M-24, 18 M-3A1 lt tks; 10 M-3A1 scout cars;
  15 M-113 APC; 25 105mm how.

Navy: 4,000 (incl naval air, naval infantry, coastguard).
3 frigates (1 ex-US *Dealey*-, 2 *Cannon*-class).
2 escorts (ex-US minesweepers).
1 large and 6 coastal patrol craft (under 100 tons).
3 S-2A MR ac, 3 SNB-5 (C-45) tpts; 1 T-34B, 4
  SNJ-4, 4 T-6 trainers, 2 Bell 47G, 2 SH-34J hel.
(2 Type 209 submarines on order.)

Air Force: 3,000; 30 combat aircraft.
1 fighter/trg sqn with 6 AT-33A.
1 COIN sqn with 8 A-37B.
1 recce/trg sqn with 10 T-6G, 6 U-17A.
Tpts incl 10 C-47, 2 F-27, 3 FH-227, 2 *Queen Air*,
  5 EMB-110C.
Hel incl 6 Bell UH-1H, 2 Hiller UH-2.
2 Cessna 182, 2 Piper *Super Cub* liaison ac.
Trainers incl 6 T-41, 2 C-45.
(1 EMB-110B1 tpt on order.)

Para-Military Forces: 2,200.

VENEZUELA

Population: 13,090,000.
Military service: 2 years, selective.
Total armed forces: 44,000.
Estimated GNP 1977: $36.1 bn.
Defence expenditure 1978: 2.64 bn bolivares
  ($615 m).
  $1 = 4.29 bolivares (1978), 4.29 bolivares (1977).

Army: 28,000.
2 med, 1 lt tk bns.
2 mech, 11 inf bns.
13 ranger bns.
1 horsed cav bn.
7 arty gps.
5 AA arty and engr bns.
142 AMX-30 med, 40 AMX-13 lt tks; 12 M-8
  armd cars; AMX-VCI, 20 UR-416 APC; 75mm
  pack, 105mm how; 20 AMX 155mm SP guns;
  81mm, 120mm mor; 35 M-18 76mm SP ATK guns;
  106mm RCL; SS-11 ATGW; 40mm AA guns; some
  20 *Alouette* III and Bell 47G hel.

Navy: 8,000, incl 4,000 Marines.
4 submarines (2 *Guppy* II, 2 Type 209).
4 destroyers (1 with *Seacat* SAM).
4 frigates.
3 FPBG with *Otomat* SSM, 3 FPB.
10 patrol craft (6 in reserve).
10 coastal patrol craft (11 on order).
6 landing ships (1 LST, 4 med, 1 tpt).
6 S-2E *Tracker*, 4 HU-16 SAR ac, 3 C-47 tpts,
  2 Bell 47J hel.
(6 *Lupo*-class frigates with *Albatros* SAM, 6 AB-212
  ASW hel, *Otomat* SSM on order.)

MARINES: 3 bns.

Air Force: 8,000; 99 combat aircraft.
1 lt bbr sqn with 18 *Canberra* B2, 7 B(I)8, 2 PR3,
  2 T4.
3 fighter sqns: 1 with 15 CF-5A, 4 CF-5B; 1 with 9
  Mirage IIIEV, 4 VV, 2 VDV; 1 with 20 F-86K.
1 COIN sqn with 16 OV-10E.
2 tpt sqns with 5 C-130H, 1 Boeing 737, 1 DC-9, 20
  C-47, 12 C-123B *Provider*, 3 HS-748, 1 Cessna
  Citation.
Hel incl 13 *Alouette* III, 12 UH-1D/H, 10 UH-19.
Trg ac incl 12 *Jet Provost* T52, 24 T-2D, 25 T-34,
  2 Beech 95, 9 *Queen Air*, 12 Cessna 182.
R.530 AAM.
1 para bn.
(1 *Mirage* IIIEV fighter, 8 A-109 hel on order.)

Para-Military Forces: 10,000 National Guard.

---

* Rapid inflation makes defence expenditure and GNP
figures in local currency and dollars unreliable.

For the armed forces of smaller countries see table overleaf.

ARMED FORCES OF OTHER LATIN AMERICAN COUNTRIES*

Country	Estimated population (000)	Estimated GNP 1977 ($m)	Total armed forces	Army — Manpower and formations	Army — Equipment	Navy — Manpower and equipment	Air Force — Manpower and equipment	Para-military forces
El Salvador	4,470	2,550	7,130	6,000 3 inf 'bdes'; 1 arty 'bde'; 1 mixed cav bn; 1 engr bn; 1 AD bn; 1 para 'bn' (coy); 2 cdo/ranger coys	12 AMX-13, 3 M-3 lt tks; 20 UR-416 APC; 30 105mm how	130 4 small patrol boats	1,000 17 *Ouragan*, 4 *Magister* FGA; 6 C-47, 5 *Arava* tpts; 1 *Alouette* III, 3 *Lama* hel; 3 T-34, 10 T-6, 6 T-41, 3 *Magister* trg ac	3,000
Guyana	840	498	2,000†	2 inf bns	4 *Shorland* armd cars; 12 81mm mor	1 large, 3 coastal patrol craft	8 BN-2A, 1 *King Air*, 1 Cessna U206 lt tpts; 2 Bell 206B, 3 Bell 212, 2 *Alouette* III hel	2,250
Haiti	4,820	1,234	6,550	6,000 Pres Guard; 1 inf bn; garrison dets	M-113, 6 V-150 *Commando* APC; 75mm, 105mm how; 81mm mor; 37mm, 57mm ATK guns	300 4 small patrol boats; 1 LCT	250 8 O-2A COIN; 2 DC-3 tpts; 7 lt ac; 3 H-34, 2 S-58, 4 Hughes 300/500 hel; 3 Cessna 150 trg ac	14,900
Jamaica	2,130	2,970 (1976)	1,800†	1,800 1 inf bn; 1 spt bn	10 V-150 *Commando* APC; 6 81mm mor	4 patrol boats (coast-guard)	2 *Islander*, 1 DHC-6, 1 *King Air*, 2 Cessna 185 ac; 1 Bell 47, 2 Bell 206, 3 Bell 212 hel	7,200
Nicaragua	2,390	2,020	7,100	5,400 Pres Guard; 1 inf bn; 1 engr bn; 16 inf coys; 1 arty bty; 1 AA arty bty	Some M-4 med tks; *Staghound* armd, 3 M-3A1 scout cars; 4 105mm how; 12 20mm, 8 40mm AA guns	200 9 patrol craft	1,500 4 B-26K bbrs; 4 T-33A, 4 T-28D COIN; 1 HS-125, 5 CASA-212, 3 C-47, 4 C-45, 2 *Arava*, 4 DHC-3, 10 Cessna 180 tpts; 3 CH-34, 4 OH-6A, 1 Hughes 269 hel; 4 T-6, 3 *Super Cub* trainers	4,000

* Costa Rica and Panama maintain para-military forces, numbering 5,000 and 11,000 respectively.
† All services form part of the army.

2

TABLES
AND ANALYSIS

1. NUCLEAR DELIVERY VEHICLES: COMPARATIVE STRENGTHS AND CHARACTERISTICS

(A) UNITED STATES AND SOVIET UNION

(i) *Missiles and Artillery*

Category[a] and type	United States				
	Number deployed (7/78)	First deploy-ment	Max. range (mi)[b]	Throw-weight (000 lb)[c]	Warheads, max. yield[d] and notes
Land-based					
ICBM					
Titan II	54	1962	7,000	7.5	1×5–10 MT
Minuteman II	450	1966	7,000	1–1.5	1×1–2 MT
Minuteman III	550	1970	7,500	1.5–2	3×170 KT (MIRV)
M/IRBM					
SRBM					
Honest John	n.a.	1953	25	n.a.	Dual-capable. $1 \times$ KT range
Pershing	108[e]	1962	450	n.a.	Dual-capable. $1 \times$ high KT range; conventional warheads under development
Lance	36[e]	1972	70	n.a.	Dual-capable. $1 \times$ low KT range; conventional warheads under development
LRCM					
Sea-launched					
SLBM					
Polaris A3	160	1964	2,880	1	3×200 KT (MRV)
Poseidon C3	496	1971	2,880	2	10×50 KT (MIRV). Can carry up to 14 RV over reduced range
SLCM					

For notes see pp. 84–86.

(i) *Missiles and Artillery*

					Soviet Union
Category[a] and type[f]	Number deployed (7/78)	First deploy-ment	Max. range (mi)[b]	Throw-weight (000 lb)[c]	Warheads, max. yield[d] and notes

Land-based
ICBM

SS-9 *Scarp*	190	1965	7,500	12–15	Mod 1: 1 × 18 MT. Mod 2: 1 × 25 MT. Mod 4: 3 × 4–5 MT (MRV)
SS-11 *Sego*	780	1966	6,500	1.5–2	Mod 1: 1 × 1–2 MT. Mod 3: 3 × 100–300 KT (MRV). Mod 3 has replaced some Mod 1
SS-13 *Savage*	60	1968	5,000	1	1 × 1 MT. A solid-fuel successor, the SS-16, is ready for deployment; it has about twice the throw-weight and may also be deployed in a land-mobile mode
SS-17	60	1975	6,500	6	Mod 1: 4 × 900 KT (MIRV). Mod 2: 1 × 5 MT operational. Has begun deployment in modified SS-11 silos
SS-18	110	1975	6,300+	16–20	Mod 1: 1 × 18–25 MT. Mod 2: 8 × 2 MT (MIRV). Deployment has begun; reported accuracy 600 ft
SS-19 Mod 1, Mod 2	200	1975, n.a.	7,000, 6,300+	7	6 × 1–2 MT (MIRV) operational. 1 × 5 MT has been tested. Has begun deployment in modified SS-11 silos

M/IRBM

SS-4 *Sandal*	500	1959	1,200	1	1 × 1 MT
SS-5 *Skean*	90	1961	2,300	1	1 × 1 MT
SS-20	100	1977	3–4,000	1.2	3 × 150 KT (MIRV). Tested at longer range with 1 lower-yield warhead

SRBM

SS-1b *Scud* A		1957	50	n.a.	1 × KT range
FROG 7		1965	10–45	n.a.	1 × KT range
SS-1c *Scud* B	1,300	1965	185	n.a.	1 × KT range
SS-12 *Scaleboard*		1969	500	n.a.	1 × MT range
SS-21		1978	65	n.a.	n.a.

LRCM

SS-N-3 *Shaddock*	(100)	1962	450	n.a.	1 × KT range

Sea-launched
SLBM

SS-N-4 *Sark*	27	1961	350	n.a.	1 × 1–2 MT
SS-N-5 *Serb*	54	1964	750	n.a.	1 × 1–2 MT
SS-N-6 *Sawfly* Mods 1,2, Mod 3	528	1969	1,750, 2,000	1.5	1 × 1–2 MT, tested. 3 × KT range (MIRV)
SS-N-8	370	1972	4,800	1.5	1 × 1–2 MT
SS-NX-17	16	1977	3,000+	3	1 × MT; also tested with MIRV. Solid-fuel successor for SS-N-6
SS-N-18	n.a.	1978	5,000+	5	3 × 1–2 MT (MIRV). Solid-fuel successor for SS-N-8

SLCM

SS-N-3 *Shaddock*	324	1962	450	n.a.	1 × K T range.

	United States				
Category[a] and type	Number deployed (7/78)	First deploy-ment	Max. range (mi)[b]	Throw-weight (000 lb)[c]	Warheads, max. yield[d] and notes
Air-launched					
ALCM					
Hound Dog	(400)	1961	600	n.a.	1 × KT range
ALBM					
SRAM	1,250	1972	150	n.a.	1 × KT range
Artillery					
M-110 203mm SP how	215	1962	10	—	Dual-capable. 1 × KT range
M-109 155mm SP how	300	1964	10	—	Dual-capable. 1 × 2 KT

(ii) *Aircraft*

	United States				
Category[h] and type	Number deployed (7/78)	First deployment	Max. range (mi)[i]	Max. speed (Mach)	Weapons load (000 lb)
Bombers					
Long-range					
B-52D	366[j]	1956	10,000	0.95	60
B-52G/H		1959	12,500	0.95	70
Medium-range					
FB-111A	66	1969	6,000	2.5	37.5
Strike Aircraft					
Land-based (incl short-range bombers)					
F-4C/D/E	(556)[e]	1962	1,400	2.4	16
F-111A/E		1967	2,925	2.2/2.5	28
Carrier-based					
F-4J/N		1962	1,400	2.2	16
A-6E	(100)[e]	1963	2,000	0.9	18
A-7E		1966	2,800	0.9	20

(iii) *Historical Changes in Launcher Strength*

	United States										
	1968	1969	1970	1971	1972	1973	1974	1975	1976	1977	1978
ICBM	1,054	1,054	1,054	1,054	1,054	1,054	1,054	1,054	1,054	1,054	1,054
SLBM	656	656	656	656	656	656	656	656	656	656	656
Long-range bombers	545	560	550	505	455	422	437	432	432	432	432

For notes see pp. 84–86.

	Soviet Union				
Category[a] and type[f]	Number deployed (7/78)	First deploy- ment	Max. range (mi)[b]	Throw- weight (000 lb)[c]	Warheads, max. yield[d] and notes
Air-launched					
ALCM					
AS-3 *Kangaroo*	n.a.	1961	400	n.a.	1 × MT range
AS-4 *Kitchen*	(800)	1962	450	n.a.	1 × KT range
AS-6 *Kingfish*	n.a.	1977	160	n.a.	1 × KT range
ALBM					
Artillery					
M-55 203mm towed gun/how	n.a.	1950s	18	—	Possibly dual-capable. If so, 1 × KT range

(ii) *Aircraft*

	Soviet Union			
Category[h] and type[f]	Number deployed (7/78)	First deployment	Max. range (mi)[i]	Max. speed (Mach)	Weapons load (000 lb)
Bombers					
Long-range					
Tu-95 *Bear*	100	1956	8,000	0.78	40
Mya-4 *Bison*	35[k]	1956	7,000	0.87	20
Medium-range					
Tu-16 *Badger*	585[l]	1955	4,000	0.8	20
Tu-? *Backfire* B[m]	80[l]	1974	5,500	2.5	17.5
Strike Aircraft					
Land-based (incl short-range bombers)					
Il-28 *Beagle*		1950	1,400	0.8	4.85
Su-7 *Fitter* A		1959	900	1.7	5.5
Tu-22 *Blinder*		1962	1,400	1.5	12
MiG-21 *Fishbed* J/K/L	(1,000)	1970	1,150	2.2	2
MiG-27 *Flogger* D		1971	900	1.7	7.5
Su-17/-20 *Fitter* C		1974	1,100	1.6	11
Su-19 *Fencer* A		1974	900	2.3	8
Carrier-based					

(iii) *Historical Changes in Launcher Strength*

	Soviet Union										
	1968	1969	1970	1971	1972	1973	1974	1975	1976	1977	1978
ICBM	858	1,028	1,299	1,513	1,527	1,527	1,575	1,618	1,527	1,477	1,400
SLBM	121	196	304	448	500	628	720	784	845	909	1,015
Long-range bombers	155	145	145	145	140	140	140	135	135	135	135

(B) OTHER NATO AND WARSAW PACT COUNTRIES

(i) *Missiles and Artillery*

	NATO (excluding USA)				
Category[a] and type[n]	Number deployed (7/78)	First deployment	Max. range (mi)[b]	Warheads and max. yield[d]	Countries equipped
Land-based					
IRBM					
SRBM					
SSBS S-2	18	1971	1,875	1×150 KT	France
Honest John	(99)	1953	25	Dual-capable. $1 \times$ KT range	Germany, Greece, Netherlands, Turkey[o]
Pershing	72	1962	450	$1 \times$ KT range	Germany[o]
Pluton	30	1974	75	1×15–25 KT	France
Lance	(48)	1976	70	$1 \times$ KT range	Belgium, Britain, Germany, Italy
Sea-launched					
SLBM					
Polaris A3	64	1967	2,880	3×200 KT (MRV)	Britain
MSBS M-2	16	1974	1,900	1×500 KT	France
MSBS M-20	48	1977	3,000	1×1 MT	France
Artillery					
M-110 203mm SP how	n.a.	1962	10	Dual-capable. $1 \times$ KT range	Belgium, Britain, Denmark, Germany, Greece, Italy, Netherlands, Turkey[o]
M-109 155mm SP how	n.a.	1964	10	Dual-capable. 1×2 KT	Belgium, Britain, Canada, Denmark, Germany, Greece, Italy, Netherlands, Norway, Turkey[op]

(ii) *Aircraft*

	NATO (excluding USA)					
Category[h] and type[s]	Number deployed (7/78)	First deployment	Max. range (mi)[i]	Max. speed (Mach)	Weapons load (000 lb)	Countries equipped
Bombers						
Medium-range						
Vulcan B2	48	1960	4,000	0.95	21	Britain
Strike Aircraft						
Land-based (incl short-range bombers)						
F-104	n.a.[t]	1958	1,500	2.2	4	Belgium, Canada,[u] Germany, Italy, Netherlands, Norway, Turkey[o]
F-4	n.a.[t]	1962	1,400	2.4	16	Germany, Greece, Turkey
Buccaneer	64	1962	2,300	0.95	12	Britain
Mirage IVA	37	1964	2,000	2.2	16	France
Jaguar	177	1973	1,000	1.4	1	Britain, France

Figures in parentheses are estimated.

[a] ICBM = range over 4,000 mi; IRBM = 1,500–4,000 mi; MRBM = 500–1,500 mi; SRBM = under 500 mi; LRCM = over 350 mi.

[b] Statute miles. Use of maximum payload may reduce operational range by up to 25 per cent of these figures.

[c] Throw-weight is the weight of post-boost vehicle (warheads, guidance systems, penetration aids) that can be delivered over a given range. At maximum range, throw-weight will be less than shown.

[d] Warhead yields vary greatly; figures given are estimated maxima. KT range = under 1 MT; MT range =

(i) *Missiles and Artillery*

	Warsaw Pact (excluding USSR)				
Category and type*fn*	Number deployed (7/78)	First deployment	Max. range (mi)*b*	Warheads and max. yield*d*	Countries equipped

Land-based
IRBM

SS-1b *Scud* A	(132)	1957	50	Dual-capable. 1 × KT range	All*q*
SRBM					
SS-1c *Scud* B		1965	185	Dual-capable. 1 × KT range	All*q*
FROG 3–7	(206)	1957–65	10–45	Dual-capable. 1 × KT range	All*q*

Sea-launched
SLBM

Artillery

(ii) *Aircraft*

	Warsaw Pact (excluding USSR)					
Category and type*fs*	Number deployed (7/78)	First deploy-ment	Max. range (mi)*i*	Max. speed (Mach)	Weapons load (000 lb)	Countries equipped

Bombers
Medium-range

Strike Aircraft
Land-based (incl short-range bombers)

Il-28 *Beagle*q	6*t*	1950	1,400	0.81	4.85	Poland
Su-7 *Fitter* A*q*	110*t*	1959	900	1.7	5.5	Czechoslovakia, Poland
Su-20 *Fitter* C*q*	28	1974	1,100	1.6	4	Poland

over 1 MT. Yield figures for dual-capable weapons (which can deliver conventional or nuclear warheads) refer to nuclear warheads only.

e Figures for systems in Europe only.

f Names of Soviet missiles and aircraft (e.g. *Scarp*, *Bear*) are of NATO origin. Numerical designations of Soviet missiles (but not aircraft) are of US origin.

g All the types listed are dual-capable, but some in the strike categories are not presently configured for the nuclear role.

h Long-range = over 6,000 mi; medium-range = 3,500–6,000 mi; bomber = aircraft primarily designed for bombing missions.

[i] Statute miles. Theoretical maximum range at optimum altitude and speed. Higher speeds, lower altitudes and full weapons loads reduce range, especially in the case of strike aircraft; for instance, an F-104 flying at operational height and speed and with typical weapons load has a combat *radius* of some 420 mi, compared with a maximum *range* of 1,500 mi.

[j] Excluding aircraft in storage or reserve.

[k] Excluding some 44 configured as tankers.

[l] Including Naval Air Force aircraft (some 280 Tu-16 *Badger* and 30 Tu- *Backfire* B) but excluding Tu-16 *Badger* tankers.

[m] Listed as a medium-range bomber on the basis of reported range characteristics.

[n] All NATO missiles are of American origin, except SSBS, *Pluton* and MSBS, which are French. All Warsaw Pact missiles are of Soviet origin.

[o] Nuclear warheads held in American custody. No nuclear warheads held on Danish or Norwegian soil.

[p] In few of these cases is the M-109 likely to have a nuclear role, and certainly not in the case of Canada.

[q] Nuclear warheads held in Soviet custody. It is not known how many are earmarked for a nuclear role.

[r] All aircraft listed are dual-capable, but many would be more likely to carry conventional than nuclear weapons. Certain other strike aircraft, such as the French *Mirage* III, may also be capable of carrying tactical nuclear weapons.

[s] *Vulcan* and *Buccaneer* are of British origin, F-104 and F-4 American, *Mirage* French and *Jaguar* Anglo-French. All Warsaw Pact aircraft are of Soviet origin.

[t] It is uncertain how many of these aircraft have a nuclear role. NATO (less US) deploys a total of about 500 F-104s and 150 F-4s in the FGA role.

[u] Canadian aircraft have no nuclear role.

2. COMPARATIVE STRENGTHS OF ARMED FORCES 1957–1978 (in thousands)

Year	USA	Japan	Germany	France	Britain[a]	USSR
1957	2,800	202	122	836	700	4,200
1958	2,637	214	175	797	615	4,000
1959	2,552	215	249	770	565	3,900
1960	2,514	206	270	781	520	3,623
1961	2,572	209	325	778	455	3,800
1962	2,827	216	389	742	445	3,600
1963	2,737	213	403	632	430	3,300
1964	2,687	216	435	555	425	3,300
1965	2,723	225	441	510	424	3,150
1966	3,123	227	455	500	418	3,165
1967	3,446	231	452	500	417	3,220
1968	3,547	235	440	505	405	3,220
1969	3,454	236	465	503	383	3,300
1970	3,066	259	466	506	373	3,305
1971	2,699	259	467	502	365	3,375
1972	2,391	260	467	501	363	3,375
1973	2,253	266	475	504	352	3,425
1974	2,174	233	490	503	345	3,525
1975	2,130	236	495	503	345	3,573
1976	2,087	235	495	513	335	3,650
1977	2,088	238	489	502	330	3,675
1978	2,069	240	490	503	313	3,638

[a] Excluding forces enlisted outside Britain.

3. INDICES OF NATO DEFENCE EXPENDITURE, CURRENT AND CONSTANT PRICES[a] (in local currency, 1970 = 100)

Country	1960	1967	1968	1969	1970	1971	1972	1973	1974	1975	1976	1977[b]	% Growth[c] 1960-70	1971-7
Belgium	53.9	81.1	87.1	90.4	100.0	105.6	117.7	130.5	153.0	186.5	218.8	243.6	6.4	14.90
	72.5	*89.8*	*93.9*	*94.0*	*100.0*	*101.5*	*107.0*	*140.0*	*115.4*	*124.7*	*134.1*	*159.4*	*3.3*	*5.46*
Britain	67.7	93.1	95.4	94.2	100.0	115.2	133.3	143.4	172.1	211.3	252.1	279.2	4.0	15.90
	100.6	*100.8*	*100.9*	*100.2*	*100.0*	*105.2*	*113.7*	*112.0*	*115.9*	*114.6*	*117.3*	*112.1*	*0*	*1.03*
Canada	80.3	95.3	92.5	92.1	100.0	103.4	108.6	116.7	158.9	151.7	174.1	200.5	2.2	11.67
	105.3	*107.2*	*101.1*	*95.2*	*100.0*	*100.6*	*100.8*	*100.6*	*108.0*	*106.6*	*113.6*	*121.2*	*-0.5*	*3.15*
Denmark	40.4	81.6	94.0	95.8	100.0	115.9	122.8	127.7	161.0	191.3	206.0	226.7	9.5	11.82
	71.4	*97.3*	*103.7*	*102.0*	*100.0*	*109.4*	*108.9*	*103.6*	*113.2*	*122.9*	*121.3*	*120.3*	*3.4*	*1.6*
France	57.7	87.1	91.0	95.5	100.0	105.4	110.8	121.2	147.4	171.3	195.6	219.9	5.6	13.03
	85.7	*102.3*	*102.3*	*101.1*	*100.0*	*99.8*	*99.2*	*101.1*	*108.1*	*112.5*	*117.2*	*120.7*	*1.6*	*3.22*
Germany	53.7	94.8	85.5	95.6	100.0	112.7	127.2	141.4	157.9	166.5	172.4	181.1	6.4	8.22
	70.2	*102.6*	*91.1*	*99.2*	*100.0*	*107.2*	*114.6*	*119.0*	*124.2*	*123.6*	*122.4*	*123.8*	*3.6*	*2.42*
Greece	36.0	66.1	77.4	89.8	100.0	109.0	121.1	139.8	169.8	309.1	291.9	418.8	10.8	25.15
	44.2	*70.0*	*81.7*	*92.6*	*100.0*	*105.8*	*112.6*	*112.9*	*108.1*	*172.6*	*144.1*	*184.2*	*8.5*	*9.68*
Italy	45.5	87.0	89.8	90.4	100.0	118.6	138.4	153.1	182.6	198.7	231.0	268.6	8.2	14.60
	67.0	*95.0*	*96.8*	*94.8*	*100.0*	*113.1*	*125.0*	*124.7*	*124.8*	*116.7*	*115.8*	*114.8*	*4.1*	*0.24*
Luxembourg	63.2	99.3	89.9	94.0	100.0	106.3	124.3	144.5	170.7	201.0	236.3	251.0	4.7	15.40
	81.5	*109.1*	*96.3*	*98.3*	*100.0*	*101.6*	*112.9*	*124.1*	*133.5*	*141.8*	*131.9*	*151.2*	*2.1*	*6.84*
Netherlands	43.5	80.6	82.7	92.8	100.0	112.6	125.4	137.7	161.9	182.6	197.0	216.4	8.7	11.50
	65.6	*93.1*	*92.0*	*96.1*	*100.0*	*104.7*	*108.2*	*110.0*	*117.9*	*120.7*	*119.7*	*123.3*	*4.3*	*2.76*
Norway	38.1	75.6	82.9	90.2	100.0	108.9	116.8	126.4	142.0	171.0	192.2	219.0	10.1	12.35
	59.2	*89.3*	*94.5*	*99.8*	*100.0*	*102.5*	*102.6*	*103.3*	*106.0*	*115.0*	*117.8*	*123.1*	*5.4*	*3.10*
Portugal	24.1	76.4	85.3	86.0	100.0	117.2	128.0	133.5	200.3	158.0	150.3	168.2	15.3	6.20
	37.3	*93.7*	*98.7*	*91.0*	*100.0*	*104.7*	*103.3*	*95.4*	*114.4*	*78.6*	*61.5*	*54.0*	*10.4*	*-11.66*
Turkey	38.6	73.7	82.7	86.5	100.0	136.1	159.7	195.5	253.8	271.4	427.3	764.8	10.0	32.91
	68.4	*87.7*	*93.0*	*92.6*	*100.0*	*114.3*	*123.6*	*131.1*	*147.0*	*131.9*	*177.3*	*249.1*	*3.9*	*13.87*
United States	58.3	96.9	103.7	104.6	100.0	96.2	99.7	100.8	110.3	116.8	116.9	133.9	5.5	5.66
	76.5	*112.7*	*115.7*	*110.8*	*100.0*	*92.3*	*92.6*	*88.1*	*86.9*	*84.3*	*79.7*	*85.8*	*2.7*	*-1.21*

[a] To produce constant price series (in italics) defence expenditures are deflated by consumer price indices. These reflect general rates of inflation, not rates in the defence sector.

[b] 1977 figures are provisional, those for Greece and Turkey being estimates; hence 1971-77 growth rates are approximate.

[c] Average annual compound growth rates over periods shown.

4. COMPARISONS OF DEFENCE EXPENDITURES 1975-1978

Country	$ million				$ Per head				% Government spending[a]				% of GNP[b]			
	1975	1976	1977	1978	1975	1976	1977	1978	1975	1976	1977	1978	1974	1975	1976	1977
Warsaw Pact[c]																
Bulgaria	457	438	408	438	52	50	46	49	6.0	5.3	5.2	5.1	2.7	2.7	2.4	2.5
Czechoslovakia	1,706	1,805	1,823	1,818	116	121	122	121	7.3	7.0	7.0	7.1	3.8	3.8	3.9	3.8
Germany, East	2,550	2,729	2,900	n.a.	148	158	168	n.a.	7.9	7.8	7.8	n.a.	5.4	5.5	5.7	5.9
Hungary	506	551	590	658	48	52	56	62	3.5	3.6	3.6	3.7	2.4	2.4	2.5	2.6
Poland	2,011	2,252	2,455	2,545	59	66	71	73	7.0	7.4	8.5	8.6	3.0	3.1	3.0	3.0
Romania	707	759	824	923	33	35	38	43	3.7	4.0	4.0	3.8	1.7	1.7	1.7	1.7
Soviet Union[a]	124,000	127,000	133,000	n.a.	490	492	508	n.a.	n.a.	n.a.	n.a.	n.a.	11–13%	11–13%	11–13%	11–13%
NATO[e]																
Belgium	1,971	2,013	2,476	n.a.	200	204	253	n.a.	10.0	10.2	10.4	n.a.	2.8	3.0	3.0	3.4
Britain	11,118	10,734	12,103	13,579	198	190	214	239	11.6	11.0	12.7	11.2	5.1	4.9	5.2	5.0
Canada	2,965	3,231	3,348	3,635	130	140	144	153	11.9	10.0	8.8	8.9	2.1	2.2	1.8	1.8
Denmark	939	861	1,085	1,320	185	168	213	259	7.3	7.4	6.7	6.5	2.2	2.2	2.5	2.5
France	13,984	12,857	13,666	17,518	264	241	254	325	20.2	20.6	19.2	20.3	3.6	3.9	3.7	3.6
Germany*	16,142	15,220	17,130	21,355	259	242	271	337	24.4	23.5	23.9	22.9	3.6	3.7	3.5	3.4
Greece	1,435	1,249	1,328	1,523	159	138	146	164	25.5	26.0	20.2	18.3	4.0	6.9	5.0	5.0
Italy	4,700	3,821	4,730	5,610	84	68	83	98	9.7	8.6	8.9	7.9	2.9	2.6	2.5	2.4
Luxembourg	22	23	29	37	65	68	80	100	3.0	2.9	2.8	2.9	0.9	1.1	1.0	1.1
Netherlands	2,978	2,825	3,716	4,208	218	205	266	301	11.0	9.8	10.9	9.5	3.4	3.6	3.3	3.6
Norway	929	902	1,130	1,291	232	223	241	316	8.2	7.6	9.3	9.6	3.1	3.1	3.2	3.1
Portugal	1,088	748	545	568	124	85	62	62	35.2	n.a.	13.3	10.6	6.6	6.0	4.0	3.3
Turkey	2,200	2,800	2,652	2,286	55	70	65	54	26.6	29.4	20.8	22.0	3.7	9.0	5.5	5.7
United States	88,983	91,000	104,250	113,000	417	423	480	517	23.8	23.8	22.7	23.0	6.1	5.9	5.4	6.0
Other Europe																
Austria	410	433	534	718	54	57	68	91	3.7	3.7	3.8	3.9	0.9	1.0	1.2	1.1
Eire	128	134	149	193	41	43	47	59	4.3	3.5	3.6	3.5	1.4	1.6	1.6	1.6
Finland	388	364	427	454	83	77	90	95	5.0	5.1	4.9	6.1	1.4	1.4	1.3	1.3
Spain	1,701	1,766	2,154	2,363	48	49	59	64	14.5	14.9	15.3	13.2	1.9	1.8	1.7	1.7
Sweden	2,483	2,418	2,833	2,946	303	294	343	355	10.5	12.5	11.6	11.7	3.4	3.4	3.4	3.4
Switzerland	1,047	1,221	1,153	1,547	160	184	172	240	19.3	18.8	18.3	18.0	1.8	1.8	2.0	1.9
Yugoslavia[c]	1,705	1,798	2,086	2,332	80	84	96	106	49.9	40.9	40.8	52.9	5.1[f]	5.6[f]	5.4	5.2
Middle East																
Algeria	285	312	397	456	17	18	23	25	4.7	n.a.	5.9	5.7	1.8[f]	2.2[f]	3.4	3.9
Egypt	6,103	4,859	n.a.	n.a.	163	128	112	n.a.	42.0	n.a.	n.a.	n.a.	22.8	n.a.	n.a.	n.a.
Iran	8,800	9,500	7,894	9,942	268	281	224	273	24.9	28.9	23.5	23.8	14.0[f]	17.4[f]	12.0	10.9
	19,540	18,758	21,263	26,731	313	299	337	422	29.2	28.9	29.6	28.7	4.3	4.4	4.3	4.2

* Incl aid to W. Berlin

Iraq	1,191[g]	1,417	1,660	n.a.	107	123	141	n.a.	43.7	26.8	29.7	n.a.	18.7	n.a.	9.6	10.2
Israel	3,552	4,214	4,259	3,310	1,045	1,201	1,176	887	50.1	56.7	32.4	30.4	31.8	35.9	36.3	29.9
Jordan	155	155	201	304	57	55	70	103	22.0	19.4	20.1	25.6	12.1	12.2	12.9	15.5
Libya	203	229	338	448	83	90	130	162	13.7	n.a.	17.4	19.5	1.4	1.7	n.a.	1.8
Morocco	224	258	346	681	13	15	19	37	4.5	6.0	7.8	11.6	3.0	2.8	3.3	3.6
Saudi Arabia	6,771	9,038	7,539	13,170	1,153	1,506	1,005	1,704	20.0	29.0	24.0	35.1	7.3	18.0	17.7	13.6
Sudan	120	146	237	n.a.	7	8	12	n.a.	15.1	8.1	10.4	n.a.	4.3	n.a.	3.6	5.4
Syria	706	1,003	1,068	1,121	96	132	138	138	25.3	22.3	23.0	24.1	11.0[f]	15.1[f]	16.3	16.4
Africa																
Ethiopia	84	103.4	149	165	3	4	5	6	19.4	n.a.	21.1	21.6	3.3	2.9	3.6	n.a.
Nigeria	1,786	2,434	2,670	n.a.	28	38	40	n.a.	11.8	15.5	16.6	n.a.	2.9	n.a.	7.7	7.8
Rhodesia	102	130	159	242	16	21	24	35	12.3	14.1	16.5	17.1	2.6	3.0	5.2	7.7
South Africa	1,332	1,619	2,231	2,622	53	62	83	95	18.5	17.0	19.0	19.7	3.2	5.3	4.9	5.1
Asia																
Australia	2,492	2,803	2,678	n.a.	184	204	191	n.a.	8.6	9.4	9.1	n.a.	3.6	3.2	3.0	2.9
China[e]	n.a.	32,400	29,750	34,380	n.a.	35	32	36	n.a.	n.a.	n.a.	n.a.	n.a.	n.a.	10.0	8.5
China (Taiwan)	1,007	1,597	1,672	3,571	61	93	95	n.a.	n.a.	54.7	48.3	n.a.	7.2	n.a.	9.3	8.3
India	2,660	2,812	3,117	3,571	4	5	5	6	21.1	19.6	16.3	16.0	2.7	3.0	3.1	3.1
Indonesia	1,108	1,024	1,513	1,691	9	8	11	12	16.7	12.1	14.8	14.5	2.6	3.8	3.5	3.5
Japan	4,620	5,058	6,135	8,567	42	45	54	74	6.6	6.2	5.9	5.9	0.9	0.9	0.9	0.9
Korea, North[e]	n.a.	n.a.	1,000	1,030	n.a.	n.a.	60	60	n.a.	16.7	15.4	n.a.	n.a.	n.a.	11.2	10.5
Korea, South	943	1,500	2,033	2,600	28	42	58	72	29.2	34.6	34.3	35.4	4.3	5.1	6.2	6.5
Malaysia	385	353	542	699	31	27	43	54	17.3	16.9	12.5	13.4	3.8	4.0	3.8	4.4
New Zealand	243	217	242	n.a.	79	69	76	n.a.	4.3	4.2	4.2	n.a.	1.8	1.8	1.7	1.8
Pakistan	725	807	808	938	10	11	11	12	12.3	17.2	39.4	42.7	8.4	7.2	5.5	4.6
Philippines	407	410	680	793	10	9	15	17	19.3	18.3	18.3	17.2	2.1	2.6	3.0	3.4
Singapore	344	315	410	n.a.	152	138	175	n.a.	18.1	15.3	18.5	n.a.	5.1	5.3	5.4	6.3
Thailand	542	601	748	n.a.	13	14	17	n.a.	25.7	18.0	18.8	n.a.	3.2	3.7	3.7	4.1
Latin America																
Argentina	1,031	1,287	1,415	1,659	41	49	54	63	9.7	11.7	14.7	14.9	1.9	0.9	2.8	n.a.
Brazil	1,283	1,780	2,071	2,039	12	16	18	18	9.3	9.7	9.4	8.6	1.3	1.3	1.2	1.1
Colombia	106	133	140	173	n.a.	5	5	6	n.a.	9.2	8.3	7.6	0.8	0.8	1.1	1.1
Cuba[e]	n.a.	n.a.	n.a.	784	n.a.	n.a.	n.a.	80	n.a.	n.a.	n.a.	8.6	n.a.	n.a.	n.a.	n.a.
Mexico	586	591	544	557	10	9	8	8	2.4	4.4	3.9	2.9	0.7[f]	0.7[f]	0.8	0.6
Peru	383	n.a.	406	n.a.	24	24	n.a.	n.a.	15.3	n.a.	13.5	n.a.	2.4	3.1	2.4	3.1
Venezuela	494	423	512	615	41	34	40	47	5.4	5.5	6.1	5.9	1.6	1.7	1.4	1.4

[a] This series is designed to show national trends only; differences in the scope of the government sector invalidate international comparisons.

[b] Based on local currency. GNP estimated where official figures unavailable.

[c] The difficulty of calculating suitable exchange rates makes conversion to dollars imprecise.

[d] See p. 11.

[e] Defence expenditures based on NATO definition, but some 1978 figures estimated from nationally-defined data. Figures from 1977 are provisional.

[f] Gross domestic product at market prices, not GNP, in 1974 and 1975.

[g] Nine-month figure only.

5. COMPARISONS OF MILITARY MANPOWER 1974–78 (in thousands)

Country	Numbers in armed forces 1974-78					Armed forces 1978			% of men 18-45	Estimated reservists[a]	Para-military forces
	1974	1975	1976	1977	1978	Army	Navy	Air			
Warsaw Pact											
Bulgaria	152.0	152.0	164.5	148.5	150.0	115.0	10.0	25.0	8.4	235.0	189.0
Czechoslovakia	200.0	200.0	180.0	181.0	186.0	140.0	—	46.0	6.1	350.0	132.5
Germany, East	145.0	143.0	157.0	157.0	157.0	105.0	16.0	36.0	4.6	305.0	571.5
Hungary	103.0	105.0	100.0	103.0	114.0	91.0	—	23.0	5.2	143.0	75.0
Poland	303.0	293.0	290.0	307.0	306.5	222.0	22.5	62.0	4.0	605.0	445.0
Romania	171.0	171.0	181.0	180.0	180.5	140.0	10.5	30.0	4.1	345.5	737.0
Soviet Union	3,525.0	3,575.0	3,650.0	3,675.0	3,638.0	1,825.0[b]	433.0[b]	455.0[b]	6.7	6,800.0	450.0
NATO											
Belgium	89.7	87.0	88.3	85.7	87.1	63.4	4.3	19.4	4.5	54.4	16.5
Britain[c]	354.6	345.1	344.2	339.2	313.3	160.8	67.8	84.7	3.0	237.5	—
Canada	83.0	77.0	77.9	80.0	80.0	29.3	14.2	36.5	1.6	19.1	—
Denmark	37.1	34.4	34.7	34.7	34.0	21.0	6.1	6.9	3.3	154.9	—
France	502.5	502.5	512.9	502.1	502.8	324.4	68.2	100.8	4.7	350.0	83.3
Germany	490.0	495.0	495.0	489.0	489.9	336.2	36.5	106.2	3.9	760.1	20.0
Greece	161.2	161.2	199.5	200.0	190.1	150.0	17.5	22.6	11.0	290.0	129.0
Italy	421.0	421.0	352.0	330.0	362.0	251.0	42.0	69.0	3.3	693.8	195.5
Luxembourg	0.6	0.6	0.6	0.6	0.7	0.7	—	—	0.9	—	0.4
Netherlands	113.9	112.5	112.2	109.7	109.7	75.0	17.0	17.7	3.7	175.0	8.2
Norway	34.9	35.0	39.0	39.0	39.0	20.0	9.0	10.0	5.1	245.0	—
Portugal	217.0	217.0	59.8	58.8	63.5	40.0	14.0	9.5	3.9	—	29.4
Turkey	453.0	453.0	460.0	465.0	485.0	390.0	45.0	50.0	5.8	525.0	110.0
United States	2,174.0	2,130.0	2,086.7	2,088.0	2,068.8	774.2	723.8	570.8	4.7	819.7	—
Other European											
Austria	37.3	38.0	37.3	37.3	37.0	33.0	—	4.0	2.6	113.7	11.3
Eire	12.3	12.1	14.0	14.7	14.6	13.2	0.7	0.7	2.5	18.7	—
Finland	35.8	36.3	35.8	39.9	39.9	34.4	2.5	3.0	3.8	690.0	4.0
Spain	284.0	302.3	302.3	309.0	315.5	240.0	40.0	35.5	4.6	1,000.0	103.0
Sweden	72.2	69.8	65.4	68.6	65.7	40.6	11.8	13.3	4.1	684.0	—
Switzerland	18.5	18.5	18.5	18.5	18.5	18.5	—	—	1.4	606.5	—
Yugoslavia	230.0	230.0	250.0	260.0	267.0	200.0	27.0	40.0	5.6	500.0	1,016.0

[a] Reservists with recent training. [b] Excludes *PVO-Strany* and Strategic Rocket Forces. [c] Includes men listed outside Britain.

Middle East											
Algeria	63.0	63.0	69.3	75.8	78.8	70.0	3.8	5.0	2.6	100.0	10.0
Egypt	323.0	322.5	342.5	345.0	395.0	350.2	20.0	25.0	5.0	515.0	50.0
Iran	238.0	250.0	300.0	342.0	413.0	285.0	28.0	100.0	5.9	300.0	74.0
Iraq	112.5	135.0	158.5	188.0	212.0	180.0	4.0	28.0	10.1	250.0	79.8
Israel	145.5	156.0	158.5	164.0	164.0	138.0	5.0	21.0	23.3	460.0	9.5
Jordan	74.9	80.2	67.9	67.8	67.9	61.0	0.2	6.7	14.2	30.0	10.0
Libya	32.0	32.0	29.7	29.2	37.0	30.0	3.0	4.0	7.7	n.a.	n.a.
Morocco	56.0	61.0	73.0	84.7	89.0	81.0	2.0	6.0	2.6	n.a.	30.0
Saudi Arabia	43.0	47.0	51.5	61.5	58.5	45.0	1.5	12.0	n.a.	—	41.5
Sudan	43.6	48.6	52.6	52.1	52.1	50.0	0.6	1.5	n.a.	—	3.5
Syria	137.5	177.5	227.0	227.5	227.5	200.0	2.5	25.0	16.1	102.5	9.5
Africa											
Ethiopia	44.6	44.8	50.8	53.5	93.5	90.0	1.5	2.0	1.8	n.a.	129.0
Nigeria	210.0	208.0	230.0	230.5	231.5	221.0	4.5	6.0	n.a.	2.0	—
Rhodesia	4.7	5.7	9.2	9.6	10.8	9.5	—	1.3	0.8	55.0	44.0
South Africa	47.5	50.5	51.5	55.0	65.5	50.0	5.5	10.0	1.3	173.5	165.5
Asia											
Australia	68.9	69.1	69.4	69.7	70.1	32.1	16.3	21.7	2.4	24.3	—
China	3,000.0	3,250.0	3,525.0	3,950.0	4,325.0	3,625.0	300.0	400.0	2.4	n.a.	n.a.
China (Taiwan)	491.0	494.0	470.0	460.0	474.0	330.0	74.0	70.0	n.a.	1,170.0	100.0
India	956.0	956.0	1,055.5	1,096.0	1,096.0	950.0	46.0	100.0	0.8	240.0	300.0
Indonesia	270.0	266.0	246.0	247.0	247.0	180.0	39.0	28.0	1.0	n.a.	112.0
Japan	233.0	236.0	235.0	238.0	240.0	155.0	41.0	44.0	0.9	39.6	—
Korea, North	467.0	467.0	495.0	500.0	512.0	440.0	27.0	45.0	n.a.	n.a.	1,540.0
Korea, South	625.0	625.0	595.0	635.0	642.0	560.0	52.0	30.0	8.1	1,240.0	1,000.0
Malaysia	66.2	61.1	62.3	64.0	64.5	52.5	6.0	6.0	2.6	27.0	213.0
New Zealand	12.6	12.7	12.5	12.5	12.6	5.7	2.7	4.2	1.9	11.5	—
Pakistan	392.0	392.0	428.0	428.0	429.0	400.0	11.0	18.0	3.7	513.0	109.1
Philippines	55.0	67.0	78.0	99.0	99.0	63.0	20.0	16.0	1.1	45.0	65.0
Singapore	21.7	30.0	31.0	36.0	36.0	30.0	3.0	3.0	6.6	45.0	37.5
Thailand	195.0	204.0	210.0	211.0	212.0	141.0	28.0	43.0	2.6	500.0	66.0
Latin America											
Argentina	135.0	133.5	132.8	129.9	132.9	80.0	32.9	20.0	2.5	250.0	42.0
Brazil	208.0	254.5	257.2	271.8	273.8	182.0	49.0	42.8	1.2	n.a.	200.0
Colombia	63.2	64.3	54.3	56.5	75.5	60.0	9.0	6.5	1.6	425.0	50.0
Cuba	116.5	117.0	175.0	189.0	159.0	130.0	9.0	20.0	8.4	90.0	113.0
Mexico	82.0	82.5	89.5	95.5	97.0	72.0	19.0	6.0	1.0	250.0	n.a.
Peru	54.0	56.0	63.0	70.0	89.0	65.0	14.0	10.0	2.7	n.a.	20.0
Venezuela	39.5	44.0	42.0	44.0	44.0	28.0	8.0	8.0	1.8	n.a.	10.0

6. GUIDED MISSILES[a]

(A) LAND AND AIR SERVICES[b]

Air-to-surface

Country of origin	Designation	Length (cm)	Launch weight (kg)	Warhead		Range (km)	Guidance		Launch aircraft and remarks
				Type[c]	Weight (kg)		Missile	Warhead	
France	AS. 11	120	29.9	HE/frag/AP	n.a.	3	WG	—	hel
	AS. 12	187	77		28.4	5.5	WG	—	Alizé, Atlantic
	AS. 20	259	143		30	7	O/CG	IR	Mirage III, G-91, F-104G
	AS. 30	390	520		230	12	CG	IR	Mirage III, Erendard
	Exocet AM.39	460	650		165	50–70	inertial SAHR	AHR	Super Frelon
France/Britain	Martel AS. 37	412	530		148	60	PHR	PF	Mirage III, Jaguar, Atlantic
	Martel AJ. 168	387	550		150	60	TV/CG	PF	Buccaneer Mk 2
Germany	Kormoran	440	600		160	37	inertial	A/PHR	F-104G
Sweden	Rb05A	360	305		n.a.	9	CG	PF	AJ-37 Viggen, Saab 105
	Rb04E	445	600		300	23	CG	AHR	AJ-37 Viggen
USA	Bullpup A AGM-12B	320	258	HE/frag	133	16	CG	rad alt	F-105, F-4, A-6, A-7; AR
	Bullpup B AGM-12D	407	812	HE/nuc	453	17	CG	laser	F-4G, A-6, A-7, F-14, F-15; AR
	Shrike AGM-45	305	182	HE/frag	66	16	CG	A/PHR	F-4, A-7, A-10, F-5
	HARM AGM-88A	417	354		n.a.	16+	PHR	n.a.	A-6, F-105, F-4; AR
	Maverick AGM-65	246	210		59	22	o/TV	TV/aut, laser	F-4, A-7
	Standard AGM-78	457	816		n.a.	25	RH	P/AHR	A-6
	Harpoon AGM-84	384	522		225	110	inertial	AHR	
	Condor AGM-53B	422	966		286	111	TV	TV	
	SRAM AGM-69	427	1,010	nuc	n.a.	160	inertial	—	B-52, FB-111
	Quail ADM-20C	391	545	decoy	n.a.	400	aut	n.a.	B-52
	Hound Dog AGM-28	1,319	4,350	nuc	n.a.	965	inertial	n.a.	B-52
USSR	AS-8	n.a.	n.a.		n.a.	10	n.a.	n.a.	n.a.
	AS-7 Kerry	n.a.	n.a.		n.a.	10	BR	n.a.	Su-19, Su-7, Su-17
	AS-1 Kennel	820	3,000		n.a.	100	BR	SAHR	Tu-16
	AS-9	n.a.	n.a.		n.a.	100	—	PHR	
	AS-5 Kelt	945	4,800	nuc	n.a.	160	n.a.	AHR	Tu-16
	AS-2 Kipper	950	6,000	HE/nuc	n.a.	180	CG	RH	Tu-16
	AS-6 Kingfish	4,000	4,800	HE/nuc	n.a.	300	inertial	AHR	Tu-16
	AS-4 Kitchen	1,100	6,000	HE/nuc	n.a.	450	inertial	n.a.	Tu-22, Backfire
	AS-3 Kangaroo	1,490	14,000	nuc	n.a.	650	CG	n.a.	Tu-95

Air-to-air

Country of origin	Designation	Length (cm)	Launch weight (kg)	Warhead weight (kg)	Range (km)	Guidance	Launch aircraft and remarks
Britain	*Red Top*	327.7	150	31	11	IR	*Lightning*
	Sky Flash	366	192.8	30	50	SAR	F-4
France	R. 550 *Magic*	293	90	12.5	8	IR	*Mirage III, F1, Crusader F-8E*
	R. 530	328.4	195	27	18	SAR/IR	
	Super 530	354	200	n.a.	35	SAR	*Mirage F1*
Israel	*Shafrir*	247	93	11	5	IR	F-104
Italy	*Aspide*	370	270	35	50–100	SAR	F-104
Japan	AAM-1	250	76	n.a.	5	IR	F-86, F-104
	AAM-2	220	74	n.a.	5	IR	F-104
Sweden	Rb72	260	110	n.a.	4	IR	
USA	*Sidewinder* AIM-9B	283	72	4.5	3.5	IR	F-106
	Falcon AIM-4F	201	63	n.a.	9	SAHR	F-102, F-4
	Super Falcon AIM-26B	207	115	n.a.	9–11	SAHR	F-101, F-106
	Genie AIM-2A	288	362	nuc	11	unguided	
	Sidewinder AIM-9H	287	83	10	10–18	IR	A-7, F-4, F-14
	Sidewinder AIM-9L	287	84	n.a.	10–18	IR	
	Sidewinder AIM-9D	287	83	10	20	IR	
	Sidewinder AIM-9E	299	74	4.5	n.a.	IR	
	Sidewinder AIM-9G	287	86	10	n.a.	IR	
	Sidewinder AIM-9J	304	77	4.5	n.a.	IR	
	Sparrow AIM-7E	365	205	30	25–50	SAHR	F-4, F-14
	Sparrow AIM-7F	365	228	40	50–100	SAHR	F-4, F-14, F-15
	Phoenix	396	446	n.a.	200+	SA/AHR	F-14
USSR	AA-1 *Alkali*	200	90	8	2–6	SAR	MiG-17/-19, Su-9
	AA-2 *Atoll*	280	70	10	4–10	IR or SAR	MiG-17/-21/-23
	AA-3 *Anab*	360	275	30	8–20	IR or SAR	Su-9/-11/-15, Yak-28
	AA-5 *Ash*	520	200	n.a.	22	SAR	Tu-28
		550	200	n.a.	22	IR	
	AA-6 *Acrid*	590	650–750	60–100	35	IR	MiG-25, Su-19
		630	7–800	60–100	45	IR	
	AA-7 *Apex*	420	320	40	14	SAR	MiG-21/-23
		450	320	40	32	IR	
	AA-8 *Aphid*	200	55	6	6.5	IR	MiG-23
		214	55	6	14	SAR	

Anti-tank

Country of origin	Designation	Length (cm)	Launch weight (kg)	Warhead Type^c	Warhead Weight (kg)	Range Min. (m)	Range Max. (m)	Guidance Missiles	Guidance Warhead	Carriage	ASM version
Britain	*Vigilant*	107	14	HC	6	200	1,600	WG/o	—	veh/hel	
	Swingfire	117	38	HC	6.8	150	4,000	WG/o	—	man/veh	*Hawkswing*
France	*ENTAC*	82	12.2	SC	4.1	400	2,000	WG	—	man/veh	
	Harpon	121.5	30.4	AP/frag	5.8	500	3,000	WG/aut	IR	veh	
	SS. 11	120	29.9	AP/frag	5.8	350	3,000	WG/o	IR	veh	AS. 11
	SS. 12	187	75	SC/frag	28.5	800	5,000	WG/o	IR	veh	AS. 12
France/ Germany	*Milan*	75	6.7	SC	3	25	2,000	WG/o	IR	man/veh	
	HOT	127.5	23.5	HC	6	75	4,000	WG/o/aut	IR	veh/hel	
Germany	*Cobra 2000*	95	10.3	HC	2.7	400	2,000	WG/o	—	man	
	Mamba	95.5	11.2	SC/frag	2.7	300	2,000	WG/o	—	man/veh	
Italy	*Mosquito*	111	14.1	HC	4	360	2,375	WG/o	—	man/veh/hel	
Japan	*KAM-3D*	102	15.7	HC	n.a.	350	1,800	WG/o	—	man/veh/hel	
	KAM-9	150	n.a.	SC	1.9	n.a.	2,000	WG/o	IR	man/veh/hel	
Sweden	*Bantam Rb53*	84.8	7.6	HC	1.9	250	2,000	WG	—	man/veh/hel	
USA	*Dragon M-47*	74.5	12.25	SC	2.4	50	1,000	WG/o	—	man	
	TOW BGM-71A	117	19	SC	3.6	65	3,000	o/WG	—	veh/hel	
	Shillelagh MGM-51C	114	27	SC	6.8	n.a.	5,200+	IRCG	—	AFV	
USSR	*Swatter AT-2*	116	29	HC	n.a.	500	2,200	o/WG	IR	veh/AFV/hel	
	Snapper AT-1	113	22.3	HC	3.2	500	2,300	o/WG	IR	veh/AFV	
	Sagger AT-3	88	11.3	HC	2.7	500	3,000	o/WG	—	man/AFV/hel	

Surface-to-air

Country of origin	Designation	Length (cm)	Launch weight (kg)	Slant range (m)	Effective height Min. (m)	Effective height Max. (m)	Guidance Missile	Guidance Warhead	Carriage and remarks
Britain	*Blowpipe*	140	12.7	3,000	n.a.	1,500	CG/o	PF	man/naval (SLAM)
	Tigercat	148	60	3,500	50	n.a.	CG/o/TV	PF	towed/naval
	Rapier	224	65	5,500	50	5,000	CG/TV	IF	towed/SP
	Thunderbird Mk 2	635	n.a.	75,000	n.a.	n.a.	CWSAHR	PF	towed
	Bloodhound Mk 2	846	2,300	80,000	300	n.a.	CWSAHR	PF	Sweden = Rb68

Country of origin	Designation								
France	Crotale	289	80	8,500	500	8,500	IR/SAHR	IR/PF	veh. South Africa = *Cactus*, S. Arabia = *Shahine*
France/ Germany	Roland I	240	63	n.a.	500	6,500	CG/IR	PF	SP
	Roland II	240	63	n.a.	500	6,500	aut/radar/o	PF	SP
Italy	Indigo	320	121	10,000	1,000	5,000	CG/BR	IR/PF	towed/naval
Sweden	RBS70	160	22	5,000	n.a.	n.a.	BR	PF	man
USA	Redeye FIM-43A	120	13	2,000	n.a.	1,500	o	IR	man. Sweden = Rb69
	Stinger FIM-92	152	15.1	n.a.	n.a.	n.a.	o	IR	man
	Chapparal MIM-72A	291	84	n.a.	n.a.	n.a.	o	IR	sp/towed/naval
	HAWK MIM-23A	503	584	35,000	30	11,000	CWSAHR	IR	towed/AFV
	Improved HAWK MIM-23B	508	625	41,000	n.a.	n.a.	SAHR	n.a.	towed
	Nike-Hercules MIM-14	1,270	4,800	140,000	n.a.	45,000	CG	CD/CG	HE or nuc, fixed
USSR	SA-7 Grail	150	15	3,500	50	1,500	o	IR	man/veh
	SA-9 Gaskin	170	n.a.	5,000	15	4,500	o	IR	twin-quad mountings on BRDM
	SA-8 Gecko	320	n.a.	12,000	50	6,000	CG	IR	4 msls on 6-wheel veh
	SA-3 Goa	670	n.a.	30,000	n.a.	12,200	CG	n.a.	veh/naval (SA-N-1)
	SA-6 Gainful	620	550	30,000	100	18,000	CG/o	SAHR	triple-mounted sp
	SA-2 Guideline	1,070	2,300	45,000	n.a.	18,000	CG/aut	PF/CD	towed/naval (SA-N-2) possibly nuc
	SA-4 Ganef	880	1,800	70,000	n.a.	24,400	CG	n.a.	twin-mounted sp
	SA-5 Gammon	1,650	10,000	250,000	n.a.	29,000	radar	AHR	HE or nuc

(B) NAVAL SERVICE

Anti-submarine

Country of origin	Designation	Length (cm)	Launch weight (kg)	Warhead Weight (kg)	Warhead Type	Range Min. (km)	Range Max. (km)	Guidance Missile	Guidance Warhead
Australia	*Ikara*	335	n.a.	n.a.	US Mk 44 torpedo	n.a.	n.a.	CG	AC
France	*Malafon*	615	1,500	n.a.	21-in. torpedo, 525 kg	2.2	13	CG	AC
USA	*SUBROC* UUM-44A	457	435	n.a.	Mk 46 torpedo/nuc	2	10	nil	AC
	ASROC I RUR-5A	625	1,853	n.a.	nuc	40	56	inertial	nil
USSR	SS-N-14	n.a.	n.a.	n.a.	Acoustic homing torpedo	n.a.	70	auto-pilot CG over-ride	n.a.

Naval surface-to-air

Country of origin	Designation	Length (cm)	Launch weight (kg)	Warhead Type	Warhead Weight (kg)	Slant range (km)	Effective height Min. (km)	Effective height Max. (km)	Guidance Missile	Guidance Warhead	Remarks
Britain	*Seacat*	148	60	n.a.	n.a.	n.a.	n.a.	3.5	CG/O	PF	also SSM
	Sea Dart	436	550	n.a.	n.a.	30	n.a.	n.a.	SAHR	PF	also SSM
	Sea Slug Mk 1	600	n.a.	n.a.	n.a.	45	n.a.	15	BR	PF	also SSM
	Mk 2	610	n.a.	n.a.	n.a.	58	n.a.	n.a.	BR	PF	also SSM
	Sea Wolf	n.a.	n.a.	n.a.	n.a.	n.a.	n.a.	n.a.	aut/radar	n.a.	
Canada	*Sea Sparrow*	365	205		27	13	n.a.	n.a.	SAHR	PF	
France	*Masurca* Mk 2 Mod 2	860	1,850		48	40	n.a.	n.a.	BR/CG	PF	
	Mod 3	860	2,080		48	50	n.a.	n.a.	SAHR	SAHR	
Italy	*Sea Indigo*	320	121	HE/frag	n.a.	10	1	6	BR/CG	IR/PF	used in *Albatros* system
	Aspide	370	220		35	n.a.	n.a.	n.a.	CWSAHR	n.a.	
USA	*Tartar* RIM-24	457	646		n.a.	16	n.a.	n.a.	SAHR	PF	
	Standard MR RIM-66A	457	590		n.a.	24	n.a.	20	SAHR	PF	also SSM
	Talos RIM-8G-AAW	953	3,175	HE/nuc	n.a.	26.5	n.a.	112	BR	SAHR	SSM (ARHM)
	Terrier RIM-2F	800	1,350	HE/nuc	n.a.	35	n.a.	20	SAHR	PF	
	Standard ER RIM-67A	823	1,060		n.a.	56	n.a.	20	SAHR	PF	also SSM
USSR	SA-N-1 *Goa*	590	n.a.		n.a.	24	1	12	CG	radar	(SA-3)
	SA-N-2 *Guideline*	1,070	2,300		130	45	3	18	CG/aut	PF/CD	(SA-2)
	SA-N-3 *Goblet*	n.a.	n.a.		n.a.	60	n.a.	n.a.	n.a.	n.a.	
	SA-N-4	n.a.	n.a.		n.a.	n.a.	n.a.	n.a.	n.a.	n.a.	

Naval surface-to-surface

Country of origin	Designation	Length (cm)	Launch weight (kg)	Warhead Type	Warhead Weight (kg)	Range Min. (km)	Range Max. (km)	Guidance Missile	Guidance Warhead	Remarks
France	*Exocet* MM.38	520	735		165	5	38	inertial	AHR	also coastal
	MM.39	470	650		165	5	50	inertial	AHR	
	MM.40	565	825		165	5	70	inertial	AHR	
Israel	*Gabriel* Mk 1	335	400		150	2	22	BR/O	SAHR	
	Mk 2	355	500		150	2	41	BR/O	SAHR	

Country	Missile			warhead[c]				guidance	fuse	remarks
Italy	Sea Killer Mk 1	375	170	frag	35	n.a.	10	BR/CG	PF	
	Mk 2	470	300	semi-AP	70	n.a.	25	BR/CG	PF	
	Mk 3	530	550	semi-AP	150	n.a.	45+	AHR	AHR	also ASM, coastal
Italy/France	Otomat	440	700	semi-AP	210	6	100	inertial	AHR	
Norway	Penguin	300	330		120	n.a.	20	inertial	IR	*Bullpup* warhead, coastal
Sweden	Rb08A	572	1,215		225	n.a.	150	aut/radar	AHR	also coastal
USA	Harpoon RGM-84A-1	457	667		225	n.a.	110	inertial	AHR	
USSR	SS-N-2 *Styx*	650	2,495		360	11	42	AHR	IR	*Osa, Komar*
	SS-N-7	760	n.a.		n.a.	n.a.	56	RH	n.a.	C-class sub
	SSC-2b *Samlet*	700	3,000		n.a.	n.a.	92	BR/CG	SAHR	coastal
	SS-N-9	n.a.	n.a.	HE/nuc	n.a.	n.a.	275	n.a.	n.a.	*Nanuchka, Sarancha*
	SS-N-12	n.a.	n.a.	HE/nuc	n.a.	n.a.	480	n.a.	n.a.	*Kiev*

[a] Missiles listed here are those *in production or about to enter production*. For the purpose of this Table a missile is defined as a weapon having its own propellant and a guidance system for the vehicle, warhead, or both. Nuclear missiles (listed in Table 1) and anti-ballistic-missile missiles are not included.
[b] Includes Naval Air.
[c] High-explosive, unless otherwise stated.

ABBREVIATIONS (applicable to this Table only).

AC	acoustic	CG	command guidance	PF	proximity fuse
AHR	active homing radar	CW	continuous wave	PHR	passive homing radar
AP	armour-piercing	HC	hollow charge	rad alt	radar altimeter
AR	anti-radiation	HE	high explosive	RH	radar homing
ARHM	anti-radar (radiation)	frag	fragmentation	SC	shaped charge
	homing missile	IF	impact fuse	SAHR	semi-active homing radar
aut	automatic	IR	infra-red	TV	television optical
BR	beam-riding	nuc	nuclear	veh	vehicle
CD	command detonation	o	optical	WG	wire-guided

7. COMPARISON OF MISSILE-ARMED PATROL CRAFT HOLDINGS 1968–1978

User	Type	Country of origin	No. held 1968	No. held 1978	On order
Algeria	*Komar*	USSR	6	6	—
	Osa-I	USSR	3	3	—
	Osa-II	USSR	—	4	—
Argentina	Type 148	Germany	—	—	2
Brunei	Vosper	Britain	1[a]	3	—
Bulgaria	*Osa*-I	USSR	—	4	—
China	*Komar/Hoku*	USSR/China	3	70	10?
	Osa/Hola	USSR/China	7	70	10?
Cuba	*Komar*	USSR	18	18	—
	Osa-I	USSR	—	5	—
	Osa-II	USSR	—	3	—
Denmark	*Willemoes*	Germany	—	10	—
Ecuador	*Jaguar* II	Germany	—	3	—
Egypt	*Komar*	USSR	8	4	—
	Komar (Egyptian)	Egypt	—	6	—
	Osa-I	USSR	12	6	—
	Vosper (*Ramadan*)	Britain	—	—	6
Ethiopia	*Osa*-II	USSR	—	2	—
Finland	*Osa*-II	USSR	—	4	5
France	*Trident*	France	—	4	—
	La Combattante I	France	1	1	—
Gabon	CNE 42m Type	France	—	1	—
West Germany	Type 162 (*Pegasus*)	USA	—	—	4
	Type 143	Germany	—	10	—
	Type 148	Germany	—	20	—
East Germany	*Osa*-I	USSR	12	12	—
	Osa-II	USSR	—	3	—
Greece	*La Combattante* III	France	—	4	—
	La Combattante II	France	—	4	6
	CNE 32m Type	France	—	2	—
India	*Osa*-I	USSR	—	8	—
	Osa-II	USSR	—	8	—
Indonesia	PSMM Mk 5	USA/S. Korea	—	—	4
	Komar	USSR	12	9	—
Iran	*La Combattante* II	France	—	5	7
Iraq	*Osa*-I	USSR	—	6	—
	Osa-II	USSR	—	8	—
Israel	*Reshef*	Israel	—	6	4
	Saar	France	6	12	—
Italy	*Sparviero*	Italy	—	1	6
Ivory Coast	P-48	France	1	2	—
North Korea	*Komar*	USSR	—	10	—
	Osa-I	USSR	—	8	—
South Korea	PSMM Mk 5	USA	—	7	—
	Asheville	USA	—	1[b]	—

User	Type	Country of origin	No. held 1968	No. held 1978	On order
Libya	*La Combattante* II	France	—	—	10
	Osa-I/II	USSR	—	5	7
	Vosper (*Susa*-class)	Britain	—	3	—
Malaysia	*La Combattante* II	France	—	4	—
Nigeria	*La Combattante* III	France	—	—	3
	Type 143	Germany	—	—	3
Norway	*Hauk*	Norway	—	—	14
	Storm	Norway	20	20	—
	Snogg	Norway	—	6	—
Oman	Brooke Marine 37.5m	Britain	—	3	6
Peru	*La Combattante*	France	—	—	6
Poland	*Osa*	USSR	5	13	—
Romania	*Osa*	USSR	5	5	—
Saudi Arabia	PGG	USA	—	—	4
Singapore	*Jaguar* II	Germany	—	6	—
Somalia	*Osa*-II	USSR	—	3	—
South Africa	*Reshef*	Israel	—	3	3
Sweden	*Jägaren*	Norway	—	2	14
Syria	*Komar*	USSR	10	6	—
	Osa	USSR	—	6	—
Taiwan	PSMM Mk 5	USA	—	—	2
Thailand	*Jaguar* II	Germany/Singapore	—	3	—
	CNB 270-ton	France	—	—	3
Tunisia	P-48	France	—	3	—
Turkey	*Jaguar* III	Germany	—	4	—
	Kartal (*Jaguar*)	Germany	—	4[c]	—
USA	*Asheville*	USA	—	4[a]	—
	PHM (*Pegasus*) hydrofoil	USA	—	1	5
USSR	*Komar*	USSR	50	—	—
	Osa-I	USSR	75	70	—
	Osa-II	USSR	—	50	—
	Sarancha	USSR	—	1	—
Venezuela	Vosper (*Constitución*-class)	Britain	—	3	—
Vietnam	*Komar*	USSR	—	2	—
Yugoslavia	*Spica*	Sweden/Yugoslavia	—	—	10
	Osa	USSR	—	10	—

[a] Missiles fitted 1971. [b] Missiles fitted 1975–6. [c] Missiles fitted 1975.

8. CHARACTERISTICS OF MISSILE-ARMED PATROL CRAFT

Country of origin	Class type	Displacement full load (tons)	Length (m)	Engines Type	Engines No.	Engines HP	Max. speed (kt)	Range at cruising speed (nm)	Complement	Missiles	Secondary armament
Britain	Vosper *Brave/Susa*	114	30.3	GT	3	12,750	50	2,300	20	8 SS-12	1×40mm, 1×20mm
	Vosper *Constitución*	150	36.9	D	2	7,200	27	1,350	18	2 *Otomat*	1×40mm
Denmark	*Willemoes*	240	46	GT*	3	12,000	40	n.a.	34	4–8 *Harpoon*	1×76mm
France	CNE	80	32	D	2	2,700	30	1,500	17	4 SS-12	2×40mm
	Trident	145	37	D	2	4,000	28	1,500	18	6 SS-12	1×40mm
	CNE	155	42	D	2	7,200	33	1,000	25	4 SS-12	2×40mm
	La Combattante I	202	45	D	2	3,200	23	2,000	25	4 SS-11	2×40mm
	P-48	250	48	D	2	4,220	21.5	2,000	25	8 SS-12	2×40mm
	Saar	250	44.9	D	4	13,500	40	2,500	35–40	6–8 *Gabriel*	1×76mm or 1–2 40mm
	La Combattante II	260	47	D	4	12,000	40	1,600	40	4 *Exocet*	4×35mm
	La Combattante III	425	56	D	4	18,000	36	2,000	42	4 *Exocet*	2×76mm, 4×30mm, 2×534mm TT
West Germany	*Jaguar II*	255	45	D	4	14,400	40	1,850	35	4 *Exocet*	1×76mm, 2×35mm
	Type 148	265	47	D	4	14,400	38	n.a.	30	4 *Exocet*	1×76mm, 1×40mm
	Type 143	378	57.5	D	4	18,000	38	2,600	40	4 *Exocet*	1×76mm, 1×40mm, 2×533mm TT
Israel	*Jaguar III*	410	58.1	D	4	18,000	38	n.a.	35	8 *Harpoon*	1×76mm, 2×35mm
	Reshef	450	58	D	4	10,600	32	4,000	45	7 *Gabriel*	2×76mm, 2×20mm
Italy	*Sparviero*	62.5	23	GT	1	5,000	50	1,050	8	2 *Otomat*	1×76mm
	CNB	270	49.8	D	3	13,500	38	2,000	45	4 *Exocet*	1×76mm, 1×40mm
Norway	*Snogg*	125	36.5	D	4	7,200	36	550	20	4 *Penguin*	1×40mm, 4×533mm TT
	Storm	125	36.5	D	2	7,200	36	n.a.	26	6 *Penguin*	1×76mm, 1×40mm
	Jägaren	140	36	D	2	7,000	35	n.a.	20	6 *Penguin*	1×76mm, 4×533mm TT
	Hauk	150	36.5	D	2	7,000	34	n.a.	22	4 *Penguin*	1×40mm, 4×533mm TT
USA	PHM-1	235	40	GT*	1	26,000	50	1,000	21	8 *Harpoon*	1×76mm
	Type 162 (*Pegasus*)	235	40	GT*	1	26,200	50	n.a.	21	4 *Exocet*	1×76mm
	Asheville	240	50	GT	1	12,500	40	1,700	25	4 *Standard*	1×76mm
	PSMM Mk 5	270	50.2	GT*	3	13,800	40	2,700	34	4 *Otomat*	1×76mm, 2×30mm
	PGG	320	56.2	GT*	1	16,500	38	n.a.	35	4 *Harpoon*	1×76mm, 2×20mm, 1×81mm mor, 2×40mm mor
USSR	*Komar*	80	25.5	D	4	4,800	40	400	25	2 SS-N-2	2×25mm
	Osa I	230	37	D	3	13,000	36	800	25	4 SS-N-2	4×30mm
	Osa II	230	37	D	3	13,000	36	800	25	4 SS-N-11	4×30mm
	Sarancha	300	43	GT	2	n.a.	45	n.a.	n.a.	4 SS-N-9	4×23mm, 2 SA-N-4
Yugoslavia	*Spica*-type	240	45	GT*	2	11,600	40	n.a.	30	2 *Exocet*	1×57mm

GT = gas turbine. D = diesel. TT = torpedo tubes. *Diesel engines provide power under cruising conditions.

9. ORGANIZATION OF US ARMOURED/MECHANIZED DIVISION

	Armd div*	Mech div*
Manpower	16,850	17,800
M-60A1/2 med tks	324	216
M-60 dozers	18	12
M-551 lt tks	27	27
M-114A1 recce	179	176
M-577A1 comd	132	127
M-113A1 APC	376	406
M-109A1 155mm sp how	54	54
M-110A1 8-in. sp how	12	12
M-106A1 107mm mor	53	49
M-125A1 81mm mor	45	54
M-163 20mm sp AA guns	24	24
Chaparral SAM carriers (M-730)	24	24
TOW ATGW carriers (M-113A1)	90	108
Dragon ATGW launchers	254	294
M-578 ARV	62	64
M-88 ARV	37	27
M-728 CEV	8	8
M-60 AVLB	18	14
OH-58 hel	66	66
UH-1H hel	54	54
AH-1G hel	9	9
AH-1S hel (*TOW*)†	42	42

ARV = armoured recovery vehicle
CEV = combat engineer vehicle
AVLB = armoured vehicle-launched bridge

* Armd div has 6 tk, 5 mech inf bns, as shown. Mech div has 4 tk, 6 mech inf bns. New armd divs will have 3 bdes (17,800 men in 9 tk, 6 mech inf bns), 360 med tks, 16 8-in., 96 155mm how, extra ATGW. New mech divs will have 1 armd, 2 mech inf bdes (18,000 men in 7 tk, 8 mech inf bns), 288 med tks, how, extra ATGW.

† Each AH-1S carries 8 *TOW* ATGW.

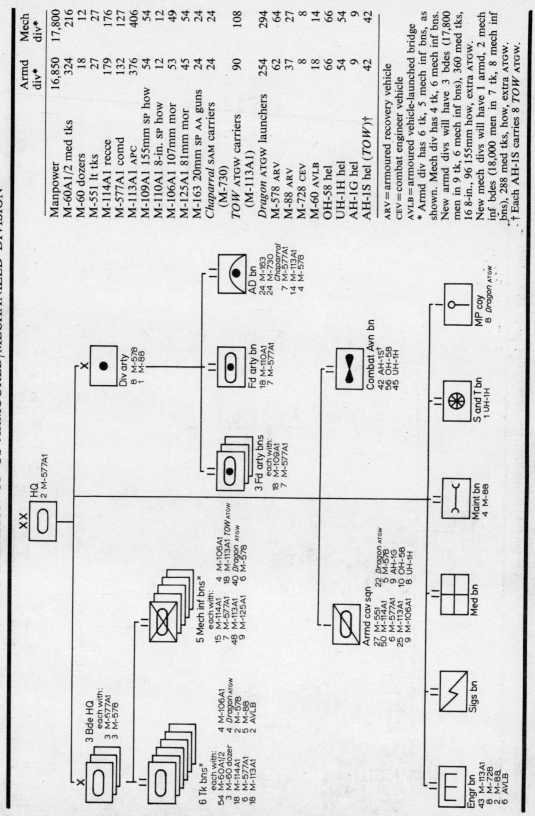

10. ORGANIZATION OF SOVIET TANK DIVISION

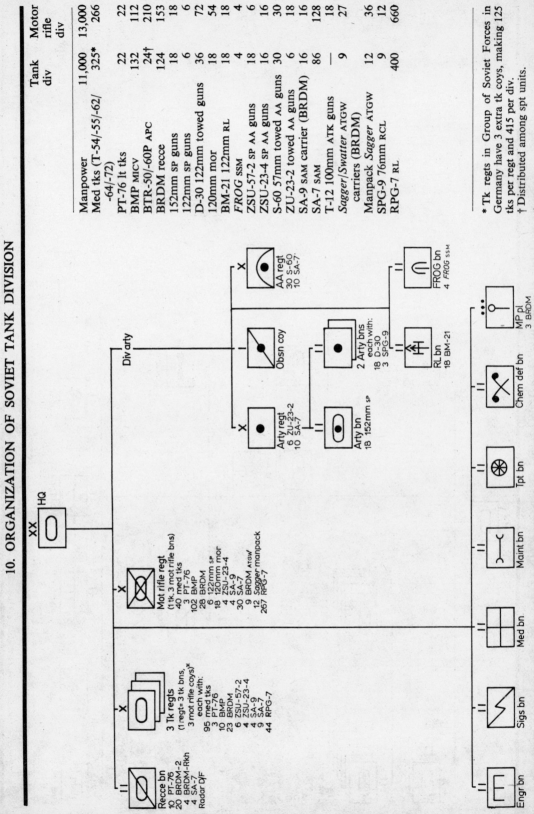

	Tank div	Motor rifle div
Manpower	11,000	13,000
Med tks (T-54/-55/-62/-64/-72)	325*	266
PT-76 lt tks	22	22
BMP MICV	132	112
BTR-50/-60P APC	24†	210
BRDM recce	124	153
152mm SP guns	18	18
122mm SP guns	6	6
D-30 122mm towed guns	36	72
120mm mor	18	54
BM-21 122mm RL	18	18
FROG SSM	4	4
ZSU-57-2 SP AA guns	18	6
ZSU-23-4 SP AA guns	16	16
S-60 57mm towed AA guns	30	30
ZU-23-2 towed AA guns	6	18
SA-9 SAM carrier (BRDM)	16	16
SA-7 SAM	86	128
T-12 100mm ATK guns	—	18
Sagger/Swatter ATGW carriers (BRDM)	9	27
Manpack Sagger ATGW	12	36
SPG-9 76mm RCL	9	12
RPG-7 RL	400	660

* Tk regts in Group of Soviet Forces in Germany have 3 extra tk coys, making 125 tks per regt and 415 per div.
† Distributed among spt units.

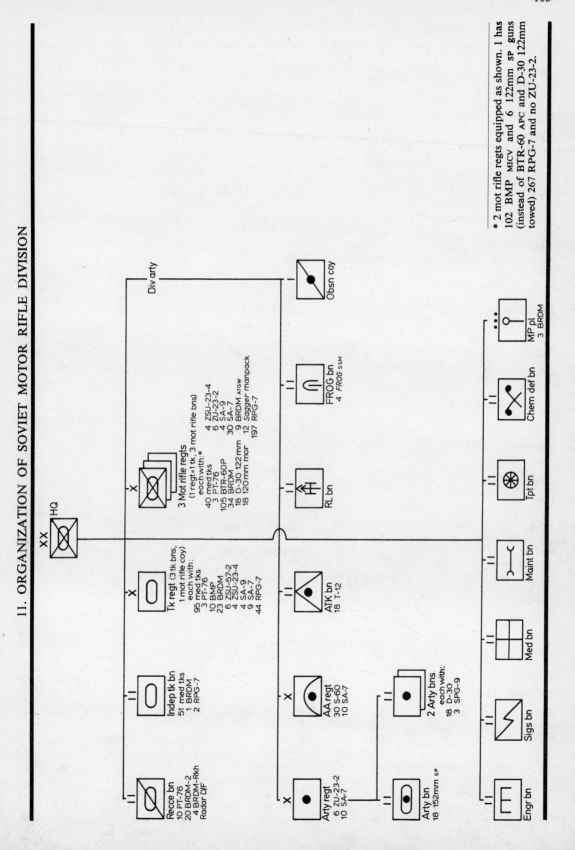

11. ORGANIZATION OF SOVIET MOTOR RIFLE DIVISION

* 2 mot rifle regts equipped as shown. 1 has 102 BMP MICV and 6 122mm SP guns (instead of BTR-60 APC and D-30 122mm towed) 267 RPG-7 and no ZU-23-2.

12. MAJOR IDENTIFIED ARMS AGREEMENTS, JULY 1977–JUNE 1978

Recipient	Primary supplier	Date of agreement	System	Quantity	Cost ($m)	Expected delivery
(a) Western Europe and NATO						
Austria	Italy	Mid-1978	AB-212 hel	12	n.a.	1979-80
Britain	Australia	July 1977	*Ikara* ASW system	n.a.	9.15	n.a.
	.USA	Aug 1977	*TOW* ATGW	n.a.	8.5	n.a.
		Feb 1978	Mk 46 torpedoes	500	72	n.a.
Canada	USA	Mar 1978	*TOW* ATGW	1,728	13	n.a.
Denmark	France/Britain	Sept 1977	*Lynx* hel	7	17	1979
Finland	Britain	Dec 1977	*Hawk* trg ac	50	240	n.a.
	USSR	Jan 1978	MiG-21bis fighters	30	n.a.	n.a.
		Jan 1978	*Osa*-II FPBG	5	n.a.	n.a.
		n.a.	Mi-8 hel	1	n.a.	1978–79
Germany	USA	Mar 1978	*Sea Sparrow* SAM	96	7.1	n.a.
		June 1978	*Harpoon* SSM	132	80	n.a.
Greece	Canada	Aug 1977	CL-215 tpt ac	2	n.a.	Aug 1977
	France	n.a.	AMX-10P APC	n.a.	n.a.	n.a.
	USA	Early 1978	TA-7H trg ac	6	26	1980
Netherlands	Britain	Early 1978	*Lynx* ASW hel	8	22	n.a.
	USA	Aug 1978	*Dragon* ATGW	2,300	37.1	n.a.
Norway	Britain	Late 1977	*Sea King* ASW hel	1	n.a.	1978
Portugal	USA	Aug 1977	C-130H tpt ac	4	20	1978
		Late 1977	M-113 APC	66	n.a.	n.a.
			TOW ATGW	16	n.a.	n.a.
Spain	France	Early 1978	*Mirage* F-1 fighters	58	800	n.a.
	Netherlands	Late 1977	F-27 MR ac	3	n.a.	n.a.
	USA	Late 1977	Hughes 300C hel	17	n.a.	n.a.
Sweden	USA	Late 1977	*TOW* ATGW msls	6,700 ⎫	50.7	1979
			TOW ATGW launchers	340 ⎭		
Switzerland	USA	Mar 1978	*Dragon* ATGW	8,580	50	n.a.
Turkey	USA	Late 1977	RF-4E recce ac	8 ⎫	93.7	n.a.
			F-4E fighters	32 ⎭		
		Aug 1978	*Sparrow* AAM	240	17.3	n.a.
(b) Middle East and North Africa						
Egypt	Britain	n.a.	*Swingfire* ATGW	n.a.	35	n.a.
		Early 1978	*Lynx* hel	50	595	n.a.
		Late 1977	FPBG	6	270	n.a.
		1977	SRN-6 hovercraft	3	n.a.	n.a.
	France	Late 1977	*Mirage* V fighters	14	n.a.	n.a.
	Italy	n.a.	*Lupo*-class frigates	2	230	1980–81
	USA	May 1978	F-5E fighters	42 ⎫	400	1978 on
			F-5F trg ac	8 ⎭		

Recipient	Primary supplier	Date of agreement	System	Quantity	Cost ($m)	Expected delivery
Iran	Britain	Mid-1977	Spt vessels	4	93.5	Mid-1981
	Germany	Mar 1978	Type 209 subs	6	500	n.a.
	Italy	Early 1978	*Lupo*-class frigates	6	n.a.	n.a.
	USA	1977	RF-4E recce ac	5	n.a.	n.a.
		Late 1977	E-3 AWACS ac	7	n.a.	1981
Iraq	France	Mid-1977	*Mirage* F-1 fighters	36 ⎫	n.a.	n.a.
			Mirage F-1B trg ac	4 ⎭		
	USSR	Sept 1977	Modernization of air force, incl MiG-21/-23	n.a.	n.a.
		1977	Il-76 tpt ac	n.a.	n.a.	n.a.
Israel	USA	Mid-1977	AH-1J hel	18	64	n.a.
			Flagstaff II hydro-foils	2	n.a.	n.a.
		Mar 1978	Hughes 500 hel	30–40	n.a.	n.a.
		May 1978	F-15 fighters	15	n.a.	1981–82
			F-16 fighters	75	n.a.	1981–83
Jordan	USA	Mid-1977	M-110A1 SP how	n.a.	12.6	n.a.
		Late 1977	AH-1 hel	10	n.a.	n.a.
Libya	France	Mid-1977	FPBG	10	600	n.a.
	USSR	1977	'F'-class subs	6	n.a.	1978 on
Morocco	France	Early 1978	*AlphaJet* trg ac	24	144	1979/80
		May 1978	*Crotale* SAM	n.a.	n.a.	n.a.
	Italy	July 1978	CH-47C hel	6	n.a.	1980
	Spain	1977	Large patrol craft	4	n.a.	n.a.
	Switzerland	Mid-1977	AS. 202/18A trg ac	10	n.a.	1977
	USA	Late 1977	AD system	1	200	n.a.
Qatar	France	Late 1977	*Mirage* F-1 fighters	30	16.4	n.a.
	USA	1977	*HAWK* SAM	n.a.	n.a.	n.a.
Saudi Arabia	Germany	1977	*Marder* MICV	n.a.	n.a.	n.a.
	Italy	Mid-1977	AS-61A4 hel	2	n.a.	n.a.
	Japan	Mid-1977	KV-107 hel	6	100	1978
	USA	Mid-1977	Boeing 747 tpt ac	1	n.a.	n.a.
		1977	*Redeye* SAM	n.a.	n.a.	n.a.
		Late 1977	FPBG	4	52.5	1987
		May 1978	F-15 fighters	45 ⎫	n.a.	1981–84
			TF-15 trg ac	15 ⎭		
Sudan	Brazil	Late 1977	EMB-111P2 tpt ac	6	n.a.	n.a.
	France	Late 1977	*Mirage* 50 fighters	24	n.a.	n.a.
			Mirage III fighters	14	n.a.	n.a.
	USA	Late 1977	F-5E fighters	10 ⎫	80	n.a.
			F-5B trg ac	2 ⎭		
Syria	France	1977	ATGW	n.a.	240	n.a.
	Italy	Mid-1977	AB-212 hel	18	n.a.	n.a.
	USA	Late 1977	*HOT* ATGW	n.a.	n.a.	n.a.
	USSR	1977	T-62 tks	60	n.a.	1977
		1977	MiG-23 fighters	12	n.a.	1978
		1977	SA-6/-8/-9 SAM	n.a.	n.a.	n.a.

Recipient	Primary supplier	Date of agreement	System	Quantity	Cost ($m)	Expected delivery
Tunisia	USA	1977	F-5E fighters	10 ⎫	53.6	n.a.
			F-5F trg ac	2 ⎭		
		1977	*Sidewinder* AAM	n.a.	n.a.	n.a.
United Arab Emirates	Britain	Early 1978	*Scorpion* lt tks	n.a.	n.a.	n.a.
	Germany	1977	*Jaguar* II FPB	4	n.a.	n.a.

(c) Sub-Saharan Africa

Recipient	Primary supplier	Date of agreement	System	Quantity	Cost ($m)	Expected delivery
Gabon	USA	Mid-1977	C-130H tpt ac	1	n.a.	Dec 1977
Ivory Coast	France	Late 1977	*AlphaJet* trg ac	12	n.a.	n.a.
		1977	FPB	2	n.a.	1978
Kenya	Canada	Mid-1977	DHC-5D tpt ac	4	n.a.	n.a.
Mauritania	Canada	Sept 1977	DHC-5D tpt ac	2	n.a.	1977
	Spain	1977	Patrol craft	2	n.a.	n.a.
Nigeria	Britain	Sept 1977	*Bulldog* 123 trg ac	12	1.27	Mar 1978 on
	France	Late 1977	*La Combattante*-class FPBG	3	104	n.a.
	Germany	Late 1977	Type 143 FPBG	3	n.a.	n.a.
		Late 1977	GW frigate	1	n.a.	n.a.
	USA	Late 1977	CH-47C hel	6	45.5	n.a.
Tanzania	Canada	Dec 1977	DHC-5D tpt ac	4	29	n.a.
Zambia	Italy	Mid-1977	AB-47G hel	10	n.a.	1977

(d) Asia and Australasia

Recipient	Primary supplier	Date of agreement	System	Quantity	Cost ($m)	Expected delivery
Australia	USA	Early 1978	Type FFG-7 frigate	1	198	n.a.
Bangladesh	Britain	Early 1978	Frigate	1	3.6	n.a.
	France	Early 1977	*Magister* trg ac	6	n.a.	n.a.
India	Britain	Mid-1977	*Sea King* ASW hel	3	15	n.a.
		Sept 1977	*Sea Harrier* V/STOL fighters	8	n.a.	n.a.
	USSR	1977	T-72 tks	70	n.a.	n.a.
		1977	*Kashin*-class destroyers	2	n.a.	1978/79
		1977	Ka-25 hel	5	n.a.	n.a.
		1977	Il-38 MR ac	2	n.a.	n.a.
	Australia	Mid-1977	*Nomad* tpt ac	5	gift	Nov 1977
Indonesia	Britain	April 1978	*Hawk* trg ac	8	50	n.a.
	France	Late 1977	*Puma* tpt hel	6	n.a.	n.a.
	Netherlands	Late 1977	F-27 400 tpt ac	4	n.a.	Mid-1978
	USA	Late 1977	F-5E fighters	12 ⎫	80	n.a.
			F-5F trg ac	4 ⎭		
Japan	USA	June 1978	*Harpoon* SSM	n.a.	15.3	n.a.

Recipient	Primary supplier	Date of agreement	System	Quantity	Cost ($m)	Expected delivery
South Korea	Italy	1977	Fiat 6614m APC	150	n.a.	1977 on
	USA	Late 1977	F-4E fighters	18	n.a.	n.a.
			C-130H tpt ac	6	76.2	n.a.
			CH-47C hel	6	40.1	n.a.
Malaysia	Britain	Late 1977	AT-105 APC	n.a.	4.7	n.a.
Pakistan	China	1977	*Hainan*-class FPB	3	n.a.	n.a.
	USA	1977	*TOW* ATGW	n.a.	n.a.	n.a.
		Early 1978	Mk 46 torpedoes	40	9.5	n.a.
Philippines	USA	Late 1977	F-8H fighter ac	25	11.7	n.a.
Taiwan	USA	Early 1978	PSMM FPBG	15	n.a.	n.a.
Thailand	Britain	Sept 1977	*Scorpion* lt tks	n.a.	17	1978–79
	Canada	Late 1977	CL-215 amph ac	2	n.a.	n.a.
	France	1977	FPBG	3	n.a.	n.a.
	USA	Sept 1977	*Merlin* IVA tpt ac	2	3.5	1977–78
		Late 1977	OV-10C COIN ac	6	13.4	n.a.
		Late 1977	UH-1H hel	13	10.5	n.a.

(e) Latin America

Recipient	Primary supplier	Date of agreement	System	Quantity	Cost ($m)	Expected delivery
Argentina	France	Aug 1977	*Mirage* IIIEA fighters	7	n.a.	n.a.
	USA	1977	T-34C trg ac	16	9.0	1978
		Early 1978	Bell-212 hel	8	n.a.	1978
		Early 1978	CH-47 hel	6	n.a.	n.a.
Bolivia	Switzerland	Aug 1977	PC-7 *Turbo-Trainer* ac	16	n.a.	n.a.
Brazil	Britain	Late 1977	*Wasp* ASW hel	3	n.a.	Nov 1977
	France	Aug 1977	*Mirage* III fighters	4	n.a.	n.a.
Chile	Brazil	July 1977	18m FPB	10	n.a.	n.a.
		1977	EMB-111N lt MR ac	5	n.a.	n.a.
Colombia	Portugal	Sept 1977	*Joao Coutinho*-class frigates	4	n.a.	1977
Ecuador	France	Mid-1977	Corvettes	4	n.a.	n.a.
		Late 1977	*Mirage* F-1 fighters	18 ⎱	105	n.a.
			Mirage F-1B trg ac	2 ⎰		
	Germany	Sept 1977	Type 209 subs	2	n.a.	1980
	Italy	Mar 1977	*Lupo*-class frigate	1	n.a.	n.a.
Honduras	Britain	Mar 1978	*Scorpion* lt tks	n.a.	n.a.	n.a.
Peru	Germany	Mid-1977	Type 209 subs	2	n.a.	n.a.
	USA	Mid-1977	T-34C trg ac	6	n.a.	n.a.
	USSR	1977	An-26 tpt ac	6	n.a.	1977
Uruguay	Brazil	Mar 1978	EMB-110B tpt ac	1	n.a.	July 1978
	Germany	1977	Type 209 subs	2	n.a.	n.a.
Venezuela	France	Aug 1977	*Mirage* IIIEV fighter	1	n.a.	n.a.

The East–West Theatre Balance in Europe

Any assessment of the military balance between NATO and the Warsaw Pact involves comparison of the strengths of both men and equipment, consideration of qualitative characteristics, factors such as geographical advantages, deployment, training and logistic support, and of differences in doctrine and philosophy.* It must be set within the context of the strategic nuclear balance, of military forces world wide and of the relative strengths of the navies of the two sides. The last is discussed on pp. 114–18.

Certain elements in the equation are of special importance. Warsaw Pact equipment is relatively standardized, whereas that of NATO is not and is therefore subject to limitations on interoperability and thus flexibility. NATO has certain strengths, such as the striking power of its tactical air forces, but there is little depth in the NATO central sector, which presents problems in its defence. On the other hand, the Warsaw Pact has its own vulnerabilities, and there may be doubts about the reliability of some of its members and the value of their forces. It must be borne in mind that Soviet land and air forces in particular are designed for offensive operations; NATO forces are primarily designed for defence, and thus are designed to deter by creating a reasonable Soviet doubt about the possibility of the speedy success of a conventional attack and the nuclear consequences that might follow.

Land and Air Forces

Although divisions on both sides are often of different size and have different organizations, it is sometimes useful to compare numbers of divisions, but quite substantial numbers of combat manpower are not held on divisional establishments. When making a divisional comparison, it is most useful to compare the divisions available in two geographical regions: first, Northern and Central Europe (taken together); and, second, Southern Europe. For obvious reasons, it is not easy to distinguish between Warsaw Pact forces of the Central Region. The Southern Flank, on the other hand, is distinctly separate from the other regions, for both political and geographical reasons. There are three areas of deployment on this flank: eastern Turkey, Greek and Turkish Thrace and north-east Italy. It would be difficult, if not impossible, for forces in any one of these areas to be moved to another. Table I has therefore been divided into two parts, with NATO listed as a whole (because US ground forces do not constitute a major part of the total) and the Warsaw Pact divided into two – the Pact as a whole and Soviet forces.

Table I: Ground Forces

Ground Forces Available in Peacetime (div equivalents)[c]	Northern and Central Europe[a]			Southern Europe[b]		
	NATO	Warsaw Pact	(of which USSR)	NATO	Warsaw Pact	(of which USSR)
Armd	10	32	22	4	6	2
Mech	13	33	20	7	24	7
Inf and AB	4	5	3	26	3	2

[a] NATO figures are for AFCENT and AFNORTH combined. As neither of the commanders of these forces can be assured of the support of ground forces in Portugal or Britain, these are not included. French forces likewise are not included, although two divisions (being reorganized – see p. 23) are currently deployed in Germany. Forces in Berlin are included. Warsaw Pact forces include all divisions of East Germany, Czechoslovakia and Poland, and Soviet divisions deployed in those countries in peacetime, together with those Category 1 and 2 divisions (see p. 9 for definitions) in the Western Military Districts of the Soviet Union which are presumed to be earmarked for employment on the Northern and Central Fronts.

[b] NATO forces include Italian, Greek and Turkish land forces and, on the Warsaw Pact side, the land forces of Bulgaria, Hungary, and Romania, together with Category 1 and 2 Soviet divisions stationed in Hungary and south-western USSR which are assumed to be earmarked for operations on the Southern Fronts.

[c] Divisions, brigades and similar formations aggregated on the basis of three brigades to a division.

MANPOWER

A comparison of front-line combat manpower deployed on the ground in normal peacetime circumstances (as distinct from total manpower, which is referred to later) fills out the picture further. The figures shown reflect the variations in divisional establishments mentioned above but also include combat troops in formations higher than divisions. They take some account of under-manning as well – many NATO and Warsaw Pact divisions are kept well below strength in peacetime. Figures calculated on this basis, which

---

* For full coverage of the comparative methods used, see *The Military Balance* 1977–1978, pp. 102–110.

Table II: Manpower in Combat Units (thousands)

	Northern and Central Europe			Southern Europe		
	NATO	Warsaw Pact	(of which USSR)	NATO	Warsaw Pact	(of which USSR)
Combat manpower in all types of formations	626	943	638	550	388	147

can only be very approximate, are shown in Table II. The figures do not include French forces; if those stationed in Germany are counted, the NATO figure for Northern and Central Europe might be increased by perhaps 40,000.

REINFORCEMENTS

Judgment on the rate at which reserve forces can be mobilized, moved to the theatre and put into action is far from easy and involves many complex factors and qualifying assumptions. Some general points can be made:

- Warning time is only useful if there is the political will to mobilize. It depends crucially upon how early an attacker's preparations can be detected. This in turn will depend upon whether the attack is based upon reinforced forces or upon those in place.
- The success or failure of an unreinforced attack will largely depend upon the defender's ability to move rapidly from barracks into defensive positions.
- Reinforcement varies greatly from country to country. It should be rapid for Central European states. It should be quite rapid for the Soviet Union although her East–West transport systems are not particularly good (change-of-gauge stations will tend to delay rail movement). The United States faces great difficulties over reinforcement.
- Any Western reinforcement by sea will become much more uncertain if it has to take place after the outbreak of hostilities. Air reinforcement will also be contested. Transit facilities are likely to come under attack. By contrast, it may be less easy for the West to interfere with Soviet reinforcement, although here too there are some vulnerabilities.
- Many Warsaw Pact divisions are not at a high state of readiness, especially those listed as Category 3 (see note on p. 13 for definitions). The size of the Soviet Union and her relative lack of good internal communications will make concentration of reserve manpower rather difficult.
- Most Western reinforcement does not involve the raising of complete formations but rather is intended to fill out the establishments of formations already deployed forward in peace.

Tables III and IV summarize the present position.

A fair summary of the initial reinforcement position might be that the Warsaw Pact is intrinsically capable of a much faster build-up of formations in the first two or three weeks, particularly if local surprise

Table III: Warsaw Pact Reinforcing Formations

	Armd divs			Mech divs			Other divs		
	Category			Category			Category		
	1	2	3	1	2	3	1	2	3
Czechoslovakia	3	—	2	3	—	2	—	—	—
East Germany	2	—	—	4	—	—	—	—	—
Poland	5	—	—	3	2	3	—	2	—
Soviet divs									
In above area	14	—	—	13	—	—	—	—	—
Elsewhere[a]	4	11	11	6	13	46	8	—	—
Soviet totals	18	11	11	19	13	46	8	—	—

[a] Included here are four Category 1 divisions in Hungary and a number of divisions that might reinforce Southern Europe rather than the central sector. Soviet naval infantry are not included. It is assumed that Soviet divisions facing China (about 43 of all categories) would not be available to reinforce Warsaw Pact operations in Europe. There may be a number of 'equipment divisions' to provide a ready reserve, in addition to the divisions shown.

Table IV: Western Reinforcing Formations

	Divs			Bdes/regts			Marines
	Armd	Mech	Other	Armd	Mech	Other	Divs
Active Formations							
United States[e]	2	3	5	1	1	1	2
Britain	—	—	1	—	—	2	—
Canada	—	—	—	—	—	1	—
Germany	—	—	—	—	—	—	—
France	—	3	2	—	—	—	—
Totals	2	6	8	1	1	4	2
Reserve Formations[f]							
United States[e]	2	1	5	3	6	13	1
Belgium	—	—	—	—	1	1	—
Britain	—	—	—	—	—	—	—
Canada	—	—	—	—	—	—	—
Germany	—	—	—	—	—	6	—
Netherlands	—	1	—	—	—	1	—
Norway	—	—	—	—	—	11	—
Totals	2	2	5	3	7	32	1
Grand Totals	4	8	13	4	8	36	3

[e] Including light divisions (infantry and airborne) and armoured cavalry regiments.
[f] Some countries, particularly Britain, Canada, the Netherlands and France, have plans to mobilize battalion-sized units in some numbers in addition to the formations shown here. France also has formations earmarked for territorial defence.

is achieved, having a large pool of reserves on which to draw and the formations to absorb them; that NATO can only attempt to match such a build-up if it has, and takes advantage of, sufficient warning time; and that the subsequent rate of build-up of formations also favours the Warsaw Pact. Only if the crisis develops slowly enough to permit full reinforcement could the West eventually reach a better position. Apart from having greater economic resources, Alliance countries, including France, maintain rather more men under arms than the Warsaw Pact. For Army/Marines the figures (in thousands) are: NATO 2,845; Warsaw Pact 2,660. And the Soviet Union has a large number of her divisions and men on her border with China. Clearly, Soviet plans will put a premium on exploiting a fast build-up of forces, and NATO plans depend on having adequate standing forces to meet any attack and on augmenting them in good time.

EQUIPMENT

In a comparison of equipment one point stands out: the Warsaw Pact is armed almost completely with Soviet or Soviet-designed material and enjoys the flexibility, simplicity of training and economy that standardization brings. NATO forces have a wider variety of everything from weapons systems to vehicles, with consequent duplication of supply systems and some difficulties of interoperability; they do, however, have some weapons qualitatively superior. As to numbers of weapons, there are some notable disparities, of which that in tanks is perhaps the most significant. The relative strengths are given opposite. Tanks in French formations are not included in these figures. If the two divisions stationed in Germany are taken into account, 325 tanks should be added to the NATO total; if the three divisions in eastern France are also counted, a further 485 should be added.

It will be seen that in Northern and Central Europe NATO has only a third as many operational tanks as the Warsaw Pact, though NATO tanks are generally superior (not, perhaps, to the T-64 and T-72 now being issued to the Soviet forces). This numerical weakness in tanks (and in other armoured fighting vehicles, where the Soviet forces are notably well-equipped both in numbers and quality) reflect NATO's essentially defensive role and has in the past been offset to some extent by a superiority in heavy anti-tank weapons, a field in which new air- and ground-launched missiles rapidly coming into service could increasingly strengthen the defence. NATO is introducing large numbers of such weapons, but so is the Warsaw Pact.

Table V: Main Battle Tank Comparison

	Northern and Central Europe			Southern Europe		
	NATO	Warsaw Pact	(of which USSR)	NATO	Warsaw Pact	(of which USSR)
Main battle tanks in operational service[g]	7,000	21,100	13,650	4,300	6,800	2,500

[g] These are tanks with formations or earmarked for the use of dual-based or immediate reinforcing formations (some 600). They do not include those in reserve or small stocks held to replace tanks damaged or destroyed. In this latter category NATO has perhaps 2,500 tanks in Central Europe. There are tanks in reserve in the Warsaw Pact area, but the figures are difficult to establish. The total Pact tank holdings are, however, materially higher than the formation totals shown in the table.

The Warsaw Pact has also built up a marked advantage in conventional artillery in Northern and Central Europe: counting field, medium and heavy guns, mortars and rocket launchers with formations, NATO has only some 2,700 against a Warsaw Pact total of over 10,000. In Southern Europe the position is more nearly equal, NATO having 3,500 against some 4,000 in the Warsaw Pact, though about one-third of the NATO total is in Italy.

LOGISTICS

NATO has an inflexible logistic system, based almost entirely on national supply lines with little central co-ordination. It cannot now use French territory and has many lines of communication running north to south near the area of forward deployment. Certain NATO countries are, furthermore, short of supplies for sustained combat, but some Warsaw Pact countries may be no better off. The Soviet logistic support has been greatly augmented in recent years. The organization has been improved, and formations have been given more support. The former NATO superiority in forward-area logistics has probably now gone, though there is some inherent advantage in operating on home territory.

AIR POWER

If NATO ground formations are to be able to exploit the mobility they possess by day as well as by night, they must have a greater degree of air cover over the battlefield than they now have. Such cover is provided by a combination of rapid warning and communications systems, fighter aircraft and air defence weapons both for defence of key areas or in the hands of forward troops. In numbers of aircraft NATO is inferior but, although the margin is being reduced, may still have a higher proportion of multi-purpose aircraft of good performance over their full mission profiles, especially in range, payload and all-weather capability; considerable power can be deployed in the ground-attack role in particular. Both sides are modernizing their inventories. The Soviet Union is producing multi-role fighters to replace the large numbers of aircraft at present used only in an air defence role, thus giving increased ground-attack capacity. In addition, fighters have for the first time been specifically designed for deep strike and interdiction.[h] NATO is also bringing into service new fighter aircraft of many types, and the United States has recently substantially augmented her F-15 and F-111 squadrons in Europe. US aircraft in particular can now be assumed to have available very advanced air-delivered weapons, such as laser-guided air-to-surface missiles and other precision-guided munitions.

The air forces of the two sides have tended to have rather different roles; long range and payload have in the past had lower priority for the Warsaw Pact, while NATO has maintained a long-range deep-strike tactical aircraft capability. (The Soviet Union has chosen to build an MRBM force which could, under certain circumstances, perform analogous missions – though not in a conventional phase of any battle.) The introduction of more advanced, longer-range Soviet aircraft now presents a much greater air defence problem for NATO, and NATO strike aircraft must face the increased air defence capability that Soviet forces have built up. The Soviet Union has always placed heavy emphasis on air defence, evident not only from the large number of interceptor aircraft in Table VI but from the strength of her deployment of high-quality surface-to-air missiles and air defence artillery both in the Soviet Union and with units in the field. These defences would pose severe problems for NATO strike aircraft, drawing off much effort into defence sup-

[h] The latest versions of the MiG-23/-27 *Flogger*, Su-17/-20 *Fitter* and Su-19 *Fencer* are reported to have substantially improved range, payload, avionics and ECM capabilities. This may well be at the expense of overall numbers in future, since there has been an increase of some 1,300 tactical aircraft in the Warsaw Pact during the last seven years or so.

Table VI: Tactical Aircraft

Tactical Aircraft in Operation Service	Northern and Central Europe[i]			Southern Europe[i]		
	NATO	Warsaw Pact	(of which USSR)	NATO	Warsaw Pact	(of which USSR)
Light bombers	160	130	125	—	50	50
Fighter/ground-attack	1,400	1,350	925	628	375	125
Interceptors	435	2,025	900	220	1,000	425
Reconnaissance	380	550	350	90	220	150

[i] The area covered here is slightly wider than for ground troops as described in note *a*. Many aircraft have a long-range capability and in any case can be redeployed very quickly. Accordingly, the figures here include the appropriate British and American aircraft in Britain, American aircraft in Spain and Soviet aircraft in the western USSR. They do not, however, include the American dual-based squadrons, which would add about 100 fighter-type aircraft to the NATO totals, nor French squadrons with perhaps another 450 fighters. Carrier-borne aircraft of the US Navy are excluded, but so are the medium bombers in the Soviet Air Force, which could operate in a tactical role.

pression. NATO territory and forces are much less well provided with air defence, but heavy expenditure is now going into new systems of many sorts, both low- and high-level, missiles and artillery (and into electronic warfare equipment for aircraft).

The Warsaw Pact enjoys the advantage of interior lines of communication, which makes for ease of logistics. It has in the past had a relatively high capability for operating from dispersed natural airfields serviced by mobile systems, but the introduction of new high-performance fighters will reduce this. It does, however, have more airfields with protective shelters and the great advantage of standard ground-support equipment which stems from having only Soviet-designed aircraft. These factors make for greater flexibility than NATO has, with its wide variety of aircraft and support equipment. NATO suffers from having too few airfields, which are thus liable to be crowded, and has been slow to build shelters. It un-doubtedly still has superiority in sophistication of equipment, but this technological edge is being eroded as the newer Soviet aircraft are brought in. The capability of NATO air crews (which in general have higher training standards and fly more hours) and the versatility of its aircraft, gives all-weather operational strength, and the quality of Western electronic technology is such that ground and airborne control equip-ment is almost certainly superior to that of the Warsaw Pact. The introduction of AWACS will give NATO an airborne control system that offers significant advantage. Since squadrons can be moved quickly, the NATO numerical inferiority shown above could rapidly be redressed regionally if enough airfields were available. While the total tactical aircraft inventories of the two sides are not dissimilar in size, the Soviet Union keeps about a third of her force of some 7,400 combat aircraft on the Chinese front.

CHANGES OVER TIME

The comparisons above begin to look rather different from those of a few years ago. The effect of small and slow changes can be marked, and the balance can alter. In 1962 the American land, sea and air forces in Europe totalled 434,000; now the figure is around 300,000. There were 26 Soviet divisions in Eastern Europe in 1967; now there are 31, and they are larger in size (despite the increase of some 25 divisions on the Chinese front over the same period). The numerical pattern over the years so far has been a gradual shift in favour of the East, with NATO relying on offsetting this by a qualitative superiority in its weapons that is now being eroded as new Soviet equipment is introduced. While NATO has been modernizing its forces, the Warsaw Pact has been modernizing faster and expanding as well. In some areas (for example, SAM, certain armoured vehicles and artillery) Soviet weapons are now superior, while in other fields (such as tactical aircraft) the gap in quality is being closed. The advent of new weapons systems, particularly precision-guided munitions and new anti-tank and air defence missiles, may again cut into the Warsaw Pact's advantage in tank and aircraft numbers, but in general the pattern is one of a military balance moving steadily against the West. As a result of this perception of a shifting balance, NATO set in train in 1977 a major review of defence policy.

It is too early to say whether this Long Term Defence Programme (LTDP), which was presented to NATO heads of State in Washington in May 1978, will in fact produce the greater readiness and savings through co-operation that are called for, but the objectives were relatively limited in scope, could be attained in practice for the small increases in budgetary outlays to which most Alliance members committed themselves in 1977 and 1978, and should serve to redress the worst of the imbalances. The ten 'task forces' addressed the following subjects:

1. Short-term readiness, including rapid outloading of ammunition and chemical protection.
2. Rapid reinforcement by US, UK and Canadian Strategic Reserves, including the use of civil air and sea lifts and the addition of three sets of divisional equipment for US reinforcements in Europe (POMCUS).[j]
3. Increased reserves and improved mobilization techniques.
4. Co-operative measures (including command, control and communications) at sea and national naval force increases, particularly in ASW, mine-warfare and defence against air and surface attack.
5. Air defence integration and qualitative improvement.
6. Command, Control and Communications (C3).
7. Electronic Warfare improvement on land, at sea and in the air.
8. Logistics, including an improvement in war reserve stocks and greater alliance co-ordination of logistic support.
9. Rationalization of the research, development and production of armaments in the direction of standardization and interoperability.
10. Theatre nuclear modernization.

Broadly speaking, these measures respond either to a specific and increasing Warsaw Pact threat – short-warning attack, increasing weight of air attack or interdiction of sea routes – or to an awareness that NATO has for many years either been wasting a proportion of the resources allotted by the members of the Alliance to the common defence or, through failures in co-ordination, not using what there is available in the most efficient way. While some of this wastage is clearly endemic in an alliance of sovereign nations of widely different size, economic strength and geographical disposition, it should be possible to make a more efficient use of resources. The only task force to be overtaken to some extent by events is the last; the moves to introduce the neutron warhead as a part of nuclear weapon modernization have, for the time being, been shelved. The political will to press ahead with improvements and modernization in general may be difficult to sustain in the face of domestic and economic difficulties besetting the Alliance. Nevertheless, in terms of the arithmetic of the East–West balance, strong and well-equipped reserve forces capable of rapid mobilization and movement into battle positions could do much to offset imbalances. US plans to increase the number of divisional stockpiles in Europe, together with an extensive overhaul of air transport resources, should give US forces in Europe the capability of moving five divisions in ten days (together with 60 tactical air squadrons) as against a current figure of only one division in that time and 40 squadrons.

SUMMARY

It will be clear from the foregoing analysis that a balance between NATO and the Warsaw Pact based on comparison of manpower, combat units or equipment is an extraordinarily complex one, acutely difficult to measure. In the first place, the Pact has superiority by some measures and NATO by others, and there is no fully satisfactory way to compare these asymmetrical advantages. Second, qualitative factors that cannot be reduced to numbers (such as training, morale, leadership, tactical initiative and geographical positions) could prove dominant in warfare. However, three observations can be made by way of a summary:

First, the overall balance still appears to make military aggression seem unattractive. NATO defences are of such a size and quality that any attempt to breach them would require major attack. The consequences for an attacker would be incalculable, and the risks, including that of nuclear escalation, must impose caution. Nor can the theatre be seen in isolation: the central strategic balance and the maritime forces (not least because they are concerned to keep open sea lanes for reinforcements and supplies, and because of their obvious role in the North and the Mediterranean) play a vital part in the equation too.

Second, NATO has emphasized quality, particularly in equipment and training to offset numbers, but this is now being matched. New technology has strengthened the defence, but it is increasingly expensive. If defence budgets in the West are maintained no higher than their present level and manpower costs continue to rise, the Warsaw Pact may be able to buy more of the new systems than NATO. Soviet spending has been increasing steadily, in real terms, for many years. Furthermore, technology cannot be counted on to offset numerical advantages entirely.

Third, while an overall balance can be said to exist today, the Warsaw Pact appears more content with the relationship of forces than is NATO. It is NATO that seeks to achieve equal manpower strengths through 'balanced' force reductions while the Pact has sought in the past to maintain the existing correlation, although recent developments in the Mutual and Balanced Force Reductions (MBFR) negotiations may indicate a substantial alteration in Soviet attitudes towards a concept of parity in conventional strengths. Nevertheless, agreement on force data has still to be reached, and, until it is, 'parity' will remain an elusive goal.

---

[j] Pre-positioned Overseas Materiel Configured in Unit Sets.

The East–West Balance at Sea

Setting aside the historical background to Soviet naval development, there is little doubt that Soviet naval forces now pose a threat to NATO which must be taken into account in making any judgment as to the state of the global balance between East and West. Quite specifically the role of NATO naval forces in controlling the sea for purposes of reinforcement and force projection, including sea-based deterrent forces, is being challenged by the Warsaw Pact. This essay establishes the criteria on which to base a judgment and then makes a comparison of naval forces which takes account of the many rather complex factors which affect naval force planning.

METHODS OF COMPARISON

There are three main ways of aggregating totals, all more or less imperfect. The first directly compares numbers of naval vessels by type; the second compares competing systems – but still on a numerical basis; the third examines the functions that each side must perform and the resources available for them.

Numerical Comparison. This is the least satisfactory method. Little can usefully be derived from numbers alone. The fact that such a comparison shows the United States with 13 aircraft carriers and the Soviet Union with none of anything like comparable performance only illuminates the way each country allocates resources but sheds little light on their relative overall naval strengths. Nor is it any more useful to compare total numbers of surface combatants, for that can conceal gross disparities in ship size and performance. It also ignores a very large number of qualitative and geographical factors, constraints which may inflate or degrade relative performance. Above all, it ignores the fact that the outcome of war at sea is no longer (if it ever was) calculable solely on the basis of individual ship performance. To an ever increasing extent, other systems – such as land-based aircraft and missiles, satellite reconnaissance and world-wide command and control facilities using communication satellites – have their impact on the war at sea. Indices based upon measurement (size, tonnage, gun calibre) and numbers are rather unhelpful except in attempting to predict the outcome of the most limited of engagements. Technology has reached a point where it is no longer possible to single out vessels and compare like with like in isolation, because the range and adaptability of modern weapon systems allow almost all weapons platforms some offensive and defensive capability against all other platforms existing in an increasingly large air and sea space. The reach and destructive capability of land-based systems (aircraft and missiles) have now grown to the point where naval units may be under continuous threat in, for example, the Eastern Atlantic and the Mediterranean. Under these conditions, direct comparison of numbers of vessels tells us little or nothing about the likely outcome.

Competing Systems Comparison. This is more useful in that it at least avoids comparing like with like but tries to compare vessels which are trying to survive with vessels (or other systems) that are trying to destroy them; for example, numbers of aircraft carriers can be compared with numbers of general-purpose (GP) attack submarines (i.e. all those which do not have a strategic missile capability), or ASW frigates with submarines. But this method too has drawbacks. It assumes that systems are competing directly and exclusively with each other, whereas the carrier faces a threat from surface-to-surface missiles (from land or sea) and from aircraft, as well as from systems delivered by submarine, while the submarine is threatened by mines and aircraft (fixed-wing and rotary-wing) and submarines, as well as by surface ASW vessels. The second major drawback concerns the context in which the ratio is applied. What may be useful in a relatively enclosed sea (such as the Mediterranean) will be meaningless in the Atlantic, the size of which may mean that only in a protracted war could all ASW units (say) actually compete directly with all submarines. Very many simplifying assumptions have to be made before this approach is particularly useful – except in comparisons over time. Here at least one can identify the rate of change of specific ratios in order to detect trends, but it would be misleading to expect an analyst to be able to say that there is a particular ratio which is comforting and another which is not.

Mission Comparison. This method will in most cases involve functional groupings of vessels under a single tactical command, rather than individual ships. Given that tactical groupings will be normal, one can begin to see whether there are enough escorts for carrier strike groups, convoys and fleet replenishment groups, for example. At the end of this essay is a balance drawn up using this methodology, but first it is appropriate to look at some of the qualitative factors which affect any balance based upon numbers, however they are put together, and to attempt some definition of missions.

MISSIONS

In general terms, NATO is much more dependent on the sea than the Warsaw Pact. Its strongest member is separated from all the others (except Canada) by the Atlantic, and although air transport can alleviate the difficulties inherent in carrying men across the 3,000 miles of sea (see below), it will never be able to make more than a small dent in the total tonnage of materiel to be ferried. The great bulk of replacement warlike stores to sustain European defence over a period must come by sea. The map of Europe shows clearly that the Northern and Southern flanks of NATO are difficult or impossible to reinforce by land. As with the transatlantic lift, air transport cannot by itself carry all the planned reinforcement to the flanks; sea transport will have to use the North Sea, the English Channel and the Mediterranean.

NATO must also use the sea for the more classical role of force projection. First, tactical air reinforcement will rely upon forward air bases which, at least in the flank countries, are few and inadequate for the sustained operation of large numbers of modern aircraft. Carriers, provided they can be defended, could provide substantial air support without overloading local facilities. Second, Norway, because of her reluctance to have foreign troops stationed permanently on her soil in peacetime, is almost wholly reliant upon external reinforcement, and certain Atlantic islands (particularly Iceland) must have their negligible peacetime garrisons augmented in order to guard against a Soviet air or amphibious landing. Third, in a war of any duration, European dependence upon oil and other imported commodities will bring sharply into focus the need to provide safe passage for merchant shipping.

In marked contrast, the Soviet Union is a continental power able to move troops and materiel to almost all possible zones of conflict by land. Therefore the Warsaw Pact is mainly concerned with sea denial, whereas NATO must think much more in terms of sea control and the projection of force by sea. The exceptions to an unambiguous sea denial role for the Pact are the need to protect strategic submarines from attack by NATO forces and (more tentatively) to move forces eastwards in a war with China via the Indian Ocean. Part at least of Soviet naval forces will be needed to guard Soviet SSBN operating areas in order to keep out NATO hunter-killer submarines and ASW aircraft – particularly in the North Norwegian and Barents Seas.

The importance of the sea for NATO depends upon certain assumptions. In a short war, lasting only a few days, the control of the sea may matter little, except so far as the security of Western SSBN is concerned; but the longer the war continues, the more vital will sea control be to the Allied defence effort. As long as the Warsaw Pact can be denied its European objectives on land in the opening days of a major conflict, the sea and the air space above it will come to assume almost overwhelming importance as the channel for transatlantic reinforcement and, in the longer term, for the transport to Europe of essential commodities. It is also true that a prolonged period of tension before the outbreak of hostilities would permit reinforcement – given the political will – to take place safely (although not without protection against surprise attack) in which case at least part of the predicted naval warfighting role of NATO will be unnecessary. Nevertheless, NATO must plan for the following missions, though not necessarily in this order of priority:[a]

- Protect sea and air routes, so as to ensure the safe passage of reinforcements both across the Atlantic and within the theatre.
- Protect merchant shipping carrying essential commodities.
- Protect the deployment of amphibious forces.
- Project air power ashore from carriers.
- Shadow and, if nuclear escalation takes place, be ready to destroy Soviet SSBN.

QUALITATIVE FACTORS

Each of the missions listed above has become more difficult to perform in the face of growing Soviet power and naval reach. Also, technology seems to be favouring sea denial rather than sea control. Modern naval weapons, together with satellites for maritime reconnaissance, provide a greatly enhanced ability to acquire targets and to destroy them at long range, using stand-off systems such as air-to-surface missiles and submarine-launched cruise missiles. The coverage of Soviet naval land-based strike aircraft has increased continuously (especially since the introduction of *Backfire*). As a result of the emphasis on nuclear propulsion for attack submarines, Soviet capacity to threaten submarines, surface units and merchant shipping has also risen. Close to shore, small manoeuvrable missile-armed FPB, shore-based missiles and aircraft will pose a major problem for anyone wishing to project power by the use of amphibious forces or carrierborne aircraft, and, at least at the start of a conflict, the Warsaw Pact may be able to deny certain quite substantial areas of sea to NATO; the Eastern Mediterranean and the Baltic, Black and Barents Seas will probably be very hostile environments, as may be the Sea of Japan.

Warsaw Pact naval forces suffer from considerable disadvantages. If unable to get into the high seas before the outbreak of hostilities, they must pass through choke points which are either under NATO control (Dardanelles, Straits of Gibraltar, Skagerrak) or which offer considerable advantages to an intercepting

---

[a] Protection of Western SSBN is not included on the grounds that, at least for the time being, Western SSBN do not appear to be seriously threatened by Soviet ASW forces. However, that situation might change if Soviet ASW techniques improve; on the other hand, the introduction of American *Trident* missiles will greatly extend the – at present – rather restricted operating areas of US SSBN.

force (the Greenland–Iceland–UK Gap). Even if Warsaw Pact submarines are able to put to sea before war starts, their detection and tracking is less difficult for NATO, and the shadowing of surface units should present few difficulties. Warsaw Pact navies still lack assured fighter cover based at sea and, despite improved SAM cover, will be vulnerable to sustained attack by NATO maritime strike aircraft when beyond the range of shore-based fighter aircraft. This highlights the Soviet need for forward air bases. NATO, on the other hand, is well-placed, using in-flight refuelling, to extend fighter cover well into the Atlantic. Also, given the lack of facilities outside the Soviet Union and the real difficulties of returning to port for repair and replenishment (made more necessary by the fact that Soviet ASW vessels in particular tend to have less reload capacity) there are grounds for calling the Soviet navy a 'one-shot' force which would find it very difficult to sustain operations in distant waters over a period in wartime.

Recent technological trends and break-throughs can have great impact on the war at sea. Electronic defences might be able to give a very large measure of protection against cruise missiles by jamming guidance systems. Given that cruise missiles form the major part of Soviet anti-shipping systems, ECM could disrupt terminal guidance and at once effectively degrade a key part of the Soviet naval arsenal. (However, advances in missile guidance could redress this.) There are also real possibilities of using effective point defence systems against incoming missiles. ECM and resistance to ECM will therefore play a very significant part in the survivability of naval forces. The possibility remains that one side or the other will achieve a substantial lead in ASW techniques – in detection, destruction, or both. On the whole, ASW advantages lie with the West at present, as much for geographical as for technical reasons.

The crucial period is that at the beginning of hostilities. The United States does not now feel entirely confident in her ability to carry out the reinforcing mission by sea in time. By turning to airlift and pre-positioned stocks for a substantial part of her reinforcements, she is not only planning to speed reaction time but tacitly acknowledging the threat of interdiction of the sea routes for some time at least, even if the outcome were eventually favourable. By avoiding the need to sail (and therefore to protect) convoys in the early days of a war at sea, a considerable number of ASW units can be released to hunt Soviet submarines or to protect high-value units such as SSBN, carriers or amphibious forces.

Non-Soviet forces make up only a very small part of the Warsaw Pact naval strength, and the multi-national aspect of their fleet operations can be disregarded. For NATO, by contrast, there remain considerable problems in terms of interoperability and common operating procedures which must degrade the overall effectiveness of NATO sea power to some degree, despite limited joint exercising in peace and constant contact between Allied naval staffs. NATO navies tend to spend a much higher proportion of their lives at sea than those of the Warsaw Pact and have developed under-way replenishment to a much greater extent than the Soviet Union, despite the considerable advances made by the latter in recent years. It is known, for example, that many surface units in the Soviet Mediterranean Squadron spend considerable periods at rest in deep water anchorages and much replenishment takes place at anchor. It must also be noted that Soviet man-power is turned over at a faster rate than NATO's.

In the balance drawn below, certain assumptions must be made with regard to reserves and refit. It seems unwise to assume that any fleet reserve units can be made ready for a war lasting less than 30 days in time to affect the outcome in any significant way. It is also assumed that the proportion of ships undergoing refit at any one time is approximately the same for each class of ship on both sides, and a factor of a quarter has been deducted from paper totals to allow for those vessels which could not be made ready for war within ten days. FPB are not listed, although they can, as already noted, play an important sea-denial role close to shore. Aircraft totals assume 80 per cent availability on both sides, while helicopters have been excluded, although almost all surface ASW platforms deploy one or more.

FUNCTIONAL GROUPINGS

There are three distinct types of NATO surface ship formation: carrier strike groups; support groups; and escort groups. In addition, submarines, aircraft, MCM groups and mines must be taken into account. *Carrier strike groups* consist of two strike carriers and about fourteen other surface warships performing a number of different protective tasks, including ASW and air defence. A normal complement for US carrier groups would, in addition to the two carriers, be one or two SAM cruisers, six to eight SAM destroyers and several ASW frigates. This group would be able to use about half of its total number of aircraft in a conventional or nuclear strike role; the remainder (about 100) would be deployed on early warning, air defence and ASW operations in connection with the protection of the group. Next is the *support group*, defined as an ASW force capable of independent operations in deep waters distant from enemy land-based air power or when the threat of land-based air power is limited by the presence of friendly fighters. This group would be built around an ASW cruiser or ASW carrier and would consist of one major unit together with eight mixed SAM and ASW destroyers and frigates. Third in the ranking of surface groups is the *escort group*, which would be capable of sustained escort operations where the threat of overwhelming air or submarine attack is limited by the support, either close or distant, of other forces. An escort group would not have an ASW carrier or cruiser but would otherwise be similar in size and constitution to the support group – that is, some eight mixed SAM and ASW destroyers and frigates.

Turning to *submarines*, the most obvious distinction is between those which are nuclear propelled and those which are diesel powered. The former have a far greater operational capability, because of their high and sustained underwater speeds. The latter are more useful in limited areas of operation, like choke points, and are, of course, much cheaper to build. Both would normally operate as single vessels, although co-ordinated group operations may be practised against large surface forces, such as carrier groups. All submarines suffer to some extent from communications problems when submerged, so that relaying target data from reconnaissance aircraft or satellite and co-operation with ASW aircraft will not be easy. They are also noisy when travelling at speed and therefore much more likely to be detected by ASW systems. Nevertheless, submarines remain a most potent threat whether armed with homing torpedoes or cruise missiles (some of the latter have a relatively long-range capability).

It is likely that, on both sides, a large proportion of nuclear attack submarines will be deployed in an attempt to counter hostile and to protect friendly SSBN. Despite the fact that they are strategic systems, the number of SSBN is therefore relevant to the equation, so long as SLBM have not been launched. Submarines could also operate in conjunction with a surface group, and the Soviet Union may use surface groups to protect submarines, though this may confuse the groups' ASW operations and allow enemy submarines to get close. Generally, submarines are considered as individual fleet units.

Naval aircraft – whether land-based or sea-based – are normally organized into squadrons and wings but operate as individual aircraft. They are therefore listed singly and are divided into those which, like the P-3 *Orion* and the *Nimrod*, are land-based maritime reconnaissance (MR) and ASW aircraft and those land-based aircraft, like *Backfire* and *Tornado*, which may be armed with air-to-surface missiles (ASM) for use against surface units. The same division applies to carrier-based aircraft, so these are also listed separately.

The comparison of *MCM groups* and Soviet *mines* may conceal the fact that most older MCM vessels will be unable to sweep or neutralize modern Soviet mines. Each group is assumed to consist of six vessels.

Finally, a word about *amphibious forces* and replenishment groups. Each will require escorting, and the former will need a number of major surface units to establish and maintain sea control during a landing and so long as supporting craft remain offshore. Carrier-borne strike aircraft are likely to be in demand to support the assaulting forces until forward air bases can be established. Any amphibious assault – as opposed to a reinforcement operation at the invitation of any ally – will demand many scarce naval resources in a general war and could not be conducted into high-threat areas without considerable prior attrition of opposing naval and air forces.

DRAWING UP A BALANCE

Before comparing forces by mission, there is one final assumption: in a war of over 30 days, all naval units of either side *could* be in competition with all the naval units of the other, depending upon deployment decisions at the time and upon other assumptions made about warning time and how that warning time is used to alter deployments. It is impossible to predict, for example, whether the carrier task group earmarked for the Mediterranean will be on station or will have been temporarily withdrawn for safety to the Atlantic. Clearly, non-US NATO forces are likely to remain in the Eastern Atlantic for the most part, but some deployment in the Indian Ocean is possible, and some French units are already there.

It is clearly possible to draw some tentative conclusions as to the overall balance of naval forces from the figures presented overleaf. As expected, NATO sea-control forces are considerably greater by any assessment than their Soviet counterparts, due to the inclusion of the US strike groups, but they face an impressive number of sea-denial systems. The mine warfare balance is obviously not a direct comparison, since only a proportion of mines might have to be cleared in the first instance, but it is clear that NATO's mines and mine-hunters are each fewer than the Warsaw Pact's. If, for example, the Soviet Union were to deploy one nuclear attack submarine to cover every NATO on-station SSBN, she is left with five for each carrier strike group. But even if she were to place even greater emphasis on 'strategic' ASW, she could not put two 'tails' on each SSBN. NATO can deploy three ASW aircraft for every Soviet submarine, though this is a rather inadequate number, given the inherent advantages of the submarine. The number of shore-based Soviet strike aircraft is impressive and the capability it represents is growing as *Backfire* is brought into service; this force is backed by 80 *Badger* tankers, which could extend its range across the North Atlantic. Nevertheless, if their target is to be the carrier groups themselves or vessels moving within the area covered by carrier aircraft, Soviet land-based strike aircraft may be opposed by about 186 carrier-borne fighter aircraft for air defence at sea (many of them the new F-14A with *Phoenix* long-range air-to-air missiles). They may also be intercepted by land-based fighters en route to their targets.

This is as far as such a general analysis can go before specific questions begin to arise about precisely how many carrier groups will be in the Atlantic, the Mediterranean or the Pacific, and how many Soviet land-based aircraft will be deployed where at a precise moment. At this point, one moves from overall

Comparison of Forces by Mission

NATO (incl France)			Warsaw Pact		
Category	US	Total NATO	Category	USSR	Total Pact
Sea-control forces			**Sea-denial forces**		
Strike groups	5	5	GP attack sub (nuc)	64	64
Support groups	3	7	GP attack sub (diesel)	119	125
Escort groups	10	30	Strike ac (shore-based)[b]	256	264
ASW/MR ac (shore-based)	173	325	Mines[e]	400,000	
ASW/MR ac (carrier-based)	88	114			
Air defence aircraft (carrier-based)	160	186			
MCM groups (all types)	½	40			
Sea-denial forces			**Sea-control forces**		
Attack sub (nuc)	68	77	Support groups	3	3
Attack sub (diesel)	10	134	Escort groups	13	13
Strike ac (shore-based)	—	77	ASW/MR ac (shore-based)[c]	164	164
Strike ac (carrier-based)	312	384	ASW/MR ac (carrier-based)[d]	19	19
Mines[e]	n.a. (probably under 100,000)		MCM groups (all types)	40	50
SSBN	31	37	**SSBN**	52	52

[b] Tu-16 *Badger*, Tu-*Backfire* B and Il-28 *Beagle*.
[c] Tu-95 *Bear*, Il-38 *May* and Be-12 *Mail*.
[d] Yak-36 *Forger* provides a limited air defence capability.
[e] An approximate figure only.

comparisons of naval capabilities into relative strengths in particular scenarios and these depend on fundamental operational assumptions that cannot be made here.

CONCLUSIONS

Given that Western assets will be spread across the globe – at least at the outset – there seems little doubt that Warsaw Pact assets could be concentrated to produce an impressive sea-denial capability in selected areas, but it is by no means clear that the Pact has a widespread sea-denial capability given the overall balance of systems. Should the West decide to concentrate its naval assets in those same areas, continuing sea control appears not infeasible. However, it is clear that NATO will be forced to disperse assets to protect much wider areas continuously against what will only be intermittent threats. In general, sea control assets have to be spread a great deal more thinly than sea-denial assets, which can be concentrated and switched rapidly from area to area. In that sense, the initiative as to the time and the place of competition rests with the Soviet Union and not with NATO. Only when NATO naval units turn to specific force-projection tasks and threaten some land objective of their own can the Soviet Union be challenged in an area selected by the West. The obvious exception to this is the Barents Sea, which the Soviet Union clearly considers to be home waters. Any NATO move into that area would be certain to provoke a massive reaction under optimum conditions for Soviet naval and maritime air forces.

Taking a long view (i.e. assuming a war lasts more than 30 days) NATO should be able to organize its own assets better, at the same time as taking a heavy enough toll of Soviet assets to establish overall sea control. Such a war at sea seems likely to be a war of attrition in which geographical factors (primarily) would appear to favour NATO. NATO losses might be high in the early days of the struggle to establish control over areas deemed strategically important, but they should decline as Soviet sea-denial forces are destroyed.

Global force relations may only matter in a long war, and then only in a prediction of ultimate outcomes rather than in predicting the outcome of specific contests in particular areas. The results of these contests will depend – to state a most obvious truth – upon where the contest takes place and what resources each side is prepared to stake on the outcome. If NATO does not attempt all its maritime tasks at once, there should be adequate resources for a number to be successfully completed, though losses may be heavy.

Ten years ago NATO would almost certainly have attempted all its maritime tasks at once with a good expectation of success. That it cannot now expect to do so is a measure of the growth of Soviet sea-denial capability and the relative decline of the West's ability to use the sea for its own purposes.

How the balance will develop depends upon many factors, not least any overseas naval and air facilities acquired by the Soviet Union. Extended maritime operations, combined with qualitative improvements already discernible, would accelerate that detectable trend in favour of increased Soviet influence.

Index for last seven years

ADELPHI PAPERS

The following is a selection of those available. They may be ordered from the Institute at a current price of **50p ($1.50)** *per copy, post free by surface mail (air mail prices on application).*

Discount rates are available for bulk orders of 11 or more Adelphi Papers of the same title.